African American
Women Playwrights
Confront Violence

African American Women Playwrights Confront Violence

A Critical Study of Nine Dramatists

PATRICIA A. YOUNG

McFarland & Company, Inc., Publishers
Jefferson, North Carolina, and London

Portions of this book have appeared in earlier versions in the following publications and are reprinted by permission of the journals:

MELUS: The Journal of the Society for the Study of the Multi-Ethnic Literature of the United States, 26(4) (winter 2001), 25–39: "Acts of Terrorism, or, Violence on *A Sunday Morning in the South*."

Griot, 6(1) (1994), 11–25: "Mara: A Tale of Seduction and Slaughter."

Women and Language. 15(2) (1992), 25–31: "Shackled: Angelina Weld Grimké."

LIBRARY OF CONGRESS CATALOGUING-IN-PUBLICATION DATA

Young, Patricia A., 1952–
  African American women playwrights confront violence : a critical study of nine dramatists / Patricia A. Young.
    p.   cm.
  Includes bibliographical references and index.

  ISBN 978-0-7864-4455-7
  softcover : acid free paper ∞

  1. American drama—African American authors—History and criticism.   2. American drama—Women authors—History and criticism.   3. American drama—20th century—History and criticism.   4. African American women—Intellectual life.   5. African Americans in literature.   6. Lynching in literature.   7. Race relations in literature.   8. Social problems in literature.   9. Violence in literature.   I. Title.
  PS338.N4Y68 2012
  812'.509928708996073—dc23   2012021414

BRITISH LIBRARY CATALOGUING DATA ARE AVAILABLE

Front cover image © 2012 Shutterstock

Manufactured in the United States of America

McFarland & Company, Inc., Publishers
  Box 611, Jefferson, North Carolina 28640
    www.mcfarlandpub.com

To Eleanor, Nathaniel, JeanMarie, and Yvonne
who have always believed in me—thanks!

Table of Contents

Introduction

Protest against lynching (the practice of hanging, burning, shooting, stabbing, or drowning accused persons without due process of law), the lack of birth control information, and racial discrimination against returning African American World War I veterans were some of the issues that early black women playwrights, including Alice Dunbar-Nelson (1875–1935), Georgia Douglas Johnson (1877–1966), Angelina Weld Grimké (1880–1958), Mary Powell Burrill (1881–1944), and Myrtle Smith Livingston (1901–1973)—the subjects of this study—dramatized in their plays. Writing within the contexts of the anti-lynching campaign and the black women's club movement, these pioneer dramatists, like other educated women of the black middle class (e.g., Ida Wells-Barnett and Mary Church Terrell), were propelled by the twin demands for justice for the African American race and for the African American woman. In their protest dramas, these writers bore testimony to the upsurge of violence committed against blacks, representing it in its most extreme form—lynching. The threat of lynching held the African American community hostage from Reconstruction to the middle of the twentieth century. While practiced nationally, it particularly degraded and controlled blacks throughout America's southern and border states. An effective instrument of racial subjugation, lynching was nurtured by the ideology of white supremacy, which flourished and intensified in the United States following the abolition of slavery. Within the context of institutionalized white supremacy, African Americans, no longer chattel, increasingly became the targets of lynching.

Deprived of their civil and political rights, black men, women, and children were flogged, dismembered, tortured with hot irons, and put to death at the whim of whites. Castration commonly preceded their murder, which was punishment for crimes such as sheltering a fugitive, disputing a white

1

man's word, testifying or defending him/herself against whites or just acting "troublesome." Because it fit their racist beliefs and provided a convenient explanation, whites created the myth that lynching was a necessary protection for white womanhood. To safeguard white female virtue, whites also created endless rules to govern the black man's behavior toward white women. Robert Zangrando in *The NAACP Crusade Against Lynching 1909–1950* examines some of these regulations and notes that the African American male was prohibited from courting, insulting, enticing, and eloping with Caucasian females. He was forbidden to enter a white woman's room, to cohabit with her or to inadvertently frighten her. He could neither nonsexually assault her—i.e., violate her by merely being in her presence—nor fail to respectfully address her as "Ma'am" or "Miss." Violating any of these specified or unspecified behavior codes was justification for lynching a black male. African Americans suffered this widespread massacre because their murderers were confident in the assumption that as executioners they served as agents for their white peers. The mob's assumption proved true, for a survey of history shows that the lynchers committed their heinous crimes with impunity.

Black women responded to the period's rampant savageries with lynching dramas—i.e., plays "in which the threat or occurrence of a lynching, past or present, has a major impact on the dramatic action" (Stephens, 1992, 331). Following the example of Grimké, who inaugurated an anti-lynching tradition in theater with her authorship of *Rachel* (1916), they poignantly depicted in their plays the injustice of racist violence and its impact on families and communities. Their lynching plays indicate that African Americans did not react passively to the terrorism inflicted upon them, and their drama reflects the female African American writers' response to the brutality and the inhumanity of lynching. Later generations of African American women continued the theater's protest against lynching and its deleterious effect on black citizens. The plays of modern and contemporary playwrights Alice Herndon Childress (1912–1994), Endesha Ida Mae Holland, (1944–2006), Sandra Cecilia Browne Seaton (1942–), and Michon Boston (1962–)—subjects of this study—attest to this fact.

African American Women Playwrights Confront Violence is a gender-focused analysis of racist physical violence as expressed in the study's lynching dramas. More particularly, it is a scrutiny of the anti-lynching dramas and of the contributions to United States and African American literature of black female pioneer writers Alice Dunbar-Nelson, Georgia Douglas Johnson, Angelina Grimké, Mary P. Burrill, and Myrtle Smith Livingston, and an analysis of the social protest plays of modern and contemporary black dramatists Alice Childress, Sandra Seaton, Endesha Holland, and Michon Boston.

The investigation is a significant and original study for two principal reasons. The first is that it illustrates how the early plays of Dunbar-Nelson, Johnson, Grimké, Burrill, and Livingston addressed lynching from a woman-centered perspective and, in particular, dealt in complicated and emotionally charged ways with the issues of black maternity and the pervasive sexual violence against black women. This novel and unprecedented examination distinguishes my study from the more literary and dramaturgical probings of contemporary scholars such as Gloria Hull, Cheryl Wall, and Elizabeth Brown-Guillory in their respective works *Color, Sex, and Poetry: Three Women Writers of the Harlem Renaissance* (1987), *Women of the Harlem Renaissance* (1995), *Their Place on the Stage: Black Women Playwrights in America* (1988), and *Wines in the Wilderness: Plays by African American Women from the Harlem Renaissance to the Present* (1990).

This book is a significant and original study also because it illustrates how the modern and contemporary plays of Childress, Holland, Seaton, and Boston confront the same evils that were addressed more than half a century earlier, while both extending and enriching the lynching canon. For example, Holland contributes *Miss Ida B. Wells* (1983), employing in this play the experimental methodologies of bifurcated characters and multiple narratives. Boston, in *Iola's Letter* (1994), examines the issues and ideologies crucial to Ida B. Wells' times and finds a deep analogy between the activist's era and the present time. Sandra Seaton, in *The Bridge Party* (1989), brings some much needed attention to the lifestyle of middle-class African Americans living in the South during the 1940s as she highlights their confrontation with racist violence.

Following the introduction of this book, chapter 1 presents a brief history of lynching and provides a short discussion of the anti-lynching movement inaugurated by African American women as expressed in the activism of Ida Bell Wells-Barnett and in the formation of the National Association of Colored Women (NACW). Chapter 1 also includes a significant discussion of minstrelsy—with its attendant stereotyping and comical language—to illustrate the cultural backdrop to the struggle the black women dramatists confronted as they began to write for the stage at the beginning of the twentieth century.

Chapter 2 is biographical: here I discuss the women's lives in relationship to each other. I investigate their personal histories, their connections with each other, the ways in which their struggles were connected, and the impact of personal events on their literature. I also explore how financial constraints, patriarchal attitudes within their families, and the presence (or absence) of female support networks affected their personal histories. Moreover, I examine these women's own experiences with maternity and/or child-rearing because the accompanying emotions influenced the plays they produced. I also include a discussion on the little-known biographies of the contemporary writers.

Chapter 3 addresses the anti-lynching plays themselves—their plots as well as their critical receptions and performances. Where possible, I include commentary by the contemporary black press. In this section, I put the plays in conversation with each other as they deal with black maternity, sexual violence against black women, the accusations against black men, and racial injustice. More particularly, I put Grimké's *Rachel* (1916) in conversation with Johnson's *Safe* (c. 1929) and Childress' *Trouble in Mind* as I explore the problematics of black maternity and investigate the impingement of racial violence on black women's reproduction.

It is at this point of juxtaposition that the present work especially develops its own critical edge as it analyzes black women's confrontation of the period's racist and sexual violence. I also consider Grimké's *Mara* (unpublished) and put it in conversation with Johnson's *Blue-Eyed Black Boy* (c. 1930) and Livingston's *For Unborn Children* (1926), while exploring the issues of miscegenation and the sexual violation of black women by white men. In further expanding the theme of miscegenation, I analyze Childress' *Wedding Band: A Love/Hate Story in Black and White* (1966) and its treatment of forbidden liaisons. Additionally, I pair Johnson's *A Sunday Morning in the South* (1925) with Seaton's *The Bridge Party* as I explore the inefficacy of turning to the American judicial system for protection against lynching. My other pairings include Holland's *Miss Ida B. Wells* and Boston's *Iola's Letter*—plays that reflect the anti-lynching activities and ideologies of Ida B. Wells. Moreover, I investigate Dunbar-Nelson's *Mine Eyes Have Seen* (1918) and Burrill's *Aftermath* (1919)—plays that treat the peculiar dilemma of the African American soldier who fights for a nation that denies him his basic constitutional rights. The composite analysis of all the lynching plays reveals in particular how the lynching of African Americans affected their families and communities.

The conclusion reviews the matter of racist violence and the methods that early and late twentieth-century black women used to stanch it. The chapter notes the corrosive impact of prejudice on American society and ultimately concludes that racist and intra-racist violence should be both confronted and eradicated. In the wake of the present racial divide, exacerbated by numerous acts of police brutality and acts of random terrorism, including church and private home burnings as well as the persistent acts of hostility directed against Barack Obama, the nation's first African American president, the lynch dramas of both the pioneer and contemporary dramatists are relevant, warranting serious scrutiny.

History indicates that many other African American women artists and writers joined the playwrights under discussion in a formal protest against lynching. In 1915, journalist Delilah Beasley wrote a series of articles for the *Oakland Tribune* to protest the public showing of the racist movie *The Birth of a Nation.* Beasley's articles stimulated a local movement to boycott the film, which depicted vicious stereotypes of African Americans that whites used to justify their lynching of black people. In 1919, Meta Vaux Warrick Fuller sculpted an anti-lynching piece, *Mary Turner (A Silent Protest)*, in protest of the lynching of a pregnant black woman. Moreover, in 1939, vocalist Billie Holiday recorded the famous "Strange Fruit," a song that recounted lynchings in the South. The "strange fruit" she lamented were the bodies of blacks that hung from branches.

Continuing the protest tradition, choreographer Pearl Primus used dance as a medium through which she denounced the period's racist violence in a 1943 performance piece. In 1944, painter Lois Malou Jones produced *Meditation (Mob Violence)*, a painting that reveals an elderly black man, bound by the hands, passively looking up to the heavens. Employing the song "Strange Fruit," choreographer Katherine Dunham composed the ballet *Southland* in 1953. This dance dramatized the lynching of a man on stage. Writer Lorraine Hansberry penned the poem "Lynchsong" in 1951, and Nina Simone recorded the famous "Mississippi Goddam." This song referenced the 1955 murder of fourteen-year-old Emmett Till and the killing of civil rights leaders James Chaney, Michael Schwerner, and Andrew Goodman.

Lynching remains a vital issue in contemporary works by black women visual artists such as Elizabeth Catlett and Pat Ward Williams. Kathy Perkins has noted that Catlett's 1992 color lithograph *To Marry* juxtaposes a struggling lynch victim with the kiss of a marrying couple. Williams' *Accused/Blowtorch/Padlock* (1986) uses a series of close-up shots from an actual lynching. In the 1990s, rap artists such as Sister Solja focused on lynching for the purpose of reminding a younger generation of America's horrific past (Perkins 1950, 18).

CHAPTER 1

Early African American Women Confront Lynching

In *The NAACP Crusade Against Lynching 1909–1950* (1980), Robert Zangrando renders a comprehensive analysis of lynching that merits attention for the historical contextualization that it provides for the murder of the fictional lynch victims in the plays under investigation. Zangrando supplies documentation to show how each literary victim corresponds to an actual target for death by mob violence. In analyzing this barbarity, Zangrando notes that lynching is a vicious practice in which mob members take the law into their own hands. On the pretext of seeking retribution for an alleged wrongdoing, they murder a victim in summary fashion, at times with great fanfare and public acclaim. Presumptions of innocence and proof of guilt are treated as afterthoughts, if considered at all. The accused may have broken a law, violated a local custom, or merely offended prevailing sensibilities. Black or nonblack, the victim is outnumbered and overwhelmed and has no means of redress because the mob functions as self-appointed prosecutor, jury, judge, and executioner.

An examination of its history shows that lynching dates at least back to the American Revolution and that it was initially used to punish suspected criminals and Tories. This savagery proved a popular mechanism for enforcing local mores and gained a foothold in the nation's settled communities as well as in its southern and western frontiers. During the nineteenth century, lynch targets included gamblers and alleged murderers, desperadoes and horse thieves, antislavery advocates, African Americans suspected of insurrectionary plots, Native Americans, and Spanish-speaking minorities. After 1890, the circle expanded to include immigrants, political radicals, labor organizers, opponents of the First World War, and occasionally kidnappers. Yet despite its various quarries, lynching preyed mainly on African Americans and was used primarily to intimidate, degrade, and control blacks throughout the southern and border states from Reconstruction to the mid–twentieth century. This mob violence enforced a racism that proclaimed the inferiority of all life deriving from African extraction.

Turn-of-the-century Euro-Americans, from both North and South, adopted a view of African Americans that was based upon pseudoscientific pronouncements of Nordic supremacy, racial hierarchies, and "natural selection." African Americans were consequently judged subhuman exclusively on the basis of their physical characteristics. White Americans then combined their prejudices with the application of brutal force and the police power of the states to subordinate African Americans.

Data supplied by the archives at Tuskegee University disclose that 4,743 persons died at the hands of lynchers from 1882, the earliest date for reliable statistics, to 1968. Of these victims, 3,445 (72.7 percent) were African American. Although valuable, these statistics are not comprehensive because the data reflect only *recorded* lynchings and exclude the countless unrecorded murders. As opposition to this rampant slaughter mounted in the 1920s and 1930s, the number of reported lynchings declined, but more subtle forms of brutality evolved. Some murderers formed select committees that were assigned to abduct, torture, and then slay the victims without fanfare and publicity. The Southern terrorists who were worried that external pressure might produce a federal anti-lynching law not only began to suppress the news of mob violence, but they also instituted "legal lynching," whereby officials consented in advance to a sham court trial, which was promptly followed by the prisoner's execution (Zangrando 1980, 4).

Because it fit their racist beliefs and provided a convenient explanation, whites created the myth that lynching was a necessary protection for white womanhood. This fiction was so widely accepted that the security of white female virtue ranked among the most popular justifications for mob murder, according to statistics.

Journalist Ida Bell Wells (1862–1931)—the subject of two plays under scrutiny: Endesha Ida Mae Holland's *Miss Ida B. Wells* (1983)—and Michon Boston's *Iola's Letter* (1994) vigorously challenged the rape myth and its justification for murdering African Americans, particularly black men. She rendered an analysis—well worth revisiting—of the relationship among political terrorism, economic oppression, and conventional codes of sexuality and morality that remains unequaled for its castigation of the patriarchal exploitation of race and gender. Responding to the infamous 1892 lynching in Memphis, Tennessee, when her three close friends were killed for owning and operating a successful grocery store, Wells carried out an investigation into lynching. She researched the circumstances of 728 lynchings that had occurred during the last decade and found that lynching was both "an excuse to get rid of Negroes who were acquiring wealth and property" and a political tactic to create an atmosphere of terror to "keep the nigger down" (Duster 1970, 64); that only a third of the murdered black males were even accused of rape, much less guilty of it; that most African Americans were killed for crimes like public drunkenness, shoplifting, "incendiarism," "race prejudice," "quarreling with whites" and "making threats"; and that not only men, but women and children were also lynched. In the course of her investigations, Wells uncovered a significant number of interracial liaisons. She dared to print that in many cases white women had actually taken the initiative. African American men were being killed for being "weak enough," in Wells' words, to "accept" white women's favors. Interestingly, Georgia Douglas Johnson's *Blue-Eyed Black Boy* features one black man who was strong enough to resist the favors of a white woman, who nevertheless charged him with assault.

In June of 1892, Wells published the well-known pamphlet *Southern Horrors*, which contained her progressive analysis of lynching—the means through which she would deconstruct the myriad of Southern claims and pretenses—to which otherwise progressive forces in the North acceded (Carby 1987, 113). In her essay—which warrants revisitation—the journalist contended that the association of lynching and rape was a contemporary phenomenon, since "the crime of rape was unknown during the four years of the Civil War, when the white women of the South were at the mercy of the race, which is all at once, charged with being a bestial one" (Wells 1969, 5).

Touted as the "first inside story of Negro lynching," *Southern Horrors* included names, dates, places, and circumstances of hundreds of lynchings for alleged rape. The widely circulated pamphlet was prefaced by Frederick Douglass and won an invitation for Wells to make her first public speech to an assembly of African American women from Boston and Philadelphia. This lecture inaugurated Wells's career in anti-lynching activism, for which she would travel throughout the United States and Britain. Wells remarked that the meeting to organize her first anti-lynching lecture and the forum itself were "the real beginning of the club movement among the colored women" in the United States (Duster 1970, 81).

In 1895 Wells published *A Red Record: Tabulated Statistics and Alleged Causes of Lynching in the United States, 1892–1894*—a book listing every lynching that had taken place during the three previous years. By carefully recording the circumstances of each case, she proved that the justifications used by Southerners—such as the need to maintain order or to protect white women—were pure fabrications. She argued that lynching should be viewed as an attempt to recover and to exercise that former physical control, which whites lost over the bodies of African Americans at the manumission of the slaves. She then illuminated the three main pretexts that whites used to justify the slaughter of African Americans. First, was the frequently quoted necessity to repress "race riots," a reason Wells identified as being devoid of evidence of injured Caucasians or of any massacres or of any proof offered of planned insurrections.

The second reason, Wells contended, was a product of the social relations of Reconstruction, when under the rallying summons of a refusal to be dominated by blacks, organized mobs, including the Ku Klux Klan and the Regulators, butchered African Americans for endeavoring to exercise their right to vote. Wells comprehended this history of sanctioned murder as a direct consequence of granting blacks the franchise but not the protective means to maintain their political right. She stated that for African Americans, the dual concepts of manhood and citizenship were embodied in the right to vote, and therefore, disfranchisement was both a political suffocation and an emasculation.

The third strand in Wells's analysis of lynching was the mobilization of racist sexual ideologies through the cry of "rape," which in actuality was a plea for revenge and an attempt to place African Americans "beyond the pale of human sympathy" (Carby 1987, 113). Rape had come to mean "any mesalliance existing between a white woman and a colored man" (Wells 1969, 11). Wells believed that the much vaunted Southern chivalry, which exalted womanhood, was a meaningless gesture that restricted itself "entirely to the women who happen to be white," though even Northern white women, as the journalist argued, had been placed outside the chivalric code when they went south to educate blacks after the Civil War (Wells 1969, 13). Wells had a bleak vision of the annihilation of the African American community being accomplished without protest. She expressed this anxiety at a convention held in Washington, D.C., where the National Federation of Afro-American Women and the National League of Colored Women merged to form the National Association of Colored Women (NACW) in 1896.

Exploding on the scene as African American women struggled to defend black womanhood against aspersions of immorality and as black male leaders failed to protect them and the black race as a whole, the clubs were an idea whose time had come with the Wells anti-lynching campaign. Under the journalist's powerful influence, black clubwomen united to abolish lynching and to "work along the lines that make women's progress" (83).

The NACW was the first social service agency for African Americans in the nation and was founded nearly fifteen years before the better-known National Association for the Advancement of Colored People (NAACP) and the male dominated Urban League. It bears mentioning that while the black women's club movement was at the front and center of the anti-lynching movement—sponsoring rallies, boycotts, petitions, and pamphlets in an effort to secure federal anti-lynching legislation—the NAACP organized its anti-lynching work along with the NACW.

Formed as the direct result of the 1908 lynching of two African Americans in Springfield, Illinois, the NAACP under leaders James Weldon Johnson (1871–1938) and Walter Francis White (1893–1955) was instrumental in keeping the exigency of anti-lynch legislation before America. During the tenures of these chief officers, the NAACP's primary strategy against lynching involved a publicity campaign backed by pamphlets, in-depth studies, and other educational activities to mobilize public support for ending the criminal mob violence. It is to be sadly noted that African American women were not offered leadership roles in the NAACP during the tenures of Walter White and James Weldon Johnson. Women's exclusion from power seats extended for several decades, beyond the association's 1909 founding. Among those women who were deprived of leadership roles within the NAACP were cofounder Ida B. Wells and the writers and intellectuals who won most of the drama prizes in *The Crisis* and *Opportunity* magazine contests sponsored between 1925 and 1927 by the NAACP and the Urban League.

The activism of the black clubwomen and the dramatists under examination demonstrates that late nineteenth and early twentieth-century black women were dedicated to both praising and uplifting the race at a time when most African Americans were thwarted by racial prejudice and economic depression. In support of the NACW's dual platform, Grimké, Johnson, Burrill, and Dunbar-Nelson wrote protest dramas that responded to the injunctions of race and gender.

They produced plays that were written to stem the sexism and the racism that pervaded the period. Their dramas all present black women who, in some way, rebelled against hierarchies of power that were based on race, class, and gender and that brutally exposed the complex systems of oppression. As prominent feminists and civil rights activists (who supported both suffrage and anti-lynch legislation), Grimké, Johnson, Burrill, Livingston, and Dunbar-Nelson created for their characters settings that mirrored the sexist and racist conditions against which women and blacks struggled. Grimké's *Rachel* (1916), for example, illustrates one way these writers combined the fight against sexism with the fight against racism. After losing a father and a brother to the lynch mobs, the protagonist, Rachel Loving—vows not to marry and have children. She rejects her suitor, assumes complete responsibility for her life, and dedicates herself to protecting her adopted son from racial violence. Rachel's refusal of marriage and maternity becomes a weapon against early twentieth-century sexism, which required female submission to male rule, and it also becomes a weapon against racism. For in refusing to bear children, Rachel deliberately fails to provide additional lynch victims.

Within the context of the anti-lynching campaign, Grimké, Johnson, Burrill, Livingston, and Dunbar-Nelson produced plays that were conceived as literary weapons for use in the battle to win social, political, and economic equality for African Americans. In specific, these dramas—which had immediate reform as their goal—were written to support the NAACP as it labored for federal anti-lynch legislation. It is noteworthy that the anti-lynching play was a genre in which African American women predominated. Literary history indicates that black women produced more dramas in this category than African American men, white women, or white men. The convention of the anti-lynching play enabled assertive African American women, like the pioneer dramatists under scrutiny, to speak out in defense of their race and of themselves at a time when their men did not. Their protest dramas—in conjunction with the lectures, petitions, and rallies of the black clubwomen activists—reflected a radical posture that was absent on the part of black male leaders such as Booker T. Washington, who evidenced a conciliatory, go-slow attitude in attaining civil rights.

In describing the characteristics of women's lynching drama, Judith Stephens writes: "All lynching plays include a focus on the threat or occurrence of a lynching incident and the impact of this incident on the characters. The lynching plays by women share additional features; for example, the home is the most common setting, and dialogue is interspersed with alternative discourse in the form of music, poetry, or prayer" (Stephens and Perkins 1998, 8). The lynching plays by African American women bear distinct ethnic hallmarks. The principal one includes a black female character who describes the lynching event to fellow characters and thereby verbally recreates an incident that plays a central role in the drama. A second hallmark of black women's lynching drama is found in the domestic setting that prominently exhibits the tools and skills of cleaning, ironing, sewing, and food preparation, which become crucial to the play's action and to the livelihood of the characters. In giving their dramas domestic environments and crafting characters who are relatives and neighbors, African American dramatists present a view of the black home as an important site of education and resistance. Another distinguishing feature of black women's lynching drama is visible in the alternative mediums that the dramatists employ, including music, poetry, and prayer. The inclusion of alternative mediums, writes Margaret Wilkerson, "help[s] to express the rage, irony, and profundity of Black American life in tonalities and colorations absent from conventional western speech" (Wilkerson 1986, 62).

This alternative medium takes the form of complete songs, such as "Slumber Boat" in *Rachel*; sections of songs, such as the hymns from the neighboring church in *A Sunday Morning in the South*; or background music, such as "Take the A-Train" in *The Bridge Party*. Prayer emerges in the form of a brief supplication in Johnson's characters in *Blue-Eyed Black Boy* and *Safe*. In *Iola's Letter*, Ida B. Wells is pictured saying grace at the Moss family dinner table and a mourner sings a solo/prayer after Thomas Moss is lynched. In the same vein, the poetry of Claude McKay and Paul Laurence Dunbar becomes an essential element of *Miss Ida B. Wells* as the playwright attempts to express, artistically, the atrocities of lynching.

A final hallmark of black women's lynching is found in a woman's telling of events. The eleven lynching plays in this study involve an African American woman describing, or re-creating through her words, a lynching incident that has taken place in the past or is presently occurring. Examples include Mrs. Loving's long, detailed, and painful speech in *Rachel* and Matilda's terse and halting, yet equally painful, "They—done lynched him," in *A Sunday Morning in the South*. These women illustrate how African American females serve as messengers relaying the tragic news or as mediums through which the lynching is revealed or re-created. Burrill's *Aftermath* employs the power of dialogue between siblings as the sister responds to her elder brother's questions about the lynching of their father. In *Iola's Letter*, Ida B. Wells leads a group of men and women from the Memphis community as they recount the events surrounding the lynching of Moss, McDowell, and Stewart. Johnson's *Safe* and *Blue-Eyed Black Boy* employ three women (mother, daughter, and friend/neighbor) as a chorus reacting from inside the home to the sights and sounds of a lynching outside. Holland's *Miss Ida B. Wells* employs two actresses (Wells One and Wells Two) who re-create a collage of lynching incidents combined with reactions of witnesses. In Seaton's *The Bridge Party*, a group of women speaking separately produce a unified, choral effect by reciting the incidents surrounding the lynching of fourteen-year-old Cordie Cheek. This esthetic quality reinforces recognition of the important role black women play in passing on vital knowledge through an oral tradition and honors the pioneering efforts of Ida B. Wells, who through her speeches, was "possibly the first person to publicly recite the horrors of lynching" (Stephens and Perkins 1998, 11).

Literary history designates the period in which Grimké, Johnson, Burrill, and Dunbar-Nelson wrote as the Harlem Renaissance—the age of the great literary and artistic explosion that occurred in black America. Much has been said and written about this celebrated era. Many of the writers who produced its great works have been justly heralded and acclaimed. Jean Toomer, Langston Hughes, Countee Cullen, and Claude McKay—for example—are authors whose names are nearly synonymous with the term "Renaissance." Concurrently, Alain Locke and James Weldon Johnson are figures whose names are identified with the leadership and the mentorship provided for the period's intellectuals and the young black writers (e.g., Nella Larsen, Eric Walrond, Rudolph Fisher, Gwendolyn Bennett, Arna Bontemps, Willis

Richardson, Helene Johnson, Zora Neale Hurston, as well as Toomer, Hughes, Cullen, and McKay) who formed the core of the Harlem group.

However repetitive and laborious, certain facts enveloping this phenomena bear noting for the significant contextualization that they provided for the movement. Scholars such as the late Nathan Irvin Huggins in *Harlem Renaissance* (1971) and *Voices from the Harlem Renaissance* (1995) along with David Levering Lewis in *When Harlem Was in Vogue* (1981) provide priceless information about this flourishing era described as "a channeling of energy from political and social criticism into poetry, fiction, music, and art" (Huggins 1973, 9). In reviewing the movement's impact, they and fellow critics acknowledged that one of the principle effects of this fecund period was made on the character of African American literature created by black authors. Moving from quaint dialect compositions and conventional imitations of white authors to sophisticated explorations of African American life and culture, Harlem Renaissance writers produced works that revealed and stimulated a new confidence and racial pride. This production of a black ethnic-centered literature owed much to the founding of African American organizations such as the NAACP (1909), the National Urban League (1910), the Association for the Study of Negro Life and History (1915), and the Universal Negro Improvement Association (1917)—all of which promoted a developing mood of racial consciousness, racial assertiveness, and protest against racism. Mention should be made that of the four organizations, Marcus Garvey's Universal Negro Improvement Association exalted Africa and unmixed African ancestry. Unlike that of his counterparts (e.g., the NAACP's W.E.B. Du Bois and Archibald Grimké), Garvey's allure was to the common African American, to whom he appealed through his newspaper, *Negro World*, established in 1918.

Other noteworthy historical factors contributed to the birth of the Harlem Renaissance and to its production of an Afrocentric literature. More particularly, the Great Migration (1910–1930) of over one million southern blacks to northern cities and the Great War (1914–1918), which introduced black soldiers to measures of dignity, brought increased money and freedom that helped to generate a race-based self-assertion. W.E.B. Du Bois's Talented Tenth—the intellectual black elite—became the era's New Negro, who shed old debasing stereotypes and who assumed a militant new face.

The famous black metropolis Harlem was the primary locus of the Renaissance because New York offered proximity to the publishing houses and facilitated opportunities for mainstream outlets that supplemented those provided by race periodicals *The Crisis*, *Opportunity*, and *Messenger*—the official journals of the NAACP, the National Urban League, and the Association for the Study of Negro Life and History, respectively. It should be noted that *The Crisis* and *Opportunity* magazines were indispensable outlets for

Harlem Renaissance writers because they provided an important source of New Negro information and sponsored literary competitions that stimulated playwrighting by black writers. Georgia Douglas Johnson, for example, won first place in the 1927 *Opportunity* contest for her folk play, *Plumes*.

The Harlem Renaissance was contemporaneous with the Jazz Age, the Lost Generation, and certain white writers (e.g., Eugene O'Neill and DuBose Heyward) who were experimenting with African American themes. Under Sigmund Freud's influence, whites became fascinated with the potential naturalness and exoticism of blacks and with the manifestations in forms ranging from Harlem street life to the racially demeaning black musicals—like Flournoy Miller and Aubrey Lyle's *Shuffle Along* (1921)—that continued the minstrel tradition and its employment of black-face comedy. This white-constructed exoticism of African Americans, however, was paralleled by the rise of talented black art geniuses such as Aaron Douglas, Sargent Johnson, Augusta Savage and Richard Barthe who infused their creations with racial dimensions.

In literature, familiar names from the preceding era graced the roster—James Weldon Johnson, W.E.B. Du Bois, and Alice Dunbar-Nelson in particular. They were joined, however, by those of the young writers who formed the core of the Harlem group. Employing the major genres of poetry, short stories, novels, and plays, these authors produced an extraordinary and diverse collection of work. In their writings, timeless topics in traditional modes contended with more daring subject matter, approaches, and techniques. This juxtaposition of generations and concepts of art led to the critical debate between the "Genteel School" and the "Bohemian School"—a discussion that consumed much attention from the movement. Yet while the Renaissance gave voice to this pressing argument, it also gave expression to history and folklore—both rural and urban—to satire, and to issues of identity and power.

The Harlem Renaissance owed much of its richness to the toil of numerous African American women, who contributed in major ways to the activity of the period. Critics Cheryl Wall, in *Women of the Harlem Renaissance* (1995), and Gloria Hull, in *Color, Sex, and Poetry: Three Women Writers of the Harlem Renaissance* (1987), augment our knowledge about the especial roles that several women—who were fortunate to have their names and achievements preserved—played in the movement. Jessie Fauset, for example, was one of the impresarios of the Renaissance (along with prominent scholars Alain Locke and Charles S. Johnson) because of her crucial position as literary editor of *The Crisis* and her intellectual evenings, which functioned as stages for cultural happenings. Indispensable behind-the-scenes support for Renaissance artists and activities was provided by two other remarkable women, Regina Anderson and Ethel Ray Nance, in particular. Nance was Charles Johnson's secretary at *Opportunity* magazine and, as such, functioned as his scout, his assistant, his clearinghouse, and his hostess. Her personal apartment was a shelter for new arrivals like Zora Neale Hurston; an informal gathering place for authors and artists like Cullen, Walrond, and Hughes; and, like Fauset's home, a forum for meetings, people, and ideas (Hull 1987, 5, 6).

In Washington, D.C., Georgia Douglas Johnson extended the list of African American women who were hostesses to the Renaissance. Johnson was especially famous for her literary soirees, which she conducted over a ten-year period (1926–1936). The following well-known passage describes a "typical" evening at one of her parties, where various Renaissance personalities gathered:

> In the living room of her S Street house behind the flourishing rose bushes, a freewheeling jumble of the gifted, famous, and odd came together on Saturday nights. There were the poets Waring Cuney, Mae Miller, Sterling Brown, Angelina Grimké, and Albert Rice. There were the artists Richard Bruce Nugent and Mae Howard Jackson. Writers like Jean Toomer and Alice Dunbar-Nelson (former wife of Paul Laurence Dunbar) and philosopher-critic Locke came regularly to enjoy the train of famous and to-be-famous visitors. Langston Hughes used to bring Vachel Lindsay; Edna St. Vincent Millay and Waldo Frank came because of Toomer; James Weldon Johnson and W.E.B. Du Bois enjoyed their senior sage role there; occasionally, Countee Cullen and, more often the suave Eric Walrond accompanied Locke. Rebecca West came once to encourage Georgia Johnson's poetry. H.G. Wells went away from one of the Saturday nights saddened by so much talent straining to burst out of the ghetto of American arts and letters. [Lewis 127]

Johnson's role as cultural sponsor was especially important because she played it in Washington, D.C., rather than in Harlem, New York. Thus, the District, under Johnson's salon-keeping, became a nexus for the intercity connections that helped to make the movement a truly national one. Poet Anne Spencer's personal involvement helped the Renaissance to flourish in an otherwise sleepy town. Putting Lynchburg, Virginia, on the cultural map, she availed her home to visiting black artists and leaders that included Marian Anderson, Roland Hayes, Georgia Douglas Johnson, Mary McLeod Bethune, the NAACP's W.E.B. Du Bois, and Walter White.

Yet even more important than the hostessing-hostelrying provided by women like Spencer and Johnson was the wealth of literature that they added to it. Monumental and prolific talents like Jessie Fauset, Gwendolyn Bennett, Zora Neale Hurston and Georgia Douglas Johnson distinguished themselves in a range of genres. Some, like Nella Larsen, Anne Spencer, and Helene Johnson, excelled in one specific form, while others, particularly the poets Clarrisa Scott Delaney and Lucy Ariel Williams, made fewer and less spectacular contributions.

Coinciding with the flowering of the black women's clubs and the anti-lynching movement, the Harlem Renaissance was, indeed, a fertile writing period for African American women. The eleven African American women who wrote between 1916 and 1930 published a combined total of twenty-one plays. Ten of their works dramatize conflicts involving race and gender. Of the eleven remaining dramas, seven foreground issues not directly related to themes of race and gender, two portray black folk life, one concerns a black warrior poet, and one depicts an African dance.

This core of writers wrote mainly protest works that targeted inconsistencies in American life. While their plays indicate that racial violence was the primary impetus for their dramatic outbursts, three other glaring social inequities propelled these authors to write. One injustice was the earlier noted mistreatment of black World War I soldiers who suffered abuse upon returning to America. Burrill was especially incensed by this wrongdoing and authenticated the hostility confronting African American veterans in *Aftermath* (1919)—which this study subsequently addresses. The economic disparity existing between African Americans and Caucasians was another evil that stimulated black women's dramatic creativity. The drastic economic discrepancy encouraged black female writers to believe that poverty was threatening to destroy the spirit of both rural and urban blacks—a destruction to which *Rachel* alludes in its presentation of black intellectuals who are denied the well-paying professional jobs for which they are trained. The last outrage that inspired black women playwrights to pen condemnatory drama was miscegenation—or as it was most commonly fleshed out—the rape of African American women by white men. Grimké's eponymous heroine Mara (Marston) experiences such a tragedy.

The black women writing for the stage at the beginning of the twentieth century—i.e., the female Harlem Renaissance playwrights—wrote under great handicap. They (and their black male counterparts) inherited the legacy of lies that the white American stage had propagated about black people since the eighteenth century. As African American dramatists, they sought to refute the white-created stereotypes, which in white minds, justified the abuse of blacks. James V. Hatch, in *The Roots of African American Drama* (1991), details some of these distortions, which serious black dramatists like Grimké, Johnson, Burrill, Livingston, and Dunbar-Nelson labored to dismantle in their plays. In surveying the historical maligning and misrepresentation of African American character, Hatch writes, "White playwrights ... corrupted the black image in diction, thought, and character" (Hatch and Shine 1974, 18). To trace the degeneracy of African American character at the hands of white dramatists is a hurtful and a repetitious process. However, a look at a few examples is necessary both to illustrate how white playwrights perverted the black image in multiple areas and to simultaneously note how these distortions have been countered by black dramatists—specifically, the ones under discussion in the present study.

Robert Mumford's *The Candidates* (1770) provides an early example of the malapropisms white playwrights forced black actors to use for one hundred fifty years. In the play, the black servant Ralpho asks his master for a new livery. The master gives Ralpho a cast-off suit of his own and the white author has Ralpho express his enthusiasm over the secondhand livery: "Gads! This figures of mine is not reconsiderable in its delurement.... The girls I'm thinking will find me desisible" (Hatch and Shine 1974, 18). By 1845, the diction of the black actor/servant had deteriorated into jibberish. In Anna C. Mowatt's *Fashion*, for example, the opening scene shows Zeke admiring his splendid new scarlet livery before Millinette, the French maid: "Dere's a coat to take de eyes ob all Broadway! Oh! Miswy, it am de fixins dat make de natural born gemman. A libery forever! Dere's da pair ob insuppressibles to stonish de colored population." To his statement Millinette replies: "Oh, oui, Monsieur Zeke, (*aside*) I not comprend one word he say!" (19).

In commenting on the racist ramifications of Zeke's fractured diction, Hatch notes that most African languages, like French, did not employ the voiced or muted *th* phoneme of English. The African substitution of a *d* for *th* as in "dere" for "there" in the eighteenth century soon became associated with slavery and ignorance. However, to American ears, Charles Boyer's French substitution of *z* for *th* in "za Casbah" sounded romantic and chic (Hatch and Shine 1974, 19).

African American dramatists acknowledge the numerous ways in which black people speak English according to their class, their region, and their social strata. Thus, when they employ dialect, black writers (e.g., Mary Burrill and Georgia Douglas Johnson) consider these factors and consequently render an authentic folk language as opposed to the mockery and derision that whites create when they write in black idiom. For example, in *Aftermath*, which is set in a backwoods cabin in South Carolina, Burrill's characters use an initial *r* but not a final one. They also use the Middle English "hit" for "it" and, to an extent, speak in a dialect that is very similar to that of backwoods whites.

White dramatists not only distorted African American character through corrupted diction, but they also misrepresented black people by denying their use of common sense. James MacCabe's *The Guerrillas* (1862) substantiates this point. An excerpt from the play shows bondsman Jerry declining the freedom Master Arthur offers him:

JERRY. Marse Arthur, yous jokin.'

ARTHUR. No Jerry. I am serious. You are free.

JERRY. (*indignant*) A free nigger? I don't want to be free.... What I want to be free for? (*with feeling*) Marse Arthur, I been in your family eber since I was born. If youse tired of old Jerry jis' take him out in de field and shoot him, don't set him free, please don't [MacCabe 1862, 17].

Another stage lie that whites told themselves about African Americans was that the blacks were cowards. Despite the fact that more than 65,000 black soldiers had died in the Civil War, whites tenaciously clung to their fantasy of the cowardly African American. An excerpt from Laura Downing's *Defending the Flag* (1894), provides evidence:

SNOWBALL. What's dat you saying 'bout Gineral Grant? Yo' ain't gwine fer to be a sojer, aire you, Marse Rob? You'se too little fer to be a sojer.

ROBBIE. And you're too big not to be a soldier, Snowball.

SNOWBALL. (*shaking*) Me—me a sojer, Marse Rob? You don't neber cotch dis chile in no battle, no sah! I'll done git my head shot off—an' den how'll I feel? [Hatch and Shine 1974, 22, 23].

To counter this particular stage mendacity, black dramatists wrote plays to demonstrate the African American's courage. Dunbar-Nelson and Burrill are only two examples of African American playwrights who depict the black male's dilemma and gallantry in fighting for America.

Concurrent with the notion of the cowardly African American character was the lie whites propagated that blacks loved them. Hatch notes that although the basis of slavery was economic, white avarice and the guilt of that avarice were softened by lies that Euro-Americans told themselves in their theaters: whites were obsessed with the notion that African Americans loved them. Blackening their faces with hog fat and burnt cork, they repeated these prevarications to themselves until they believed them (Hatch and Shine 1974, 20, 21).

Yet of all the distortions of African Americans that white-created stereotypes forced black dramatists to refute, none confounded them to the extent that the minstrel show's "stage Negro" did. The warping of African American character as epitomized in this theatrical "darky," who defined for the nation's mind the characteristics of black personality and black theatrical type, was both prodigious and permanent. He had such a deleterious effect upon the perception and the treatment of African Americans that he warrants attention for the impetus that he supplied to serious black writers who sought his effacement and for the justification that he provided whites for their persistent abuse of blacks.

A brief review of the minstrel show—America's first original contribution to the theater form and the parent that spawned this construct—is necessary to show how the stage Negro thwarted the efforts of solemn black authors like Grimké, Johnson, Burrill, Livingston, and Dunbar-Nelson, who sought to convey both realistic images of black people and real African American life to the white public. Such a discussion, however repetitive and laborious, illustrates how this darky's entrenchment in white minds prevented the plays of sober African American dramatists from being accepted and produced by commercial theaters.

The minstrel show originated on the southern plantation. Noting its (debatable) purpose, J.V. Hatch observes that while white scholars suggest that the show was presented as an entertainment for the master, African American scholars state that the singing, dancing, and improvised dialogues were staged for the slaves' enjoyment—with much of the performance material being field hand satire on the master and his house slaves.

In the course of its evolution—as black culture was simultaneously imitated and exploited—minstrelsy incorporated white performers in black face who sang and danced black music, often passing it off as their own creation. An example of such musical appropriation is evident in the case of Picayune Butler, an African American singer, who composed a song that he titled "Old Zip Coon." Upon hearing this composition, George Nichols, a white performer in Purdy Brown's Circus, introduced the song as his own work, naming it "Turkey in the Straw."

During the early 1830s, Daddy Rice, a white showman, witnessed a jump dance performed by a black youth. Rice was so impressed with the boy's creativity, that he blackened his own face and imitated the youth's dance, calling his grotesque version "Jumping Jim Crow." Rice's act became so popular that the name "Jim Crow" became synonymous for Negro.

Minstrelsy was formalized in 1842 with the antics of Dan Emmett, the alleged composer of "Dixie." During the next forty years, myriads of white men applied hog fat and burnt cork to profit from their caricature of African Americans, whose music, speech, dance, and culture they mimicked and distorted. Nathan Huggins, in *Harlem Renaissance* (1971), mirrors whites' comic and pathetic view of African Americans and provides a detailed description of their greatest distortion. In particular, this

> theatrical darky was childlike; he could be duped into the most idiotic and foolish schemes; but like a child, too, innocence would protect him and turn the tables on the schemers. His songs were vulgar and his stories the most gross and broad; his jokes were often on himself, his wife or woman. Lazy, he was slow of movement, or when he displayed a quickness of wit it was generally in flight from work or ghosts. Nevertheless, he was unrestrained in enthusiasm for music—for athletic and rhythmical dance ... he was insatiable in his bodily appetites; his songs and tales about food would make one think him all mouth, gullet and stomach.... The stage Negro went into ecstasy over succulent foods—pork, chicken, watermelon—"lipsmacking," "mouth-watering".... This caricature was ... the antithesis of the Protestant Ethic [251].

After the Civil War, several black minstrel troupes appeared, but to succeed they had to imitate their imitators, and they too blackened their faces and drew white and red circles around their mouths and eyes. Like their white counterparts, when African American minstrels blackened their faces and assumed the character of the stage Negro, they marked the distance between themselves and the antithesis of the Protestant Ethic. A case in point is seen in the performances of Bert Williams and George Walker, perhaps the most talented team of African American minstrels to entertain at the turn of the century. Attempting to exceed the limits of the theatrical darky, these actors employed the stereotype as an instrumental satire. So when they billed themselves as Two Real Coons, Williams and Walker neither portrayed themselves nor any other actual blacks. Instead, the pair rendered style and comic dignity to a fiction that white men had created and fostered (Huggins 1973, 258). In 1879, Pauline Hopkins wrote *Peculiar Sam, or The Underground Railroad* for her family's troupe, the Hopkins' Colored Troubadours; she employed the current minstrel dialect as well as song and dance to engage her audience in the serious subject of emancipation.

By the late 1880s, the minstrel tradition was losing steam, and a number of African American composers and writers turned to creating musicals and variety shows. There were two decades of black musicals. The first was ragtime—from *Clorindy; or The Origin of the Cake Walk* (1898) by Will Marion Cook and Paul Laurence Dunbar to *The Red Moon* (1909) by Bob Cole and Rosamund Johnson. The second was the jazz decade—from *Shuffle Along* (1921) by Miller, Lyles, Sissle, and Blake to *The Blackbirds* of 1928. Because minstrel imagery died hard (if at all), these African American musicals were saturated with caricatures of black people and were racially demeaning.

Extending into the mid–twentieth century, the minstrel tradition included participants such as Al Jolson, Eddie Cantor, George Jessel, Amos and Andy, and T.S. Eliot, who employed it for his play *Sweeny Agonistes*. Minstrelsy has exerted a strong influence on American culture and figures significantly in the United States Caucasian imaginary. As Eric Lott explains in *Love and Theft: Blackface Minstrelsy and the American Working Class* (1993):

> The minstrel show has been ubiquitous, ... it has been so central to the lives of North Americans that we are hardly aware of its extraordinary influence. Minstrel troupes entertained presidents (including Lincoln), and disdainful high-minded quarterlies and rakish sporting journals alike followed its course. Figures such as Mark Twain, Walt Whitman, and Bayard Taylor were as attracted to black face performance as Frederick Douglass and Martin Delany were repelled by it. From "Oh! Susanna" to Elvis Presley, from circus clowns to Saturday morning cartoons, black face acts and words have figured significantly in the white Imaginary of the United States [4, 5].

Nathan Huggins in *Harlem Renaissance* (1971) offers an explanation for this prominent figuring. Tracing the antics and speech to the white-constructed darky, he notes that the stage Negro—whose creators resisted other theatrical representations of black people—served an important function for Euro-Americans. He provided a release for the fears and insecurities of white men "who were tied up in the knots of an achievement ethic—depending ... on self-sacrifice and self-restraint" (Huggins 1973, 253). In fact, the entire theatrical darky character—from the actual face-mask with its grotesque mouth and lips and eyes, its wool for hair, the colorful and ridiculous clothing, to the actual style of song and dance—objectified and hence

> created a distance between white men's normative selves (what they had to be) and their natural selves (what they feared but were fascinated by). With such a creation, [whites] could almost at will move in or out of the black face character ... [and] find remarkable freedom behind their black masks [Huggins 1973, 254, 257].

Moreover, white freedom depended on the restriction of African Americans who were not allowed to deviate from their stereotyped character either on the stage or in real life. The stereotype, i.e., the darky mask, defined African Americans the way whites chose to perceive them. Outside the mask, the black person was either invisible or threatening. African Americans accepted its pretense and wore the mask to move in and out of white society with profit and with safety.

Because the stage Negro performed its function so well in releasing whites from their deep-seated fears and insecurities, the task of serious black writers to dismantle the darky's ensconcement in white American minds was monumental and never thoroughly achieved. Yet to mitigate his negative effects on the perception and the treatment of African Americans, black dramatists (e.g., Grimké, Johnson, Burrill, Livingston, and Dunbar-Nelson) abandoned the stage Negro and his carefree, riotous living in their plays and substituted realistic images of upright and subjugated black people. In exhibiting virtuous, but oppressed African Americans, sober black playwrights followed in the tradition of William Wells Brown (1815–1884)—the first black dramatist to inaugurate the campaign to win racial equality with his authorship of the abolitionist plays *Experience, or How to Give a Northern Man a Backbone* (1856) and *The Escape, or a Leap for Freedom* (1858). Brown's plays were never staged, but he read them publicly. Their objective, the same as that of his speeches, was to appeal for the freedom of slaves.

Like Brown, playwrights Grimké, Johnson, Burrill, Livingston, and Dunbar-Nelson used the convention of theater as an arena for advancing social change. Their plays, written to argue for the full enfranchisement of

African Americans, were unacceptable to Broadway because it preferred the racially degrading black comedies like Miller's and Lyle's *Runnin' Wild* (1924), which employed variations of the stage Negro along with ragtime, jazz, blues and the current new dances (e.g., the Cakewalk, the Charleston, the Black Bottom, and the Lindy Hop). Unable to compete with the black playwrights whose revues were presented on Broadway and whose compositions reinforced negative black stereotypes, the serious black dramatists wrote realistic plays depicting the black experience that were performed in schools, churches, lodges, and halls—sites that W.E.B. Du Bois recommended.

It bears mentioning that Du Bois's call for a black nationalist theater was issued in response to the exploitation of black talent by white promoters, who did nothing to contribute to the development of black theatrical arts (Huggins 1973, 291). As one of the foremost intellectual forces behind the Harlem Renaissance, Du Bois felt an urgent need for an authentic Negro theater—a "folk theater." His concern with the development of an independent black dramatic theater led to the creation of black folk dramas and to his organization of Krigwa Players Little Negro Theater. Though short-lived (1925–1927), this drama group was significant because it extended Du Bois's efforts and those of intellectual Charles S. Johnson to foster formal cultural production and increase readership through contests and publication in the NAACP and Urban League magazines, *The Crisis* and *Opportunity*. Georgia Douglas Johnson was one of the mainstays of Du Bois's Krigwa Players. She contributed the folk plays *Blue Blood* (1926) and *Plumes* (1927) to the theater's repertoire. In 1928, her colleague Mary P. Burrill experienced a similar honor and witnessed the Krigwa Players' production of her play *Aftermath*.

Du Bois's notion of a black nationalist theater which was "About ... By ... and Near [African Americans]" appealed to black playwrights like Grimké, Burrill, Johnson, Livingston and Dunbar-Nelson, who desired to assert the legitimacy of their vocation, to prove the quality of their craftsmanship, and to create for African American actors viable roles that were relevant and non-alienating to their talents. To varying extents, each dramatist accomplished these artistic goals while she simultaneously found a niche for her art within the convention of theater.

CHAPTER 2

Life Stories

━━━━━━━━━━━━━━━━━━━━━━━

Alice Ruth Moore Dunbar-Nelson

Alice Ruth Moore Dunbar-Nelson was born on July 19, 1875, in New Orleans, Louisiana, to Patricia Wright, a seamstress, and Joseph Moore, a merchant marine. Of white, black, and Indian ancestry, she had reddish blonde baby curls and a white complexion that enabled her to imbibe the high culture of segregationist America. Critics note that Dunbar-Nelson suffered shame about some circumstance(s) of her birth and that she looked down on darker-skinned blacks, especially if they were also less educated and less refined than their lighter-skinned counterparts.

Alice attended public school in New Orleans, Louisiana, and enrolled in the teacher's training program at Straight (Dillard) University in 1890. Upon receiving her degree in 1892, she began her career as a teacher in the public school system of New Orleans. In 1895, Dunbar-Nelson published her first collection of short stories and poems, *Violets and Other Tales*. After moving to Brooklyn, New York, where she taught at the White Rose Mission (renamed the White Rose Home for Girls in Harlem, which she co-founded), she began corresponding with the poet Paul Laurence Dunbar. Paul had initiated the correspondence upon seeing Alice's picture, which accompanied one of her poems published in the *Monthly Review* in 1897.

Alice's family evidenced strong objections to their relationship. Specifying their reservations, Virginia Cunningham (1947), an early Dunbar critic writes:

> The Moores did not approve of Paul's having scraped an acquaintance with Alice through letters; they were ashamed of his having a washwoman for a mother and of his lack of college training. Whether they said so or not, they were also ashamed of his black skin, so much darker than Alice's.... Then,

too, the family felt the usual mistrust of poets as money earners, and it is possible that they disapproved of Paul's connection with a minstrel show like "Clorindy" [172].

Nevertheless, the two married on March 8, 1898, in a secret ceremony in New York. Following her marriage, Alice moved to Washington, D.C., with her husband.

Alice continued to write and in 1899 published *The Goodness of St. Rocque and Other Stories.* Her published fiction dealt exclusively with Creole and anglicized characters rather than with African American characters and African American culture. In eschewing the plantation and minstrel stereotypes to which the reading public was long accustomed, Alice helped to create a new short story tradition and rendered Creole sketches that solidified her in the then-popular "female-suitable local color mode." Many of Alice's manuscripts and typescripts, both short stories and dramas, were rejected when she explored the themes of racism, the color line, and oppression. This rejection coupled with the fact that *Violets* and *St. Rocque* were the only published collections of her work have made it difficult for both readers and critics to access Dunbar-Nelson's work.

When Alice's marriage ended in 1902, she moved to Wilmington, Delaware, and took a position as a teacher and administrator at Howard High School. She held these dual positions until 1920. During this period, she also directed the summer session for in-service teachers at State College for Colored Students (renamed Delaware State College), taught two years in the summer session at Hampton University and taught at Howard University. Although she never saw Paul again after their volatile separation, Alice continued to publish under the Dunbar name, even after Paul died in 1906. It bears mentioning that the poetry, essays, and newspaper articles that she published while teaching at Howard High School were also all published under Dunbar's name.

In 1907 Dunbar-Nelson took a leave of absence from her teaching position in Wilmington and enrolled as a student at Cornell University, returning to Wilmington in 1908. On January 19, 1910, Alice entered into a second marriage with Henry Arthur Callis, who was twelve years her junior. She had met him at Cornell University where he was completing his bachelor's degree before going to Howard High School to teach English. Possibly ashamed of the discrepancy between their ages, Alice kept the marriage a secret. She subsequently divorced him, and Callis went on to earn his medical degree in 1921 from Rush Medical College, University of Chicago. A co-founder of Alpha Phi Alpha Fraternity, Inc., (the first one for African American men), Callis became a prominent physician and was active in civic affairs. He died on November 12, 1974. His fraternity-sponsored biography, *Henry Arthur Callis; Life and Legacy*, states that he and Dunbar-Nelson "became friends and the friendship continued until they were married" (Wesley 1977, 44). This is the sole public statement of their marriage.

Not remaining idle after her divorce from Callis, Dunbar-Nelson served as coeditor and writer for the A.M.E. Review, one of the most influential church publications of the era, and from 1913 to 1914 she published *Masterpieces of Negro Eloquence* (1919). In April 1916, Alice married her third and final husband, Robert J. Nelson, a journalist, politician, and civil rights activist. Although Alice had been active in social, political, and cultural organizations since her youth, this involvement increased around the time of her marriage to Robert Nelson. She was extremely active in Delaware and regional politics, as well as in the emerging civil rights and women's suffrage movements. In 1915, she was field organizer for the middle Atlantic states in the campaign for women's suffrage. During World War I, Alice served as a field representative of the Woman's Committee of Delaware and helped direct political activities among African American women. In 1924 she campaigned for the passage of the Dyer Anti-Lynching Bill, and from 1928–1931, she served as executive secretary of the American Friends Inter-Racial Peace Committee.

During this busy and productive time Alice published chiefly in the periodical press. "People of Color in Louisiana" *(Journal of Negro History)* in 1917 was followed by her poetry, which was published in *The Crisis, Ebony and Topaz,* and *Opportunity* magazines. Countee Cullen also included three of her most popular poems, "I Sit and I Sew," "Snow in October," and "Sonnet," in his collection of African American poets, *Caroling Dusk* (1927). In 1920, Alice edited and published *The Dunbar Speaker And Entertainer,* a literary news magazine directed toward a black audience. From 1920–1922 Alice, together with Robert Nelson, was co-editor and publisher of the *Wilmington Advocate,* a progressive African American newspaper. From this period on, Alice maintained an active career as a journalist. She was a highly successful syndicated columnist and wrote numerous reviews and essays for newspapers, magazines, and academic journals.

Alice also continued to write stories, poems, plays and novels, much of which remains unpublished. Her press publications included "The Colored United States," *(Messenger* 1924), "From a Woman's Point of View," (later, "Une Femme Dit," column for the *Pittsburgh Courier* 1926), "As in a Looking Glass" (column for the *Washington Eagle* 1926–1930), and "So It Seems to Alice Dunbar-Nelson" (column for the *Pittsburgh Courier* 1930). Like Georgia Johnson and probably Mary P. Burrill, economic conditions precluded Dunbar-Nelson from concentrating solely on her writings; however, her corpus stands as a major achievement.

Much of the private life of Alice Dunbar-Nelson has been made known through the "recent" discovery of her diary. Gloria T. Hull, Dunbar-Nelson's biographer, studied and researched the author's diary with the assistance of Dunbar-Nelson's niece, Ms. Pauline A. Young. Although a few researchers had cursorily glanced at it, the diary had never, before Hull's investigation, been thoroughly read or studied. The original has been acquired by the University of Delaware, and a microfilmed copy is a part of the Paul Laurence Dunbar Collection at the Ohio Historical Society. In its manuscript entirety, the diary consists of almost 2,000 pages of different sizes.

Written between 1921 and 1931, the diary of Alice Dunbar-Nelson is the second journal by an African American woman to be published in the United States. Charlotte Forten Grimké's *Journal*, which was published in 1953, preceded it. The core of Dunbar-Nelson's diary discloses what it means to be an educated black woman of the middle class in early twentieth-century America. In particular, the journal recounts the experiences of one privileged African American woman whose caste and Caucasian features allowed her to enjoy rights and advantages denied most contemporary African Americans.

Dunbar-Nelson maintained her diary during a period of personal turbulence. When she initiated her writing on July 29, 1921, Dunbar-Nelson was attempting to adjust to the previous year's tragedies: the termination of her teaching position and chairmanship of the English department of Howard High School; chronic financial problems; and the death of her favorite niece, Leila Ruth Young. After she stops writing on December 31, 1931, Dunbar-Nelson enjoyed a prosperous lifestyle made possible by her husband's January 1932 appointment to the Pennsylvania Athletic Commission. Dunbar-Nelson's journalizing throughout this traumatic period of her life seems to support the maxim that diaries are frequently maintained during times of calamity.

Gloria Hull provides information about the physical features of the journal. She notes that when Dunbar-Nelson begins to keep a diary, the author wrote "Bought this book for a diary." "This book" was an 8¼" × 7" bound, unlined volume with a brown cell-patterned cover (Hull 1984, 33). It was predominantly handwritten on both sides in dark ink (now faded). Occasionally Dunbar-Nelson typed on the book pages; sometimes she wrote or typed on other blank sheets and pasted these to the book pages.

In 1926 and 1927, Dunbar-Nelson kept her diary on 6" × 3½", almost tissue-thin, loose, blank sheets prepunched with three holes at the top. Dunbar-Nelson wrote, mostly in ink, although there are a few pencil entries. Her handwriting is both small and cramped. Except for three or four weeks in 1928, Dunbar-Nelson used these same 6" × 3½" sheets for 1928 and 1929. The sheets for this period, however, are mostly lined. Dunbar-Nelson continued to write in small script using ink, but sometimes she turned the pages around and typed all the way across their vertical length.

The 1930 diary was written in ink in a purple 5¼" × 4" date book. "The Standard Daily Reminder," a slightly under 7⅝" × 5⅛", faded purple, water-stained book, served as Dunbar-Nelson's diary for 1931.

Many of her entries are mechanical or journalistic, while others reflect introspective thinking. There are only two recorded instances of her rereading what she has earlier written (the anniversary of her 1930 trip to California and her 1931 birthday).

Dunbar-Nelson wrote her diary whenever she was prompted. During the first years of the journal, she constantly vowed to write daily, but she was never able to keep her resolves. Some lapses were five to ten days long; others lasted three or four weeks; and once she stopped writing altogether for two months.

The kinds of entries that she made also varied from year to year—ranging from the leisurely sentenced ones of 1921, to the choppy ones of 1926–1927, to the intense and briefly reflective entries of 1930. She writes in every one of her many moods, only confessing once, in 1931, that she deliberately refrained "when the misery and wretchedness and disappointment and worry were so close to me that to write it out was impossible, and not to write it out, foolish" (Hull 1984, 18,19).

When Dunbar-Nelson begins her chronicling, at the end of July 1921, she writes about her and Robert's battle to continue the *Wilmington Advocate*, a liberal African American newspaper they had been publishing for two years. This publication—which was financed by the Republican party and subjected to its whims as well as to the negative effects of prejudice and pow-erlessness—consumes much of Dunbar-Nelson's attention for the year 1921. She wrote editorials and compiled news items for it; she conducted fund raisers to support it; and she participated in the all-night sessions required to get the ill-fated newspaper on the street to sell by Friday afternoon. When the newspaper officially collapsed in 1922, Dunbar-Nelson suffered a loss of standing and political clout in Delaware that was tied to her association with the *Wilmington Advocate*. She also lost her coveted chairmanship of the League of Colored Women, which no longer considered her politically sig-nificant at the demise of her newspaper.

Another concern of Dunbar-Nelson in 1921 was her involvement with the Federation of Colored Women's Club. An officer in the Delaware chapter, she also participated in other states' chapter activities. One of the opening entries in Dunbar-Nelson's diary begins with the "greetings" that she gave at a Summit, New Jersey, club meeting: "State Federation Colored Women's Clubs. Left Wilmington 6:45 ... arrived Summit 11:13. Spoke in afternoon. Tired to exhaustion" (Friday, July 29). In the course of chronicling her club activities, Dunbar-Nelson characterizes the average club woman: "Mrs. S. Joe Brown is a typical club woman of affairs, and she's on my nerves. Nervous, hurried, talking always in a low incessant monotone. Kind to a fault, but indefatigable" (Tuesday, November 1).

Dunbar-Nelson was also interested in her lecture circuit during 1921. Her journal is filled with numerous pages that give details of travel, accommodating hostesses, and the towns, churches, and schools in which she lectured. Perhaps Dunbar-Nelson's greatest speaking engagement of the year was a group project that included her participation in the delegation of prominent black citizens who presented President Harding with racial concerns. Accompanied by notables such as James Weldon Johnson and Mary Terrell, Dunbar-Nelson petitioned Harding to grant clemency for the sixty-one black soldiers serving lengthy prison terms for participation in the Houston "race riot" of August 1917 (Hull 1984, 80).

As Dunbar-Nelson examines 1921, she calls it "one of the unhappiest years I ever spent" (Saturday, December 31). She chronicled this wretchedness "in full, copious, long-sentenced entries, often writing many pages on one day, at one sitting, and sometime catching up with a week or more at a time" (Hull 1984, 44). By the conclusion of 1921, Dunbar-Nelson has introduced many of the concerns that pervade the journal in subsequent years: her financial crises, her club activities, her delight in good food, and her love of pinochle.

The next portion of Dunbar-Nelson's diary begins with an entry dated November 8, 1926. No evidence exists within the writing to provide clues about the five-year lapse in her journal. External data, however, proves that in the years between 1922 and 1926, Dunbar-Nelson led a very active life.

One of her most important projects involved her leadership of the Delaware Anti-Lynching Crusaders—a group who in conjunction with the national effort—agitated for congressional passage of the 1922 Dyer Anti-Lynching Bill. This legislation aimed to curtail the widespread lynching that assailed African Americans. The defeat of this bill was instrumental in Dunbar-Nelson's defection to the Democratic party. She and many other staunch black Republicans changed parties when the incumbent Republican congressmen did not endorse the Dyer Anti-Lynching Bill that would have made lynching a crime. An entry dated Saturday, July 16, 1926, alludes to the participation of a black politician—Perry Howard—who was instrumental in helping Republican congressmen block the passage of the Bill. "Up betimes and plan for leaving Washington.... Bobbo ... tells me we are to spend the day with Perry Howard.... Mine old enemy!"

In 1924, Dunbar-Nelson became an educator and a parole officer at the Industrial School for Colored Girls—where she remained until 1928—teaching mixed-grade classes, attending court parole sessions, directing musicals and dramatic presentations and executing other tasks. In 1924 Dunbar-Nelson and Robert began a close association with the Black Elks. Alice wrote a column, "As in a Looking Glass," for the Elk newspaper, the *Washington Eagle*, which her husband managed. Because Robert's job anchored him in Washington, D.C., Dunbar-Nelson spent much of 1925 and a great deal of 1926 in a futile effort to secure a teaching position in the District of Columbia. An entry dated Wednesday, December 15, illustrates some of the inconvenience she experienced in the process. "Reach Washington by 2:15. Straight to Franklin Building to present credentials.... Such a time as I had collecting and collating them!... I am to agree to abide by decision of Board of Education on appointment, even if I pass."

In 1927, Dunbar-Nelson invested much effort scheming for the secretaryship of the Society of Friends' American Inter-Racial Peace Committee, a subsidiary of the Friends' Service Committee, aimed at promoting interracial and international peace. She especially coveted this position because it could free her from teaching responsibilities and grant her deliverance from "the Barn" at the Industrial School for Colored Girls (Thursday, May 24). Perhaps the biggest secret of Dunbar-Nelson's life is revealed this year when she cryptically alludes to her secret marriage to Henry Arthur Callis on Wednesday, January 19. "January 19, 1910–1927. This is the date, is it not.... Seventeen years we *would have* been together."

Stylistically, the 1926–27 diary entries contrast markedly with those of 1921. Dunbar-Nelson seemingly finds fewer satisfactory opportunities to write. She does not keep her journal current and lapses in 1927 for periods ranging from a few days to two months.

At the beginning of 1928, Dunbar-Nelson was still teaching at the Industrial School for Girls. But she quit the institution when the half-time American Inter-Racial Peace Committee (AIPC) offered her full-time employment. The Philadelphia location of her new job required her to commute daily from Wilmington. Dunbar-Nelson's professional antagonist became Wilbur K. Thomas, a white executive secretary of the American Friends Service Committee. His racist attitudes and remarks made Dunbar-Nelson's tenure at the workplace challenging and uncomfortable.

While working for the AIPC, Dunbar-Nelson also wrote poems, articles, and obligatory newspaper columns. Her prescient comment that her diary is "going to be valuable one of these days" suggests Dunbar-Nelson's source of motivation in maintaining her journal (Friday, September 21). In 1928, she provided interesting disclosures about family members that bear mentioning. On Thursday, April 26, she wrote, "Leila still stays at home.... Mama still devilish. Leila too fagged to do much marketing and Mama determined not to let anyone be more ill than she" (Saturday, April 28). "Leila is always happier when she is uncomfortable" (Thursday, August 16).

Overall 1928 was rather a good year for Dunbar-Nelson. She had the job of her choice and invited speaking engagements. Still, she was not completely happy, for in an entry dated Monday, December 17, she grieved her loss of social touch. "Enjoy meeting ... lots of others. All along in the back of my mind is that constant nasty nagging of my loss of social touch everywhere, save in Manhattan." People don't invite me to parties, *anywhere.* Why?"

By 1929, Dunbar-Nelson's AIPC secretaryship became very demanding—to the point of pressuring her to raise money for its programs. While she was still a member of the Industrial School Trustee Board and was participating in club activities, Dunbar-Nelson believed she was losing friends and becoming an outsider. The entry from Saturday, February 16, reflected her concern: "Bessye Bearden is cool. Someone has told her something and she is breaking with me.... I've lost both Geraldyn and her. Something wrong with me somewhere. Can't keep friends I want and can't get rid of friends I don't want."

Personally, 1930 was a more blissful year for Dunbar-Nelson, and she described the year as "one glorious fling" (Hull 1984, 341). She began the year by taking a ten-week tour sponsored by the AIPC. Dunbar-Nelson visited thirty-seven different schools and colleges, twelve YWCAs or YMCAs, seven churches, and ten clubs or teacher's organizations, and reached a total of twenty-three thousand persons.

California was the backdrop for one of the major narratives in the diary. Here she had a "romantic fling ... with Fay Jackson Robinson, a younger newspaper woman and socialite whom she met on the trip" (Hull 1984, 341). Another woman, Helene Ricks London, a water colorist, also entered the relationship that Dunbar-Nelson and Fay shared. Hull explains that "Helene and Fay were involved with each other before Dunbar-Nelson entered the picture and that both of them were passionately interested in her. This intrigue accounts for many letters, sonnets, domestic scenes, arguments, heartaches, and tears" following Dunbar-Nelson's return from her tour (Hull 1984, 342).

Professionally, Dunbar-Nelson was suffering discouragement. Nearly every extracurricular writing that she submitted was rejected. Moreover, her niece Ethel died and her mother's health disintegrated. Dunbar-Nelson was beset with suicidal yearnings and wrote: "Life *is* a mess. I am profoundly in the D's—discouraged, depressed, disheartened, disgusted. Why does one *want* to live?" (Saturday, August 2). As she assessed 1930, Dunbar-Nelson wrote that the only good thing about the year was that it "brought me California. I shall bless you for that" (Wednesday, December 31).

Dunbar-Nelson characterized 1931 as "a year of marking time" (July 19) and so it was. She waited for her Inter-Racial Peace Committee job to dissolve—and in April, it did; she and her family waited for Mama Patricia to die—a process that took a year; and she waited for Robert to secure a political sinecure, which he did in 1932. The high points of the year included Alice bobbing her hair, changing her signature to Aliceruth, and visiting Helene London in Bermuda.

Alice's diary very obviously discloses many of her private heartaches, longings, victories, and defeat. Yet, the heart of her journal exists in what it reveals, through Dunbar-Nelson's life, about the meaning of being a black female in early twentieth-century America. Perhaps the first insight into this meaning can be gleaned from a look at the impact of Alice's marriage to the eminent poet Paul Laurence Dunbar. One observes that during her whole career, Dunbar-Nelson received attention for being Paul Laurence Dunbar's wife and widow and not primarily for her own individual achievement. When Paul was alive, she was thought of as his wife who incidentally "wrote a little herself," a secondary status that she sometimes buttressed by her deferential poses and feminine role-playing (Hull 1984, 19). After Paul died and Alice remarried, she continued carrying his name to ensure the linkage with her famous spouse. Perhaps Dunbar-Nelson did so partly because she was aware that in a racist, sexist society such a linkage could be useful, and she knew that, as an African American woman, she needed as much help as she could get. Therefore, when Alice died—after two husbands and numerous accomplishments of her own—she was still called "Wife of Poet" (20).

Dunbar-Nelson's living situation also provides insight into the meaning of being an African American woman in the United States during the first three decades of the twentieth century. At the beginning, it is apparent that Dunbar-Nelson's basic living situation is that of a woman-centered household and strong female-to-female family relationships. The core consisted of Alice; her sister, Leila; their mother, Patricia; and Leila's four children, three of whom were daughters. Even though they acquired husbands and other children, these women always remained together. Dunbar-Nelson never bore any children herself, but she became the mother of two—an elder daughter, Elizabeth, and younger son, Bobby—when she married widower Robert Nelson. Alice helped to rear Robert's two children as well as Leila's four. The women's personalities complemented each other more than they clashed with them. The result was that the ladies constituted an in-house mutual support.

Dunbar-Nelson's helping relationships with the women of her family were also part of a larger system of black female support. She knew nearly all of the active and prominent African American women of her time—Nannie Burroughs, Charlotte Hawkins Brown, Jessie Fauset, Laura Wheeler, and Bessy Bearden, to list a few—and she associated with them.

Many of her eminent contemporaries were a part of the flourishing black women's club movement, which became especially visible and effective with the 1896 founding of the National Association of Colored Women. African American women of all classes united to combat negative stereotypes about themselves and to materially and spiritually aid in the overall amelioration of the race. For Dunbar-Nelson, this work included attending local executive and full membership meetings; cooperating with other clubwomen and the public to execute official duties, tasks, and projects; and planning and participating in state, regional, and national conventions. These clubwomen made impressive accomplishments in housing, education, civil rights, women's suffrage, travel accommodations, health, and cultural affairs.

The excellence of the club movement lay in the opportunity it afforded black women of an identical mindset to work together. The diary reflects this kind of racial and sororal camaraderie in Dunbar-Nelson's relationships with three particular women. The first was Edwina B. Kruse, the founding principal of Howard High School. She provided emotional and financial sustenance for Dunbar-Nelson. Dunbar-Nelson highly esteemed Kruse and in her honor wrote an unpublished novel based on Kruse's life. Entitled *This Lofty Oak*, the manuscript is 565 typewritten pages. Dunbar-Nelson continued to be attentive to Kruse even when the founding principal retired and became senile.

The second woman, Georgia Douglas Johnson, was the most popular African American woman poet of the 1920s. The diary records these two authors sharing womanly interactions—Dunbar-Nelson teaching Johnson how to wear hats, for example, and their relating to each other as sister writers. Johnson invited Dunbar-Nelson to be a special guest at one of her Washington, D.C., literary salons, and Dunbar-Nelson in return kept up with what Johnson was producing and reviewed her work. They both benefited as women and as authors from their interaction with one another.

The third woman was Mary McLeod Bethune, who although not a close personal friend of Dunbar-Nelson, served certain role-model functions (e.g., fund raiser, school administrator) for the writer. The diary presents a few scenes that include a picture of Dunbar-Nelson styling her hair while Bethune gets a pedicure at Bethune-Cookman College. It should be noted that Dunbar-Nelson extended her strength outward, for example, to the young women at the Industrial School. She bought them watches when they excelled in their lessons, advised abortions for them, and helped to see them through college.

The next aspect of Dunbar-Nelson's life illuminated by the journal is the question of class, which becomes problematic when related to the ambiguous status of African American women. Even educated, "middle class" professional black women like Dunbar-Nelson almost always came from and/or had first-hand knowledge of working class or poorer situations. In addition, being black, they enjoyed no entrenched security or comfort even in this achieved class status—and being women, their position was rendered doubly marginal and complicated. These facts, state Hull, fostered many contradictions that the diary reveals (Hull 1984, 22).

An example of such a contradiction is seen in an entry dated March 28, 1927. Dunbar-Nelson writes grimly about having to go to the pawnshop to raise $25 on her rings and earrings to pay the water bill, and then in the next paragraph, she details a "palatial" and "very fine" gathering of the Philadelphia Professional Woman's Club at which she spoke. The white women ("wives of professional men") at this affair had no idea that they were being addressed by and were socializing with a woman who had just visited a pawnshop in order to pay her water bill. Dunbar-Nelson was dressed to look like what she termed a "certified check" and was comporting herself likewise. She had the breeding, education, culture, looks, and manners of the "higher classes" (and thought of herself in this way) but as her journal shows, she had none of the money to back it up (Hull 1984, 23).

Related to this issue of class is the notion of the "genteel tradition" in African American life and literature, with its special ramifications for black women. Scholars of the early twentieth century identify two cultural strains: the genteel and the bohemian/realistic. Dunbar-Nelson belongs to the first group and is viewed as conservative, stiff, uptight, and accommodationist. This genteel stance was basically a part of the attempt to counter negative racial stereotypes and to put the best racial foot forward. For black women, additional burdens were in place. These women were always heedful of their need to be living refutations of the sexual slurs to which black women were subjected, while also being tyrannized by the Victorian cult of true womanhood that victimized their white counterparts.

Recognizing this situation may aid in understanding why Dunbar-Nelson carried herself in a manner that the *New York Inter-State Tattler* newspaper called her "distinctively aristocratic" (December, 1928). Moreover, such recognition may provide a perspective from which to view some of her less flattering utterances and attitudes—i.e., her refusing to ride in a car with the printer's wife and "Taylor Street friends," her describing a poor black high school graduation ceremony as "very monkey," and this November 6, 1929, characterization of the president of the National Federation of Colored Women: "Sallie Stewart is a fine woman. But she offends my aesthetics. Fine woman in the sense of achievement—hopelessly, frightfully, common-place, provincial, middle class."

The truth of the matter (that is the other truth of the matter) observes Hull (1984), is that Dunbar-Nelson was a genuine down-to-earth person who, when she allowed herself, enjoyed all kinds of people and all kinds of activities. She drank bootleg whiskey, "played the numbers," bought "hot" clothes, had friends whom she dubbed "rough-necky," went to Harlem dives, and indulged what she called a "low taste" for underworld films and S.S. Van Dine novels. However, one would not have guessed any of this by her appearance (23).

Dunbar-Nelson's diary also underscores a complex duality in the area of love and sexuality. Dunbar-Nelson's marriage to Robert was apparently characterized by strong mutual respect. The two were partners and friends in life. Robert had conventional male attitudes (he liked Alice to be home when he ran in, and he scolded her for looking like a charwoman—even while she was cleaning the house), and he was jealous and rather possessive. On September 21, 1928, for example, Dunbar-Nelson wrote, "He was cross, of course, as he always is, when I show any interest in any male or female." Nevertheless, Robert admired and encouraged Alice. And she in turn felt, "I have a lot to be thankful for Bobbo, first, last and always, the best of all" (Thanksgiving 1930).

As earlier noted, prior to marrying Robert, Dunbar-Nelson secretly married Henry Arthur Callis, who was twelve years her junior. Callis affords the occasion in the journal for Dunbar-Nelson to muse about her former loves: "[Leaving him] ... I walked slowly home through the beautiful streets thinking after all, love and beautiful love has been mine from many men, but the great passion of at least four or five whose love for me transcended that for other women—and what more can any woman want?" (June 4, 1931).

Dunbar-Nelson's diary indicates that she wanted much more, and she wanted her fulfillment with women. Gloria Hull points out that the diary shows at least three emotionally and physically intimate relationships Dunbar-Nelson shared with women. Her journal explicitly records two lesbian relationships, the more profound being with Faye Jackson Robinson, a Los Angeles newspaperwoman and socialite. Dunbar-Nelson was ecstatic about their touching and commemorated their joy in a sonnet, which began: "I had not thought to open that secret room" (Thursday, March 20, 1930). And despite the misunderstandings, miscommunications, and disappointments Dunbar-Nelson experienced at the hand of Robinson, she still sighed in her diary on March 18, 1931: "Anniversary of My One Perfect Day.... And still we cannot meet again."

That the duality in Dunbar-Nelson's sexuality was representative of that experienced by many of her counterparts is substantiated by the existence and operation of an active black lesbian network of which she speaks in her diary. Dunbar-Nelson mentions that a friend of hers (Elizabeth Stubbs) tells her to "look over a Betty Linford," and that a "heavy flirtation" between two clubwomen friends of hers puts her "nose sadly out of joint" (July 25, August 1, 1928). All of these clubwomen were prominent and professional— and most had husbands and/or children. Yet somehow, they contrived to be themselves and to carry on these relationships in an extremely repressive context—with even more layers of oppression piled on by the stringencies of their roles as African American women (Hull 1984, 25).

Equally crucial for Dunbar-Nelson were the conditions and struggles of the workplace. Perhaps the most graphic revelation of what it meant to be an African American woman on the job emerges from her work with the Inter-Racial Peace Committee. Here, her white male boss questioned her executive ability and even complained about her lipstick. The Quaker board that controlled her committee also gave her a hard time, receiving her reports in silence, failing to attend her events, and begrudging the $2,000 it would have cost to keep her black-oriented program in operation while it squandered large sums of money on other projects. In addition, there were such incidents as the Quaker woman who came into the office and (not knowing Dunbar-Nelson's race because of her fair complexion) inveighed against blacks in her presence (Hull 1984, 26).

The final area of discussion focuses on what the diary reveals about Dunbar-Nelson as an African American woman writer and public figure. Fortunately for Dunbar-Nelson's posthumous reputation, she flourished throughout the Harlem Renaissance. During the height of the Renaissance, her poetry (some of which had been written earlier) was consistently published—even though Dunbar-Nelson, strictly speaking, did not belong to the group of bold, young, experimental poets and did not achieve new popularity or refurbish her basically traditional style. As a credentialed, older contemporary, she enjoyed the respect of the younger writers and was sent copies of their books and asked to judge contests. However, like many of the women writers of the period, her position as author was adversely affected by her themes and style and certainly by her gender, which automatically excluded her from male circles of prestige and power (Hull 1984, 29). It should be noted that when Dunbar-Nelson needed employment most, she was unable to find it with either *The Crisis* or *Opportunity* magazines.)

Journalism occupied most of Dunbar-Nelson's time; but none of her attempts at film scenarios, short stories, and a novel was successful. The screenplays did not suit the film companies, and the novel, a satirical one entitled *Uplift*, was damned by the author herself as "inane, sophomoric, amateurish puerility" (June 16, 1930).

Seen in relation to her other literary work, Dunbar-Nelson's diary may be the most significant and enduring piece of writing that she produced. Its revelations about African American culture and about women's existence is priceless. Her diary provides private glimpses of public figures and inside reports of major events. For example, a 1927 entry gives readers a view of Dunbar-Nelson and stellar scholar W.E.B. Du Bois cooking breakfast at Johnson's home; but the diary also affords a view of numerous national African American conventions, such as the research conference held in

Durham, North Carolina, in December 1927 and the annual assembly of the NAACP. Moreover, the diary shows that at one point, Dunbar-Nelson and Carter G. Woodson, founder of the Association for the Study of Negro Life and History, were collaborating on researching and writing a book.

In 1932, Alice moved from Delaware to Philadelphia when Robert Nelson took a position as member of the Pennsylvania Athletic Commission. By this time Alice's health had begun to decline, and she was frequently ill. In September 1935, she was admitted to the hospital with a heart ailment from which she did not recover. On September 18, 1935, Alice Dunbar-Nelson died at the age of sixty. She left behind a journal that is, indeed, invaluable in its revelations about black culture. As Gloria Hull (1984) states, it should force a radical assessment of the generalizations society has become accustomed to accepting as truth about black women writers during the early twentieth century (31, 32).

Angelina Weld Grimké

Angelina Grimké's (1880–1958) heritage has become the subject of recent scholarly attention. In *Archibald Grimké: Portrait of a Black Independent* (1993), Dickson D. Bruce, a noted Archibald Grimké specialist, augments what is known about the writer's family history and sheds important light upon relatives whose lives and legacy influenced the literature that Angelina produced. Highly significant to the writer's fiction are Nancy Weston—her slave grandmother and the likely prototype for her loving maternal characters—and Sarah Stanley, Grimké's mother, whose desertion may be a possible cause for Angelina's excessive attachment to women.

A member of the biracial Grimké family, Angelina was born in Boston, Massachusetts, on February 27, 1880, to Sarah E. Stanley, the daughter of a white Methodist minister from Ann Arbor, Michigan, and Archibald Henry Grimké, a mulatto former slave. Angelina's paternal great grandfather John Faucheraud Grimké had been a colonel in the Revolutionary War and a justice of the South Carolina State Supreme Court. A wealthy and notoriously cruel slaveholder, he married Mary Smith, the daughter of one of the richest bankers in the Charleston vicinity. The couple produced fourteen offspring, including Grimké's great aunts, Sarah Moore and Angelina Emily, two famous fighters for abolition and women's rights. Angelina Emily married the abolitionist minister Theodore Dwight Weld. Grimké's father was the eldest of three sons born to Henry Grimké, a lawyer and eminent South Carolina planter, and Nancy Weston, Henry's biracial slave.

Little is known about Weld Grimké's paternal grandmother. She was related to many of the free people of color in Charleston's free African American elite community. Possessing both the mindset and the values of this aristocratic class, she was the embodiment of black womanhood at its finest and the fundamental source of the strict upbringing that Angelina would inherit. Nancy's date of entrance into the Grimké household is uncertain, as are the date and the origin of her relationship with Henry.

At one point, she worked as a nurse to Henry's wife, Selina, and to their three children: Montague, Thomas, and Henrietta, half-siblings to Archibald and half-uncles and aunt to Grimké. Nancy was a strong presence in the master's home. She assumed much of the responsibility for child-rearing and was so powerful in the Grimké family that she once threw Henry to the floor, when at Selina's orders, he threatened to whip her (Archibald H. Grimké Collection). Upon Selina's death in 1843, Weston remained in the household and continued to tend the Grimké children and Henry. In one letter, Montague notes that when he and Thomas were students at the Citadel, Nancy fashioned and forwarded gifts to them. Moreover, she relayed news to the boys—despite her illiteracy—through Henry's letters (E. Montague Grimké Collection).

Shortly after 1847, when Nancy was in her thirties and Henry was in his mid-forties, Henry abandoned his urban law practice and became a planter. He purchased the rice plantation Cane Acre and a work force of thirty slaves. Having sent his children away to school, he relocated to Cane Acre's Colleton County with Nancy where the couple remained to manage the estate and to start their own family. Weston played a crucial role in the general operation of Cane Acre. Many years later she told Archibald that she pretty much ran things on the Grimké estate (Archibald H. Grimké Collection). One letter in the Archibald Grimké Collection recounts an instance when Nancy exerted her influence over Henry and persuaded him to countermand an order made by the plantation overseer. The result was that, at Nancy's urging, Henry canceled the overseer's directive to deny the slaves their traditional off-day (Archibald H. Grimké Collection).

During some point, Nancy assumed the Grimké surname for herself and for the three sons Henry fathered: Archibald (b. 1849, whom Henry named), Francis (b. 1850), and John (b. 1852). Perhaps Weston's adoption of the Grimké name was her attempt to seize respectability for herself and legitimacy for her children. As Henry's mistress, she was permitted to enjoy limited privileges. In particular, she was allowed to live with her sons in her own private home and to enjoy the right of proprietorship. Records indicate that she owned chickens, ducks, and pigs.

However benevolent Henry may have occasionally been to Nancy and to their biracial children (e.g., he nursed Nancy continuously during her two-week fever using "practice, little physic and a plenty of starvation," and he did not list their sons as slaves in the 1850 census of slaves on Cane Acre), he did not share his abolitionist sisters' racial enlightenment and racial toleration (Archibald H. Grimké Collection). Notorious for being a cruel slave master, he perpetrated grave barbarities against his slaves. An incident from the late 1820s illustrates his great brutality. It concerned his incessant acts of atrocity against his manservant John. When his sister Angelina confronted him about his savageries against the bondsman, Henry increased his violence toward the slave. Throughout his life, Henry remained strongly attached to slavery and to white supremacy. He specified his racist views in a letter to Montague wherein, after professing his faith in the doctrines of equality proclaimed in the American Declaration of Independence, he added, "These remarks apply exclusively to the Caucasian race" (E. Montague Grimké Collection).

Grimké would have been aware of her grandfather's racist sentiments and of how he maintained them despite his liaison with Nancy. Moreover, she would have known that the privileges her grandmother enjoyed were the spoils of an immoral and degrading union. Perhaps she was mindful of her grandmother's violation and of Nancy's precarious status as a black woman when she created the morally chaste female Marston characters who were raped by the white lascivious Carewe men.

At Henry's death, the black Grimké's lost their privileged political status. Their declining political standing was based on key events in the family, which began in the early 1850s. When Henry died in 1852, he did not emancipate the black Grimkés. Instead, he passed the ownership of Nancy and her children to Montague, who allowed them to live as quasi-free slaves (legal bond servants who lived essentially free lives) until 1860. In that year, when South Carolina seceded from the Union, Montague returned Nancy and her sons to slavery. While Nancy was "thrown upon the uncharitable world to struggle with its foaming billows alone," Archibald, Francis, and John became house slaves to Montague, who upon occasions, either severely beat them himself or ordered their brutal floggings to be administered at the infamous workhouse (Archibald Henry Grimké Collection). Archibald endured his brother's cruelty until 1862, the year he escaped from slavery, dressed in girl's apparel. Never to return to bondage, he remained a hiding fugitive for three years. In February 1865, when South Carolina fell, he emerged a free young man (Archibald H. Grimké Collection).

Due to Nancy's painstaking efforts, Archibald entered the newly freed South as a literate man. Through an industriousness anticipating that of Grimké's maternal characters, Nancy had washed and ironed for several local hotels and had earned the monthly dollar necessary to pay for the Grimké brothers' education. Her wages had enabled them to attend antebellum Charleston schools for the free black elite, with whom she had encouraged strong class and skin color-based ties. Recounting her father's early education in a biography written more than half a century later, Grimké wrote: "Before the Civil War, the three brothers learnt their 'Three Rs' in a sedate little school conducted by some white southern gentlemen of Charleston for the children of free colored people" (*Opportunity* 45). Eventually, Archibald and Francis attended Pennsylvania's Lincoln University—the pivotal site where they encountered their celebrated aunt Angelina—whose public acknowledgement of her nephews radically transformed their lives.

Dickson Bruce recounts the well-known circumstances leading to this noteworthy meeting with their sixty-three year old aunt. The scholar states that in February 1868, Angelina Emily Weld Grimké was in her Boston home reading an issue of the *National Anti-Slavery Standard* when she came upon "Negroes and the Higher Studies," an article quoting Edwin R. Bower and reprinted from the Boston *Commonwealth*. Seeking to disprove black inferiority, Bower referred to his own experiences teaching black students at Lincoln, comparing them favorably with "any class I have ever heard." He concluded by singling out one of the participants "by name of Grimkie, who came here two years ago, just out of slavery" (*National Anti-Slavery Standard*, *XXVIII*, February 8, 1868, [2]).

Despite the misspelling of the surname, Angelina Emily could not miss its similarity to her own. She initiated a correspondence with Henry's sons and shortly acknowledged Archibald and Francis as her nephews—whose welfare she vowed to ensure. In June, 1868, Angelina Emily and her son Charles Stuart Weld met with Archibald and Francis at Lincoln's commencement exercise in the presence of University President Rendall and other prominent people (Archibald H. Grimké Collection). Thereafter, Angelina Emily honored her vow, opening her home to and ultimately financing her nephews' education.

It is a certainty that Nancy Weston's inculcation of strong moral, spiritual, and intellectual values (reminiscent of those instilled by Grimké's maternal characters in their children) facilitated her boys' "adoption" by their powerful relative. Many years later as the spokesperson for her family, Grimké paid tribute to her grandmother in a "pen picture":

> I knew her for the only time, the last year of her life (she lived to be eighty four) and though I was a child, then, I can remember her perfectly. She spent her days, sitting in a large rattan rocker in her sunny room on the second floor back of my uncle's Washington home. She moved about seldom and then with the greatest effort, leaning on a cane; but there was something unconquerable, indomitable in that bent, gaunt body and in that clean-cut, eagle-like face. If she yielded to age it was only inch by inch. Her keen old eyes could flash and I never heard her speak in uncertain tones.... Sometime, somewhere, that spirit must have lived in the body of a great queen or an

empress. How else explain her? But the most beautiful thing about her was her motherly love [Angelina W. Grimké, "A Biographical Sketch of Archibald H. Grimké," *Opportunity III* (February 1925)].

While Nancy carefully groomed the character of her sons to attract success, the funding and the connections of aunt Angelina Emily secured it. With her support, Archibald graduated from Harvard Law School and became in 1874 the second African American to receive an LLB. A distinguished lawyer, diplomat, author, and editor, Archibald was also a prominent race leader. He served as president of the Washington, D.C., branch of the National Association for the Advancement of Colored People for ten years and as vice president of the national organization. He also provided leadership for the American Negro Academy, serving as its president from 1903 to 1916.

Aunt Angelina's Hyde Park home in Massachusetts, which she shared with her husband Theodore Weld, the prominent abolitionist minister, became the place where Archibald and Francis met many eminent people. It was here that the Weld couple introduced their nephews to the "Boston clique," which included the abolitionists and feminists William Lloyd Garrison, Gilbert and Parker Pillsbury, Lucy Stone, Charles Sumner, Wendell Phillips, Elizabeth Peabody, Frederick Douglass, Lewis Hayden, and Judge Sewall—all of whom substantially influenced the brothers' philosophies and careers.

It was perhaps through these Boston friends that Archibald met the white Boston University student Sarah Stanley. An examination of this important figure—as expressed in her behavior during her courtship, marriage, and divorce from Archibald—reveals an unstable woman who undermined the emotional and psychological well-being of her child. Perhaps it was Sarah's dereliction of her daughter that contributed to Grimké's insatiable craving for female intimacy and to her thwarted sexuality, which severely restricted her literary canon.

Approximately Archibald's age and also from an anti-slavery background, Sarah defied the wishes of parents and friends with her engagement and marriage to Archibald. Her father, the Rev. M.C. Stanley, was a strong advocate of racial equality, but he drew an inexorable line at interracial marriages—especially when they involved his family. The Reverend Stanley was so incensed with his daughter's engagement that he wrote letters of disapproval to the couple. Referring to their engagement, he wrote Archibald that he had "some misgivings in this case" and that he wished that he and Mrs. Stanley had been "consulted" earlier (Archibald H. Grimké Collection). However in a separate letter to Sarah, he was vitriolic in his criticism of her impending "mixed" union. He initially accused her of succumbing to the influence of the Boston "Unitarians," who had encouraged their wedlock.

Angered by their impact on Sarah's decision, Stanley remarked that her plans had "filled our hearts with mourning" (Archibald H. Grimké Collection). He then inquired how Sarah thought those same "Unitarian" friends might feel should it be one of their own daughters who stood on the brink of a mixed marriage. Finally he declared: "We look upon it as a sad day ... when you went to Boston and especially when you associated yourself with the deniers of Christ and the insane theorisers of that infidel city" (Archibald H. Grimké Collection). Apparently M.C. Stanley promoted racial equality, but he did not tolerate interracial marriages—especially those involving his family.

Ignoring the advice of her and Archibald's long-time friend Lucy Stone, Sarah married Archibald on April 19, 1879, in the Beacon Hill residence of the Welds' friend Mrs. Charles C. Curtis, where Pastor C.A. Bartol, a radical Unitarian minister officiated. Attended by only a few guests, the ceremony resulted in a union that tells a desolate story of interracial marriage. Yet their marriage warrants attention for what it shows about the formative years of Grimké, who would forever crave maternal love and would share an extremely close and powerful bond with her father.

Records indicate that initially the marriage was blissful and that their daughter's birth, which occurred ten months later on February 27, 1880, enhanced it. The proud and happy parents named their child Angelina, "Nana," in memory of Archibald's beloved aunt who died in October 1879. The couple's joy, however, was short-lived, for two years later in June 1882, Sarah left her husband with her daughter in hand. Ostensibly, mother and child left to join the Stanley family in Michigan for a summer vacation on Mackinac Island. Their summer visit, however, turned into a full year, and in May 1883, Sarah was requesting Archibald to ship her and Nana a trunkful of clothes and books.

It is interesting to speculate why the marriage failed. Perhaps Sarah had only married Archibald to deliberately outrage her family. And when the novelty of having an African American husband expired, the pressures attendant to their biracial union proved too intense and too insurmountable. Another reason could be due to Archibald's involvement with a paramour. That he was seeing another woman (in *some* capacity) is suggested by a letter Sarah wrote to him about eighteen months following her departure from their home. Warning Archibald she writes, "The one you call your good fairly is your evil genius, in that she prompts you to seek fame & power instead of Peace and Good-will" (Archibald H. Grimké Collection).

Archibald tried unsuccessfully to negotiate his wife's return. In the initial aftermath of their separation, Sarah's primary anxiety was that he might interfere with her custody of Nana. Exhibiting a maternal concern that was to disappear three years later, she wrote Archibald from Detroit, "I wish to be assured that you fully relinquish your claim to her person and freely trust her care and education in my hands." Sarah noted that Nana was "a child of unusual promise," whom a mother could bring up best (Archibald H. Grimké Collection). To secure her guardianship of Nana, Sarah also demanded guarantees that Archibald would not endeavor to kidnap their child from her, and on that condition, she allowed him to visit Angelina and to periodically let her stay with him. Archibald reluctantly agreed to Sarah's terms, and Angelina remained in her mother's and grandparents' care. In view of Sarah's subsequent abandonment of Nana, the extreme maternal anxiety herein displayed seems incredulous and suggests an unstable temperament on Sarah's behalf. Such a temperament was to replicate itself in Nana, as the child's developing character would illustrate.

After her separation from Archibald, Sarah was besieged with health and career problems. She had been sickly throughout the marriage (as her daughter would be throughout her life) and did not improve upon its dissolution. As an ailing single parent, Sarah found it difficult to give Nana the attention she deserved. And her budding career, in progress by 1884, compounded the problem of properly caring for Nana. It was during this time that Sarah began to teach correspondence courses on the theory that physical illnesses and personal difficulties were susceptible to psychological solutions. Perhaps Sarah's instruction in this discipline provided her with one means to deal with some of her personal problems that she experienced during this period. As an outgrowth of her interest in this subject, she published her works *Personified Unthinkables: An Argument Against Physical Causation, and First Lessons in Reality, or, The Psychical Basis of Physical Health* (1886). Here, Sarah's vocation as teacher/author anticipates that of her daughter who would also become an educator/writer. Eventually, Sarah—as would Angelina—became well-known in her field and began to travel fairly extensively.

While addressing the pressures stemming from her health and from her career, Sarah also sought to resolve the most urgent one that resulted from her daughter's race and its attendant domestic and social difficulties. To this purpose, on April 25, 1887, she wrote Archibald the following letter in which she relinquished all responsibility for the child whom she insisted upon rearing three years earlier:

Dear Archie;

Within the past few weeks I have been obliged to suspend all work and I now realize that ... I am quite reconciled to resign her to you.... She is really much more like you than myself and you can control her better than I have been able to do ... just now I am both physically and mentally unfit to have the care of her at all....

My own family, kind and anxious as they are ... do not give her the love she requires to make her good and happy.... It is almost impossible for her to be happy with me ... because she is now getting old enough to see and feel the thoughts of others, which the difference in race and color naturally engender regarding her. My present plan is to send her on to you by express from St. Louis or Cleveland. I will telegraph to you the moment she starts so there will be no mistake, and this letter will reach you a few hours ahead of her [Archibald H. Grimké Collection].

Sarah kept her word, and in a few days after communicating her intentions, she shipped her young unaccompanied daughter on a train from California to Boston. William Drake observes that Sarah's nerves had collapsed under the strain of facing a white world with her black daughter, and for this reason she returned her child to the husband she had deserted five years earlier (Drake 1987, 20). On Sarah's behalf, it could be said that clearly she held on to Nana as long as she could, despite the Stanley's (and society's) cool treatment of her child. However, fearing that her family would disown her because of her daughter's race, and cognizant of contemporary divorce laws and racist conventions, Sarah did what was expedient in relinquishing Angelina.

Grimké appears to have never forgiven her mother for rejecting her, but in her literature, she assigned all her female characters loving mothers or mother surrogates, attempting, perhaps to repress the pain of her abandonment. The protagonists Rachel Loving and Mara Marston of the plays bearing their names are two examples of Grimké's heroines who experience the affection of doting mothers. In their tenderness, these maternal characters suggest that Grimké revered motherhood, despite her motherlessness and her rift with the one woman she most needed. Grimké articulates her maternal reverence through Rachel Loving who exclaims: "I think the loveliest thing of all the lovely things in this world is just being a mother" (Grimké 1974, 143). Though Grimké never married or bore children, she focused on the theme of maternity—specifically the precariousness of black maternity in many of her works. Grimké's own mother eventually moved to San Diego where she committed suicide in August 1898, having ingested poison. Her works were collected in a posthumous volume, *Esoteric Lessons*, and were published in 1900. Upon Sarah's death, her estate went to Nana, as she had promised Archibald it would. However, the amount, after medical and funeral expenses were deducted was $32.70, a sum that Archibald returned to M.C. Stanley (Archibald H. Grimké Collection).

Angelina was eighteen years old when she received news of her mother's death in a letter written to her by Emma Austin Toller, Sarah's sister. Aunt Emma wrote, "She was hoping to see you once more ... and was trying so hard to make a little house to which you could come and visit. She never ceased to love you as dearly as ever and it was a great trial to have you go away from her, how great God alone knows; but it was the only thing to do" (Angelina Weld Grimké Collection). Nana conveyed the news of her mother's death in a letter to her father, who was just then completing a four-year term as American consul to the Dominican Republic. Archibald acknowledged Sarah's death in a casual sentence at the end of a cheerful, newsy letter, inadvertently giving the impression that he and Angelina had long since turned their backs on a woman who had permitted social racism to destroy bonds of love that should have grown stronger under strain (Drake 1987, 21). Indeed, Sarah's dereliction of her daughter produced devastating effects on Grimké. Robbed of important family female networks of support, she understandably formed fast and passionate relationships with women who accepted and affirmed her. That such friendships might have occasionally developed into love relations will be seen in Grimké's association with Burrill.

Angelina had shared her father's world since she was abandoned at seven and was seemingly contented there—even though it was not the African American sphere to which her mother had consciously relegated her. Unlike Georgia Johnson, Mary Burrill, and Alice Dunbar-Nelson, whose white relatives did not appear to acknowledge or accept them, Angelina became a part of the prominent Weld circle, regularly staying in the Weld home when her father had to be away. Nana's position in the Weld family became so entrenched, that in his will Theodore "assigned a bequest to 'my nephew,' Archibald Grimké, for the education" of Angelina. At his death in 1895, Weld left Archibald eighty-seven shares of stock in an insurance company, worth five dollars a share, to help provide for Angelina's future needs (Lerner 1967, 365).

Thus, from the outset, Angelina was well connected and financially well endowed. Unlike her colleagues Johnson, Burrill, and Dunbar-Nelson, she was never to experience financial hardships which handicapped her literary production, and she was never compelled to apply for literary grants or fellowships. Her wealth enabled her to attend prestigious white schools in Massachusetts that included Fairmount School in Hyde Park, the Cushing Academy in Ashurnham, the Boston Normal School of Gymnastics and Carleton Academy at Northfield Minnesota. In general, as an elementary school pupil, she excelled in grammar, history, and spelling and participated in various school activities, once dancing in a May Day's children's program. In 1894, she was described by the local Norfolk County *Gazette* as "well-known" in the community (Angelina Weld Grimké Collection).

During these student years, Nana initiated her literary career, writing at twelve her tribute to Theodore Weld, which she delivered on his ninetieth birthday celebration. The following year she published her first poem, "The Grave in the Corner," a sentimental saga of a young woman's mourning for her beloved soldier, in the May 1893 *Norfolk County Gazette*.

Nana continued her education under the guardianship of her famous uncle and aunt, the Rev. Francis Grimké and his diarist wife Charlotte Forten in Washington, D.C.—when Archibald began his American consulship in Santo Domingo. In Charlotte (1837–1914), Angelina had an important literary role model, who was both a poet and the only African American woman besides Alice Dunbar-Nelson to have a book-length journal published in the United States. Charlotte had married Francis late in life and was twelve years his senior. She became an important mother figure in Angelina's life after Archibald and Sarah separated. Having lost her own infant daughter (Theodora Cornelia) when she was 43, Charlotte might have redirected her maternal drive toward Nana. To this possible purpose, she provided Angelina and later Archibald with room and board during her student and adult years.

While Angelina and her aunt shared a mutual love—and at Charlotte's death Nana wrote her finest elegy "To Keep the Memory of Charlotte Forten Grimké"—the relationship was not without its strain. In a diary entry on October 24, 1909, for example, Nana complained about the trouble "Lottie" gave her when Francis was away, mentioning such conflicts as their arguments about who will start the fires: "Things she never dreams of doing while he is here she does when he is not. She gets real sprightly." (Angelina Weld Grimké Collection). Like her mother Sarah Stanley, Angelina was willful and rebellious; and because of these traits, her residency with Aunt Lottie and Uncle Frank was brief.

Exasperated by Nana's misconduct, Charlotte wrote to Archibald that she could not care for his daughter another year. Lottie noted that Washington had been a bad influence on Angelina who should go somewhere else. In returning Nana to her father's care, Charlotte became the second "mother" to desert Angelina.

Yet perhaps Nana's intractableness in her aunt's home becomes significant in view of the disclosure that Francis made at Archibald's death, when he revealed that throughout her life Nana had been jealously and unsuccessfully trying to come between the two brothers. This revelation suggests that Angelina's deliberate contrariness in Charlotte's household might have been simply part of her continuous ploy to sever the close fraternal tie which the Grimké brothers shared (Francis J. Grimké Collection).

Nana's misconduct in her uncle's house generated her father's ire. In response, Archibald wrote her that she could only blame herself for the decision he was forced to make, namely that of sending her away from Washington and from her friends. He remarked, "I had hoped against hope that you would disappoint this dread of mine & prove your self in every respect worthy to live in such a city as Washington, that you would try to be a comfort & joy in the home of your uncle & aunt. I know now that you have been neither." Ending his letter in frustration, he encourages Angelina to adopt new goals: "All I want you to do now is to turn over a new leaf in your dear young life & begin a noble chapter of achievement in every good thing & work, & of conquest of self" (Angelina Weld Grimké Collection).

Angelina did not immediately follow her father's advice. In fact, during much of his consulship she remained a lackadaisical student, excelling one semester and doing mediocrely the next. By 1899, she exhausted him with her scholastic underachievement. When he threatened to withdraw her from school, promising to "put you to learn some trade instead," she radically improved her performance in school (Angelina Weld Grimké Collection). She evidenced enough progress to satisfy her demanding father and graduated from the Boston Normal School of Gymnastics in 1902. That same year Grimké moved to Washington, D.C., and taught physical education at the Armstrong Manual Training School. However, dissatisfied with teaching gym, she changed to English, and in the process precipitated much controversy. She had prepared for the change in subjects by taking summer courses in English at Harvard from 1901 to 1910.

A recap of Grimké's 1907 embroilment shows that Armstrong principal Dr. W.B. Evans bore a grudge against Angelina and used his authority to give her bad performance evaluations. He stated that she had been hired to teach physical education but was, through covert maneuvering, changed to English. Denying Grimké a salary increase, Evans added that she was "unfitted by attitude to teach in a school of this kind" since she personally disliked industrial education (Angelina Weld Grimké Collection). Archibald was very supportive throughout this ordeal and encouraged Angelina to transfer to the college-preparatory M Street School. He suspected that part of the principal's harassment of Angelina was a way to target himself, because of his professional and societal position, which invited envy. It could have been also that as a biracial woman from a privileged family, Angelina was singled out and labeled with an "unfortunate temperament." Although Evans scheduled her for dismissal, he was unable to prevent Grimké from being hired at the Dunbar High School, as the M Street High School was renamed.

After Angelina's transfer from Armstrong in 1907, her evaluations radically improved, indicating perhaps, that she was better qualified to teach at an academic institution rather than at a vocational one. Her challenges with school administrators continued, however, at her new school. In a diary entry dated September 21, 1909, she records feeling "a trifle humiliated" because she was moved from second year English to first year English with the exception of a "IIa English" and expected that she might even have to do clerical work (Angelina Weld Grimké Collection). At her new school, she assigned her classes essay topics that included "My First Love," "On Being Colored," and "Vanity" (Angelina Weld Grimké Collection). She taught at Dunbar until 1926 when injuries she sustained from a 1911 train crash forced her to retire from teaching at age 46.

Grimké lived in D.C. until 1930, when she was 50 years old. While living in the nation's capital, her correspondence was sent to 1526 L Street NW and 1415 Corcoran Street NW. It was in the nation's capital that Grimké produced some of her better known writings, as she wrote in concert with the cadre of African American scholars, authors, and artists who were also there. She wrote 173 poems of which 31 were published in African American literary journals. The primary themes of her prose and drama focus almost exclusively on lynching and on the burdens of black maternity.

In her short stories "The Closing Door" (1919) and "Goldie" (1920), Grimké combines these themes in an effort to jar white readers into the realization of the devastating effects of their racist violence on black family life. Both stories were published in the *Birth Control Review* and were perceived as recommending childlessness to the black community. The protagonists of these stories dearly love children and yearn to bear them. However, they forswear motherhood in order to safeguard the lives of unborn children from lynchings, which have claimed the lives of relatives and friends. "The Closing Door" was originally used as an early draft of *Rachel*, but Grimké removed it from the play and made the story a separate work. "The Closing Door" draws attention to infanticide as the ultimate weapon against racist violence. It also anticipates Johnson's anti-lynching play *Safe*, which presents the same resolution. It bears mentioning that in her treatment of the lynching theme, Grimké, like contemporary black women writers—including Burrill, Johnson, Livingston, and Dunbar-Nelson—avoided the graphic depiction of lynching and burning rituals. She also refrained from using the sexual accusation of black males as the primary cause for lynching. Grimké had evidenced an early preoccupation with lynching at the age of nineteen. In November of 1899, the young Angelina collected signatures for an anti-lynching petition. Moreover, she wrote many of her anti-lynching works during the post–World War I lynchings and amid the controversy over the Dyer Anti-Lynching Bill of 1922—the same legislative piece Dunbar-Nelson labored to have passed.

In reviewing the circumstances of Grimké's private life, one notes that she inhabited an environment deluged with political, religious, feminist and racial liberalism—all of which helped to shape the concerns informing her serious works. Responding to the gentility of her background and to her heritage of social activism, Grimké wrote protest plays as one means to continue her family's participation in the twin campaigns for civil and women's rights. In the process of doing so, she became among the first to use the American stage to denounce social injustice, as she censored the violence committed against blacks and the cruel violation of African American women. The acceptable material that Grimké produced for publication was correct, cultured, and traditional. It focused primarily on the "talented tenth," i.e., upper class, conservative African Americans, who like herself were victimized by the "we must prove ourselves" syndrome. The acceptable works that Grimké published did not reveal her possible lesbian orientation that scholars find in her 1896 correspondence, her 1903 diary, and her manuscript poems. Coming from an elite social class, she was compelled to create characters representative of her stratum and to submit work that was devoid of any "compromising" subject. Grimké's confinement is especially underscored here, for it shows how the exertion of class mores restricted the content of her literary output. No proper lady of the black cultured milieu could allude to lesbian themes in literature with impunity *unless* the allusions were made subtly enough to be read as lesbian-directed only by the in-group.

Gloria Hull offers priceless insight into the relationship between Angelina's thwarted sexuality and her psychic/artistic imprisonment:

> Equally obvious is the connection between her lesbianism and the slimness of her creative output. Because of psychic and artistic constraints, the "lines she did not dare" went almost as unwritten as they were unspoken. Being a black lesbian poet in America at the beginning of the twentieth century meant that one wrote (or half wrote)—in isolation—a lot that she did not show and could not publish [Hull 145].

Like Dunbar-Nelson, Angelina was restrained from expressing her lesbian works in print. That Grimké left behind twenty woman-identified holograph poems at her death suggests that for publication and perhaps for social propriety, she deliberately chose "safe" works (like her protest drama) to submit to the press and consciously limited her canon. She knew that when one wrote for the press, she did so in "shackles"—chained between her lesbian reality and the literary/moral conventions that would not give her voice. Hull (1979) notes that in Grimké's day, being a lesbian writer of color meant that one "fashioned a few race and nature poems, transliterated lyrics, and double-tongued verses that sometimes got published. It meant, ultimately, that one stopped writing altogether, dying 'with her real gifts stifled within' and leaving behind the little that managed to survive of one's true self in fugitive pieces. The fact that Grimké did not write and publish enough is given as a major reason for the scanty recognition accorded her and other women poets of the Harlem Renaissance." Like her victimized counterparts, Angelina was "triply disfranchised. Black woman, Lesbian" with no space in which to move (23).

Excerpts from Grimké's "lesbian" writings merit consideration—with the provision that it be taken into account that among women, Victorian discourse allowed for abstract eroticism in the absence of the physical. Carroll Smith-Rosenberg, who studied some contemporary and representative female correspondence of the late nineteenth and early twentieth century homosocial subculture to which Grimké belonged, comments on the characteristic tenderness which women expressed in their written communications: "These letters were but an example of the romantic rhetoric with which the nineteenth century surrounded the concept of friendship. Yet they possess an emotional intensity and a sensual and physical explicitness that are difficult to dismiss" (Smith-Rosenberg 1986, 59). The following letters from Grimké's unpublished canon provide a case in point, as they express her craving for female love and female intimacy.

In particular, the Angelina Weld Grimké Collection shows that in February 1896, Mamie (Mary) Burrill, a school friend of Nana's—possibly one of the bad influences that Aunt Lottie claimed Washington exerted on her— sent Grimké a letter containing apologies, school gossip, church news, and a nostalgic recollection of their private good times:

> Dear Angie [,] do forget how I have treated you ... and blot out from the pages of your memory all that I have ever said to you....
> I am in Mr. Brown's room and while sitting in school I think quite often of you, Have you forgotten how I used to come and meet you at noon.... Could I just come to meet thee once more, in the old sweet way, just coming at your calling, and like an angel bending o'er you breathe into your ear, "I love you" ... do you love me as you used to? Answer me soon. Mamie [Angelina Weld Grimké Collection].

In response to Mamie, "Angie" wrote her a passionate letter that same year while she was attending the Carleton Academy in Northfield, Minnesota, in which she exclaimed:

> My own darling Mamie;
> I hope my darling you will not be offended if your ardent lover calls you such familiar names. Oh Mamie if you only knew how my heart overflows with love for you how it yearns and pants for one glimpse of your lovely face. How gladly if you would only allow me would I lay down this love ... and die for you if you wished it.... I hope ... that in a few years you will come to me and be my love, my wife! How my brain whirls how my pulse leaps when I think of those two words, "my wife" with joy and madness.... Now may the Almighty father bless thee little one and keep thee safe from all harm, Your passionate lover [Angelina Weld Grimké Collection].

It is not certain what happened between Grimké and Burrill. However, by some unspecified time in 1903, their relationship terminated. Burrill eventually became the life partner of Lucy Diggs Slowe but in later years alluded to her former relationship with Angie in a note (dated July 11, 1911). Referring to the train wreck injuries that compelled Angelina to retire in 1926, Mamie writes: "If I can serve you at all, for the sake of the days that are a long way behind us both, I trust you will let me do so" (Angelina Weld Grimké Collection). Grimké had shared a seven-year association with Burrill, and its demise left visible traces in her disposition. In observing one vestige of their break-up, Bruce Kellner writes in *The Harlem Renaissance: A Historical Dictionary* (1984), "Their intense relationship between 1896 and 1903 left [Angelina] somewhat withdrawn and solitary" (145). Perhaps it was this failed relationship that inspired Grimké to make her landmark vow: "I shall never know what it means to be a mother, for I shall never marry. I am through with love and the like forever" in a diary that she maintained from July 18 to September 10, 1903—the same year her relationship with Mamie ended.

The journal does not disclose the identity of Grimké's lover, but the references chronicling this failed romance indicate that her lover was female: "Whether I ever see you again or not, you have done this for me, dear, you have made a woman of me. Is that not something to do? Nor any man could have done that. I am proud that you were her, my sweet" (Angelina Weld Grimké Collection). Moreover, the manuscript poems of longing and void that Grimké wrote during this same period parallel the diary's narrative of heartbreak and sadness and indicate that her paramour was a woman.

It was possibly this same thwarted love affair that supplied the fuel for one of her fiercest conflicts with her father. Dickson Bruce writes, "Archibald Grimké knew about the romance and did not approve. Father and daughter fought several times about it;... [Archibald] gave his daughter an ultimatum, asking that she choose either him or her friend. She chose her father, but not before they had gone through some battles" (Bruce 1993, 99). Referring to one of these fights, Angelina writes in her diary in July 1903, "My father and I have been having a hard time tonight over you, dear. I guess he is right and I shall have to give you up." And in another entry from her diary, Angelina explains her reason for renouncing her paramour, indicating that it was because the relationship competed with her love for her father: "It almost hurts me to see that my love for you is nearly as great as that for my father. It hurts me to feel also that he has had a rival for I do love him so much" (Angelina Weld Grimké Collection).

This rivalry bears testimony to the strong patriarchal power to which Angelina was subjected. It is clear that her father, whom she sought to please, was the source of some restriction and oppression in her expression of her lesbian identity. And it is abundantly apparent that Grimké decided to give up Burrill [?] only because Archibald was going to disown her had she not. The turmoil between father and daughter had to be intense. One can only speculate how Archibald Grimké, a pillar of the Washington, D.C., and Old Boston communities reckoned with his daughter's sexual orientation. Nothing in the conservative, aristocratic, and Christian background that he painstakingly provided for Angelina promoted homosexuality. Rather, the privileged social status that he conferred upon his only child was one that obligated her to live as well as to write in the "shackles" of propriety.

As a result, Grimké ostensibly suppressed her sexuality and spent some of her energies fulfilling her inherited socio-political duties. A cursory look at her adult life shows both the offices she assumed to address her obligations and some rare glimpses of Grimké as a private individual. In addition to her roles as poet, playwright, and educator, Angelina functioned in her later years as the official authority and representative of her family—particularly for Archibald and Francis. On November 9, 1938, for example, she assisted with the dedication of the Archibald Henry Grimké school in Washington, D.C. And on another occasion in February 1925, she wrote a sketch of her father's life for *Opportunity* magazine. In the essay's most humorous section, she described the Grimké brothers as the champion fighters of their elite neighborhood street:

> Cummings street came to know the three Grimké boys ... not because they loved church and Sunday-school and washed their faces and hands and behind their ears and kept their clothes in spotless condition, but because of all the fighters in the street, they were the greatest. Each was adept in his line and invincible in it. My uncle John was the champion "butter," my Uncle Frank the champion "biter," and my father the champion "kicker." The trio always fought in unison, an attack upon one being an attack upon all. Against such a versatile Grimké army what could the other boys do? Nothing on the street dared to appear aggressive even. A good many years have passed since then, but the Grimké brothers are fighters to this day, pens and tongues proving as efficient weapons as teeth and feet [45].

Grimké not only found time to speak on behalf of her noted family, but she also found time to avidly read. She was particularly well read in the classics, current books, and in periodicals such as *The Nation* and *The New Republic*. In describing herself she once wrote, "I am a voracious reader and possess something of a private library" (Angelina Weld Grimké Collection). Besides reading, Angelina sewed, danced, played tennis, and took annual vacations in Massachusetts and Connecticut. Her friends and acquaintances included relatives of the "Boston Circle"—to whom her father had introduced her— as well as the contemporary educators, writers, and artists of eminence. She corresponded and visited with author Jessie Fauset (who later denounced *Rachel* as a work that advocated racial genocide), elocutionist Hallie Q. Brown, and colleague Georgia Douglas Johnson (with whom she was particularly close). Grimké even wrote a charming poem enumerating what she liked about Johnson, and in 1955 she received an invitation to visit Georgia in her Washington, D.C., home.

In physical stature, Angelina was extremely petite. She weighed 92 pounds in 1899 at the age of nineteen and 100 pounds in 1912, at the age of thirty-two. Biographers note that she was a pretty little girl and an attractive woman, and that she dressed well. As a child, her demeanor was solemn, and in succeeding years, her face acquired a "haughty sadness." It is perhaps significant that Grimké made the girls in her plays and stories petite, cute, and dark-haired, like herself (Hull 1987, 148). Her health, though, was not robust. Correspondence between her and her father and close friends frequently refers to her various ailments. She suffered from enlarged glands, nerves, headaches, and bone and bilious conditions.

As a quadroon, whose mother was white and whose father was mulatto, Grimké was extremely fair in complexion. She was acutely conscious of her mixed racial identity as well as the intra- and the interracial realities accompanying skin color. In one of her personal statements, her mixed ancestry seemingly inspires her to affirm the basic humanity of all people and to see no inherent differences between the black and the white race. She expressed this particular view in an undated letter that she sent to a Hampton University woman who was organizing a European tour: "As you probably know I am the product of both races and as far as I can make out there is little or no choice between them" (Angelina Weld Grimké Collection). However, in a journal entry dated July 31, 1903, Grimké expresses her knowledge that the matter of skin color carries great socio-political weight and that it is used by both races as a criterion for discrimination. Referring to a Miss Randolph's indifference to her dark complexion, Angelina writes:

> For as fair as I am I find I am very sensitive. How much harder it must be to be black. God pity them! They not only have the white people's prejudice to contend with [but] the light colored people's too. Light people are very small. What difference does color make anyway it is only skin-deep [Angelina Weld Grimké Collection].

Grimké was seemingly concerned about this issue of intraracism, and in *Rachel* she exposed its ravaging effects on her black-skinned African Americans—i.e., the Lanes—who experienced additional prejudice because of their skin color. Like Johnson, Burrill, and Dunbar-Nelson, Grimké was visibly mixed blood. She understood well the sorrows of inter- and intraracial prejudice and translated these sympathies into her literary work. It bears mentioning that of the three writers, Angelina appeared to be the most comfortable with her biraciality. Johnson told Arna Bontemps in 1941 that she really did not enjoy "writing racially": "Whenever I can, I forget my special call to sorrow and live as happily as I may" (Hull 1987, 19). One notable critic alleged that Johnson had "no feeling for the race" (Hull 1987, 19). Documentation, including some of her diary entries, suggests that Dunbar-Nelson (did not like and) looked down on dark-skinned, lower-class blacks. Moreover, she passed for white whenever she chose. Mary Burrill, like Dunbar-Nelson, was affiliated with a black sorority, which historically barred dark-skinned women from membership. She too, passed for white when she desired.

As a post–Victorian middle-class black woman, Angelina, like her peers, entered the acceptable female field of teaching. At one point, she, Burrill, and Johnson taught at the same institution (Dunbar High School) in Washington, D.C., where Angelina interacted both professionally and personally with them. In the area of finances, Angelina fared significantly better than Johnson, Burrill, Dunbar-Nelson and other black writers, male or female. Due to her family's wealth, she never struggled to have enough money to write or to pay bills.

In the way of personality, Grimké admitted that she possessed a quantity of traits that made hers a difficult one. Her diary entry of December 31, 1911, contains the following self-disclosure:

> My faith in myself is not profound. On this the last day of the year 1911 I am brought face to face with myself. I cannot say I am proud. My hands are not clean.... There are so many, many things I could have left undone, unkind thoughts ... so many times when I have depressed others unnecessarily because I selfishly was blue; and the shadows black of many other disagreeable and disgusting things. Remorse and regret two unpleasant visitors on the last day yet here they are beside me hugging me close and I can do nought but entertain them civilly for they are rightful guests.... I am too critical, too impatient about trifles in my friends. Help me to ... not be a cad [Angelina Weld Grimké Collection].

Corroborating Grimké's self-assessment, her friend Joseph B. Robinson writes her on January 5, 1934:

> I don't know of any friend of yours whom you have known intimately over any length of time, that you don't accuse of trying to rob you or that you don't quarrel with on some pretext or other sooner or later.... I do wish you would take hold of yourself quit suspecting everybody. You would certainly find life much more pleasant [Angelina Weld Grimké Collection].

Yet if Angelina's personality were abrasive in 1934, then it had been intolerable between 1928 and 1930, the last two years of Archibald's life. Under the strain of caring for her father—even with the help of two professional nurses and her Uncle Francis—she became litigious, irritable, and possibly neurotic. She had violent confrontations with Francis over financial matters and engaged in bitter recriminations with him that extended for sometime after Archibald's death. Apparently the tensions between niece and uncle had existed for some time. It may be useful to recall that Angelina had jealously and unsuccessfully tried to undermine the brothers' relationship for years (Francis J. Grimké Collection). However, during those final days of Archibald's illness, her anger with Francis escalated, and his very presence fueled her ire. After Archibald's death, Angelina quarreled with her uncle and threatened to disinter her father from the demeaning plot (as she perceived it) where Francis had him buried. It was also during this crisis that she exhibited additional singular behavior. She wrote haranguing letters to the physician concerning a nurse who had supposedly swindled them; charged that Francis had called her "crazy"; and procured a May 7, 1930, notarized statement from Dr. William C. McNeill declaring that she was "competent of conducting her business affairs" (Angelina Weld Grimké Collection).

Biographers note that Grimké's burden of nursing her father may have been complicated by their extremely close relationship, which was, it seems, almost incestuous. Lacking a mother for balance, she was doubly (and probably ambivalently) bound to him with the iron of affection and chastisement—even writing literature to prove her worth and win his approbation. Possibly her lack of lovers, husband, and children promoted ties between father and daughter that grew into an unhealthy, life-time dependency (Hull 1987, 149). During this tragedy, Grimké's friends, including Anna Julia Cooper, sculptor Meta Warrick Fuller and her husband Dr. Solomon Fuller, counseled Angelina to "keep the upper hand" and to "get a fresh grip on yourself" (Angelina Weld Grimké Collection).

After Archibald died in 1930, Grimké relocated to Brooklyn, New York, ostensibly for her writing, but according to Arna Bontemps, she produced little or nothing thereafter. Unlike other African American writers of that period, including Georgia Douglas Johnson, Angelina did not apply for the prestigious awards in black literature that the Harmon Foundation offered from 1926 to 1930. In her self-imposed isolation—which occurred as the American Depression dried up interest and literary markets for black writers and helped to end the Harlem Renaissance—Angelina Grimké seemingly committed artistic suicide. She appeared to have lost the requisite motivation, mentality, and industry for creating. Her colleagues mourned her "demise," and in 1955 Anna Julia Cooper wrote: "It is regrettable that in later years Miss Grimké has not kept up the line of creative work which her earlier successes foreshadowed" (Cooper 1951, 27). In commenting on Grimké's later life, Arna Bontemps remarks, she "spent the last years of her life in quiet retirement in a New York City apartment" ("Biographical Notes," *American Negro Poetry*, p. 190). She died June 10, 1958, at her home, 208 West 151st Street, after a long illness. She was 78 years old.

Mary Powell Burrill

Little is known about the personal or the public life of Mary P. Burrill (1881–1946). She was born in Washington, D.C., on August 30, 1881 to

Clara and John Henry Powell Burrill and was educated in the local schools, including Dunbar High from which she graduated in 1901. Photographs among the Archibald Henry Grimké Collection indicate that she had at least two sisters—one of whom was Clara Burrill Bruce, who was a member of the NAACP drama committee the year the association produced Grimké's *Rachel*. When Burrill's family relocated to Boston, she attended Emerson College. She received a diploma from the school in 1904, and upon returning in 1929, she earned her bachelor of literary interpretation. In 1905 Burrill was appointed to teach English in the M Street High School and was later transferred to Armstrong High School for a few years. She then returned to the new M Street High School (renamed Dunbar) to teach dramatics, English, and speech. The Charles Sumner School Museum and Archives where the DC schools' archives are housed note that Burrill is reported to have been the first teacher of dramatics in the colored schools. Burrill also served as director of the School of Expression, which was a part of the District's Conservatory of Music, headed by Harriet Gibbs Marshall. As a director from 1907 to 1911, she taught elocution, public speaking, and dramatics.

During her tenure at Dunbar—where she remained until her retirement in 1944—Burrill inspired many students to write and direct plays. Along with colleague Angelina Grimké, Burrill mentored Willis Richardson, who became the first black dramatist to have a serious play—*Chip Woman's Fortune*—produced on Broadway in 1923. She also inspired her student May Miller to write *Pandora's Box*, which won Miller a fifty-cent cash prize as well as the honor of being published in *School's Progress* magazine in 1914. An outstanding educator, Burrill was so respected among her students that upon her retirement, the Dunbar Class of 1945 dedicated its yearbook to her.

As a teacher, Burrill directed plays of great quality that were well-received by the community. Colleague Mary Gibson Hundley (1965) noted in *The Dunbar Story 1870–1955*:

> In dramatics, Miss Mary P. Burrill gave many years of outstanding service in the training of speech and acting. Boys and girls who had never entered a theater or appeared on a platform would surprise their classmates and themselves under her direction, by playing roles on the stage in the school auditorium. In the 1920s, Maeterlinck's the *Blue Bird* and J.M. Barrie's *Quality Street* were among ... her brilliant productions. Students from underprivileged homes, whose color barred them from the usual cultural contacts, found themselves developing in speech, posture, and poise. At one period, Miss Burrill persuaded Walter L. Smith, principal, to introduce a daily program of posture drill at the beginning of each class period throughout the school [133].

In an interview, Professor Emeritus Carroll Miller of Howard University, Burrill's former tenth grade student, corroborated Hundley's praise of the dramatist. He recalled that the "short, plump" educator was involved with unrecorded theatrical performances, which included a 1921 production of *Three Pillows and a Bottle* and *The Vespers*. Burrill also directed the unique, beautifully staged *Living Pictures*, "which were phrases of speech combined with Art and Music" (Woodlawn Sketches). A talented performer of some renown, Burrill was widely sought as a dramatic reader. For fifteen years, she appeared annually at Howard University's Rankin Chapel to read Van Dyke's *The Other Wise Man* with the choir.

In addition to directing plays of great quality and to producing work that endorsed the NAACP's anti-lynching campaign, Burrill wrote drama in support of the Birth Control League. In 1919, she published a one-act play, *They That Sit in Darkness*, in Margaret Sanger's *Birth Control Review*— a monthly periodical that lobbied for the right of women to have contraceptive information. The journal also featured in the same issue Grimké's short story, "The Closing Door," another pro-contraceptive work. Burrill's drama tells the story of a young African American girl who is forced to give up her plans to attend college when her mother dies after giving birth to her tenth child. The mother's death could have been averted (and the daughter could have gone to college) had the mother been given the prohibited facts of birth control. *They That Sit in Darkness* candidly illustrates the tragic consequences of denying women access to such vital information. It also reflects Burrill's sympathy with the predicament that poor, ignorant, and/or African American women were placed in as the result of their inaccessibility to contraceptive methods. In 1929, while a student at Emerson, Burrill revised *They That Sit In Darkness* and retitled it *Unto the Third and Fourth Generations*. The drama was then published in the 1930 Emersonian yearbook and awarded Best Junior Play of the Year.

An investigation of Mary Burrill's private life—the little of it that is known—shows no documentation that she ever married or bore children. It is most likely, however, that she interacted with and possibly assumed responsibility in rearing her sister Clara's children. Records indicate that Clara Washington Burrill married Roscoe Conkling Bruce, Sr., and produced at least three children from their union: Roscoe Conkling Bruce, Jr., Burrell, and Clara. Mary's family is the subject of Alice Dunbar-Nelson's journal entry dated Saturday, August 27, 1927, in which she describes a visit with the Bruces, her bureaucratic friends:

> Tessa and I proceed by taxi ... to Roscoe Bruce's place. A ground floor office and here we see Roscoe, fat and portly and happy with his life-time position of $12,000 a year, and little seventeen year old Burrell at a desk and soon Carrie, his wife, still limping from her elevator accident, but wearing her Phi

Beta Kappa and a smile of satisfaction over her $3600 position, and Clara, the senior in Radcliffe, at a desk too. What luck! And Carrie just refused a settlement of $50,000 for her accident! We talk over Roscoe's plant, the wonderful Rockefeller foundation, which he is to run for life! I ask for a job for Bobbo. [Dunbar-Nelson's husband] Of course, there is none, of course [193].

As a loving and concerned aunt, Mary would have been upset that her nephew Roscoe C. Bruce, Jr., was barred from the freshman dormitory at Harvard in 1923 because of his color; and she might have been somewhat disturbed that her niece Clara eloped in 1922 instead of having the formal wedding that her family's social status anticipated (Roscoe Conkling Bruce Sr. Collection). Thus, while Mary Burrill had no biological children, she probably had parental sensibilities toward her nieces and nephews; and much like Dunbar-Nelson, who also bore no children, Mary assisted, to some degree, in child-rearing responsibilities.

Further investigation of Mary's private life reveals that emotionally and physically intimate relationships with women were significant aspects of her life. Her ardent letter of February 23, 1896, to Angelina Grimké can be recalled, as can Grimké's passionate letter of response. Assuming that Mary/Mamie was the unnamed lover who occasioned the strife between Angelina and her father, it is likely that Burrill was devastated when, at Archibald Grimké's insistence, Angelina terminated their seven-year relationship. Disparate class standing could not have been a contributing factor to Angelina's father's ultimatum. Records indicate that Mamie was also from an aristocratic black family with ties to eminent black and Caucasian luminaries. Her sister Clara had married the aforementioned wealthy R.C. Bruce, who was the only son of Blanche K. Bruce (and Josephine), former United States senator from Mississippi. Bruce trained at Phillips Academy-Exeter, New Hampshire, studied at Harvard University and graduated magna cum laude. He married Clara on June 3, 1903, the year that Angelina repudiated her ties to Mamie. Patriarchy, intolerance, and probable embarrassment over homosexuality—on behalf of both families—were the most likely reasons for the demise of the Burrill-Grimké association.

Yet Mamie went on to seemingly find the love of her life in Lucy Diggs Slowe—educator, social reformer, clubwoman, and Howard University's first dean of women (1922–1937). Burrill shared a house with her in Washington, D.C., at 1256 Kearney Street NE. While Mary served the black Washington community as an educator, playwright, play director, and actress, her partner served it largely as a university administrator and as a women's activist. In such capacities, they were both high profile, eminent women who supported each other publicly and privately. It was at Dean Slowe's university that Burrill performed her Christmas production for fifteen years, and it was to Lucy's school that Burrill sent many of her graduating students. Documentation indicates that Burrill championed Slowe's cause during the Dean's battles against Howard University's president Dr. Mordecai W. Johnson. Points of contention included the administrative responsibility for the use of university dorms; Slowe's salary; university provision of living quarters for the dean of women; and budgetary matters.

One of the most vivid examples of Burrill's commitment to Lucy Slowe is illustrated in a letter dated May 2, 1938, that Burrill addressed to Dr. Abram Flexner, former president of the Trustee Board of Howard University. In this correspondence, which was written to vindicate her deceased friend from charges that Slowe contributed to the disturbance on Howard's campus, Burrill states:

> Among the Collection given to me just prior to her death by the late Dean Lucy D. Slowe ... for purposes of biographical information, I note in her correspondence that on May 15, 1933, when you were President of the Trustee Board of Howard University you said to Miss Slowe that you had been told by one of the Trustees of Howard University that there would be "no peace at Howard University as long as she was on the campus!"

Burrill then catalogues disturbances occurring on the Howard campus since the dean's demise. She sarcastically concludes her letter and tells Dr. Flexner: "There is another reason for the perpetual turmoil at Howard than the presence there of Howard's distinguished alumna and former Dean of Women, Lucy D. Slowe—a great woman of our race" (Lucy Diggs Slowe Collection).

In another instance illustrative of Burrill's support and commitment to Lucy Slowe, Mary writes the university official an acerbic letter in which she castigates him for unscrupulously terminating Slowe's secretary, Miss W.B. Wilson, the day after the dean's funeral. She tells Mr. Hungate, the president of the Board of Trustees of Howard University:

> The points I wish to call to your attention are as follows:
>
> 1. The day after Miss Slowe's funeral all the locks on her office doors were changed.
> 2. Miss Slowe's secretary was not given keys to the changed locks, was *never* given such keys.
> 3. Miss Wilson was told to go home and take a rest, and that she would be sent for later. This she did. Several days later she was sent a letter containing her *dismissal from her position, signed by Miss Alida Banks Acting Dean of Women.*

What I would like to know is this—Has a subordinate like Miss Banks the power to dismiss someone who has been appointed by the Trustees of the

University; and secondly, Miss Wilson, being appointed by the Trustees for the year 1937-38 to the position as secretary to the *Dean of Women*. Should she be put out of office at the death of Miss Slowe?

Such acts of injustice against a defenseless woman who has a little child to support, is [not] in keeping with the general policy of Howard under this administration.

I appeal to your sense of justice and fair play to see that Miss Wilson is reinstated in her position [Slowe Collection].

That Burrill and Slowe were viewed, acknowledged, and accepted as a lesbian couple by prominent black Washingtonia is suggested by the large number of letters and telegrams of condolence (including one from Mary McLeod Bethune) addressed to Burrill at Lucy's death on October 21, 1937. The general tone of the condolences is "spousal" in nature. Phrases such as "sympathy expressed to those nearest, left behind"; "you have my deepest ... hope that you will be sustained with the knowledge that she will live forever in ideals"; "I realize what you are going through and only wish there might be something I could do"; and "I can imagine how hard it has been for you" substantiate this impression (Slowe Collection). Moreover, the thank-you note sent by Howard University Treasurer V.D. Johnston (I thank you for your letter received today and check for $4.00 for the hauling of the effects of Dean Lucy D. Slowe, deceased) and excerpts from an undated letter to Burrill signed by a Todd and Gladys suggest the presence of a marital bond that the two women may have shared:

Dear friend:

Our thinking at this time may be a bit clearer than yours; so we say these flowers speak what is in our minds—namely:

Life must go on and abundantly so. "Our mutual friend" would say this to you. You then, must calmly and serenely find your own adjustment.... Move on [Slowe Collection].

That Burrill was emotionally devastated by the passing of her beloved friend and loyal confidante becomes abundantly clear. A letter dated February 5, 1938, indicates that Burrill moved to 1111 Columbia Road NW, possibly in an effort to escape the pain that the Kearney house may have held for her. It is uncertain whether Slowe's death precipitated the lengthy and the lingering sickness from which Burrill died nine years later. The following passage from Mabel Carney's May 17, 1938, letter, which was written to Mary seven months after Slowe's death, generates this question: "I am sorry to learn that you have been seriously ill. I trust, however, that the approaching vacation will give you needed rest and help to restore your usual health" (Slowe Collection). Investigation shows that Mary never recovered the robust health that she enjoyed prior to her friend's illness and death. In fact, Mary's obituary, which appeared in the March 1946 *Washington Star* reported that the playwright died in New York after a long illness. It can only be speculated whether Slowe's passing was the genesis of Burrill's deterioration and demise.

One year earlier, Burrill visited Georgia Johnson and precipitated some conjecture about her sexual orientation. Evidencing such questions, Johnson wrote a cryptic letter to Harold Jackman on January 10, 1945, following Burrill's visit to her home:

> Now, her [a]ddress is 1046 Hoe Ave apt 1—name Mary Powell Burrill—She's very fine in elocution and has done a fine play....
>
> Nina [Angelina Grimké] knows her but do not speak of these things, she I mean Mary may be strictly on the level and Nina may think differently. However, let the inside story remain between [u]s for now.
>
> I would like to know if she [Burrill] is doing what I naturally feel a little [n]ervous when I think of every circumstance.
>
> She [Burrill] is retired—and nice looking and elegant.
>
> When you have read this tear it up that it may never fall into thoughtless hands [Cullen-Jackman Collection].

A possible translation of Johnson's correspondence could read:

> Nina knows Mary. Nina is a lesbian and Mary, being an acquaintance or friend of Nina's could be one, too. However, Mary could be heterosexual and Nina is deceived about Mary's orientation. Let's not disclose Nina's preference to Mary. I would like to know, however, if Mary sleeps with Nina (or with any woman) because Burrill is what Nina likes. Mary is nice looking and elegant—all that Nina would want.

Apparently, Johnson was unaware of the romance that Mary and Nina had shared many years earlier. She did learn, as did later generations, that Burrill lived a life of extraordinary courage—to which her protest dramas and protest letters attest. A formidable advocate for women's and civil rights, Burrill held membership in The National Council of Negro Women and the Alpha Kappa Alpha Sorority, Inc. Under her co-leadership, the sorority sponsored a suffrage rally in 1917 and elicited the assurance of Montana Congresswoman Jeanette Rankin that she wanted all women to be given the ballot regardless of race. In concert with Alpha Kappa Alpha Sorority, Burrill sent a telegram to President Warren Harding in 1922, urging him to promote the passage of the Dyer Anti-Lynching Bill.

As a staunch feminist who advocated complete female autonomy, Burrill campaigned for the liberation of her gender—including their right to equal pay, opportunity for equal employment, unrestricted divorce, retention of maiden name in marriage, adoption of simple clothing, right of abortion, and the nineteenth amendment. She fought as a recognized crusader for women's free access to birth control information and promoted her political and gender agenda through drama.

Georgia Douglas Johnson

Unlike that of Alice Dunbar-Nelson, Angelina Grimké, Myrtle Smith Livingston, and Mary P. Burrill, the early life of Georgia Johnson (1877–1966) is enveloped by mystery and contradiction, as the conflicting years of her date of birth indicate. While 1880 and 1886 are the years commonly given as Georgia's birthdate, the year 1877 (September 10) was verified by the registrar's office at Atlanta University where Johnson attended. Two events corroborate the registrar's verification. First, Johnson, herself, writes in a 1963 letter to Dr. Robert K. Carr—then president of Oberlin College— that she was a member of the 1893 Atlanta University graduating class. "Dear President Carr: I am ... the only living graduate of the class of '93" (Johnson Collection). In addition, Atlanta University's publication, the *Alumni News* said of its alumna, in a 1952 issue, "Mrs. Johnson, a graduate of Atlanta University in the Normal Department of 1893 ... has been a teacher" (Johnson Collection).

Another discrepancy that surrounds Johnson's early years involves the identity of her progenitors. Biographers traditionally name George and Laura Jackson Camp as Johnson's parents—based on the personal history that she supplied graduate students Theresa Scott Davis and Charles Y. Freeman— who in 1931 wrote a paper entitled "A Biographical Sketch of Georgia Douglas Johnson and Some of Her Works" for the now defunct YMCA Graduate School in Nashville, Tennessee. However, in the October 1958 *Oberlin College 125th Anniversary Alumni Catalogue Report*, Johnson names Peter and Mary Ann Brown Johnson as her parents. Moreover, Johnson's son corroborates this information and supplies the same names for her forebears on the *Oberlin College Former Student Record*, a document that was made September 22, 1966, four months after the writer's death. In view of the documented identity of Johnson's parents, much of the biographical information that she supplied Davis and Freeman—which until the present study was considered definitive background data—now appears suspicious. For example, Georgia alleged: "Her paternal grandfather was an Englishman who moved to this country with his parents in the early days and settled in Marietta, Georgia. His family was wealthy and he was quite musical. He died in his middle thirties in the midst of a brilliant and ambitious career" (Davis and Freeman 1931, 3). While Johnson's extremely fair skin (Cedric Dover describes her as "being a near white") and obsession with the theme of miscegenation in her literature may attest to her European extraction, no documentation has been found to substantiate her claims about her paternal grandfather's ethnicity, economic status, or existence (*The Crisis*, December 1952, 59: 635).

On the maternal side, Georgia identified her grandmother as a Native American and her grandfather as an African American bridge builder, "both of whom died early in life leaving the care of seven young children to the oldest daughter, Laura, fourteen at the time" (Davis and Freeman 1931, 3). According to Johnson, Laura became her mother and earned her living as a maid. Georgia observed that Laura held "primitive ideas" and resented her daughter's dominating childhood personality. Yet despite their conflicting character traits, Johnson was able to describe her mother as an individual with a "great big loving heart" and was seemingly protective of her mother's privacy. To this end, Georgia requested Davis and Freeman to "step very lightly on my early history. My mother still lives and while she is uneducated, she has a great reticence and is unusually shy" (Davis and Freeman, n.d., Special Collection, Fisk University Library, Nashville, Tennessee). However, Johnson disclosed that Laura married three times and from the third marriage produced two half brothers and one half sister for Johnson. Of all the siblings Georgia claimed to have had, records indicate that she only mentioned one of them on a single occasion. In particular, in a March 31, 1945, letter to Harold Jackman, she writes that she sent an Easter card to her sister, whose husband "dropped dead and I knew she was unstabilized" (Cullen-Jackman Collection).

Records indicate that Johnson attended schools in Rome and Atlanta, Georgia, graduating, as earlier noted, from Atlanta University's Normal School in 1893. A cherished alumna, Johnson received an honorary Doctor of Literature from Atlanta University in 1965. Moreover, at some unrecorded time (probably following her 1910 move to Washington, D.C.), she studied library and social work at Howard University. The 1958 report blank for *Oberlin College 125th Anniversary Alumni Catalogue*, which contains this information, does not indicate that Johnson took a degree in either discipline.

In reviewing these student years in her discourse with Davis and Freeman, Johnson noted that throughout them, she suffered from severe loneliness and became withdrawn and isolated. She said her residence at Atlanta University provided some respite, and while there, she "experienced the first real homey sympathetic atmosphere" of her life. Yet, one particular comment to Davis and Freeman suggests that even while in the hospitable environs of Atlanta University, Johnson did not form close relationships: "There were girls in school whom I would have liked to be associated with but I was too proud to seek them and I had no material offerings to make to attract superior girls" (Davis and Freeman 1931, 2). Georgia remarked that to combat the loneliness and the estrangement, she purchased a violin and taught herself to play. Perhaps this loneliness that she experienced during her student years followed her—to some extent—throughout her adult life. And it might have been a cornerstone upon which she founded her literary salon, which provided a supporting network for black authors. Her personal experience with loneliness may have also been a reason that she nurtured a group of black writers whose unconventional lifestyles invited condemnation and social ostracism. For having once been estranged from the "in-group," herself, Johnson probably knew how other excluded people felt.

Moreover, the loneliness that playing instruments seems to have assuaged *could* have also been the reason that music became a compelling passion in Johnson's early life. In its pursuit, she studied at the Cleveland College of Music and later at Oberlin College (1902–1903) in Oberlin, Ohio, where she majored in harmony, violin, piano and voice. Johnson also desired to compose songs at this juncture in her life—an ambition that she disclosed more than twenty years later in an autobiographical statement: "Long years ago when the world was new for me, I dreamed of being a composer—wrote songs, many of them. The words took fire and the music smouldered and so, following the lead of friends and critics, I turned my face toward poetry and put my songs away" (*Opportunity*, July 1927, 204). Yet, fortunately for Johnson, her late-life collaboration with the renowned composer Lillian Evanti allowed her to return to her initial passion and to enjoy the publication of some of her songs.

Prior to becoming the poet-playwright, journalist, and short story writer for which she was ultimately known, Johnson became an educator, initiating her career in Marietta, Georgia. In all likelihood, she consistently taught music, except during the time that she mentioned in 1931 when she "once taught teachers to write, well I did more than that I did the drawing and illustrating on the choice school Collection" (Schomburg). Eventually, Georgia became an assistant principal in the Atlanta schools and remained in the city long enough to marry attorney Henry Lincoln Johnson on September 28, 1903. Perhaps Johnson's concern with federal anti-lynching legislation—an obsession that permeates her protest plays—took root during her marriage and was influenced by her husband's legalistic attitudes and practices.

Henry, or "Link" as he was commonly called, was born of former slaves in 1870 and was a graduate of Atlanta University (BA, c. 1888) and the University of Michigan (LLB, c. 1892). A prominent member of the Republican party, Link had been the Georgia delegate-at-large to the Republican National Convention since 1896. Georgia bore him two sons: Henry Lincoln Johnson, Jr., an attorney (b. 1906), and Peter Douglas Johnson, a physician (b. 1907, d. 1957). In 1910, the family moved to Washington, D.C., where Link established a law firm and where the careers of both wife and husband approached turning points. In particular, it was in the nation's capital that Johnson published her initial poems, met her early mentors, and produced her first book of poetry, which won her literary fame.

Evidence of Georgia's ascent appeared in the first decade of the twentieth century. In 1916, the same year that the NAACP produced Grimké's *Rachel*, *The Crisis* published Johnson's maiden poems: "Gossamer," "Fame," and "My Little One." Two years later, the Cornhill Company published Johnson's *The Heart of a Woman and Other Poems*—a nonracial book of poetry that expresses the tender yearnings of a woman. Johnson's early mentor, William Stanley Braithwaite, the established poet anthologist and one of Afro-America's severest critics, whose poetry first inspired Johnson to pen verse—wrote the introduction to her book—and thus helped to ensconce Georgia into the poetry arena where she was to dominate and to earn for herself the appellation "the foremost woman poet of the race." In Countee Cullen's *Caroling Dusk* (1927), Johnson recounts the experience that was instrumental in achieving her acclaim from a third-person narrative: "Dean Kelly Miller at Howard University saw some of her poetic efforts and was pleased. [William] Stanley Braithwaite was his friend and he directed her to send something to him at Boston. She did so, and then began a quickening and a realization that she could do!" (*Caroling Dusk* 74).

In *The Heart of a Woman*, Douglas did so well in expressing the love-longing of a feminine sensibility that Braithwaite wrote in its introduction:

> The poems in this book are intensely feminine and for me this means more than anything else that they are deeply human.... It is a kind of privilege to know so much about the secrets of woman's nature, a privilege all the more to be cherished when given, as in these poems, with such exquisite utterance, with such a lyric sensibility [Intro. to *The Heart of a Woman*, vii, ix].

In extolling Johnson's verses, Braithwaite enumerates the general themes, subjects, moods, and tones that the writer addresses: "nature, or the seasons, touch of hands or lips, love, desire, or any of the emotional abstractions which sweep like fire or wind or cooling water through the blood" (Intro. to *The Heart of a Woman*, ix). Braithwaite's list could be extended to include the specific topics of sorrow, death, memory, time and aging, poetry, solitude, and evanescent joy. Johnson "treats these much-handled goods," remarks Gloria Hull, "with feeling and respect, giving her renditions if not original force, then a delicate power (Hull 1987, 159). In further describing Johnson's verses, the Cornhill Company succinctly notes that her "poems are brief, holding much of music and passion in a small cup of speech" (Glen Carrington Collection).

While Johnson was preparing and producing her first book, her husband was advancing in his political career. In 1912, President William Taft had appointed Henry the recorder of deeds—a post traditionally occupied by an African American male since Frederick Douglass—for Washington, D.C. Henry maintained the post until 1921 and probably would have held it longer had not the Senate refused to confirm his renomination by President Warren Harding. In her 1921 diary, Johnson's friend and colleague Alice Dunbar-Nelson reports on the recorder of deeds situation, which formed a brief but volatile episode for the year. In particular, Dunbar-Nelson's diary provides some interesting examples of the animosity that Link's enemies expressed during his political crisis. In the first entry dated Monday, September 12, Dunbar-Nelson's husband

> Bobbo says he had a letter ... this morning saying that the Senate Committee would report unfavorably on Link Johnson's appointment. Poor fellow! coming on top of his paralytic stroke, I fear ... Terrell's [Robert Terrell, husband of educator/activist Mary Church] letter implied that Bobbo should go after the job of Recorder of Deeds. He would have ... but I stopped him. I hate to take advantage of a sick man.

On Tuesday, November 29, Dunbar-Nelson reports: "Jimmy Cobb explaining Link's rejection by the Senate, secretly rejoicing at it, I've no doubt." And finally on Saturday, December 3, Dunbar-Nelson writes:

> The refusal of the Senate to confirm Link Johnson [as recorder of deeds], of course is the most talked of thing now in the colored news Collection and elsewhere. Some of Bobbo's friends, notably Melvin Chisum, seem to think that he should go after the Recorder-ship, now that Johnson is eliminated.

Although Link lost his office, he maintained his position as Republican national committeeman from Georgia until his death in 1925.

A review of Link's professional life shows that he enjoyed a flourishing career (i.e., judge, attorney, politician). However, there are indications that suggest that he was opposed to his wife enjoying the same professional freedom that he did. Records disclose his conventional attitude on women's roles and note that Link "didn't think much of his wife's longing for a literary career" and that "he tried to discourage the idea, but would quote her poems when making some of his greatest political speeches. The 'Colonel' thought a woman should take care of her home and her children and be content with that" (*Pittsburgh Courier*, July 1928). As becomes flagrantly apparent, Link's patriarchal attitude was an iron "shackle" with which Georgia was forced to contend.

A speculation on her role as the wife of this prominent lawyer suggests that Johnson subordinated her developing career to the promotion of her husband's. Advancing Link's profession probably obligated her to entertain her husband's colleagues in an immaculate house that was commensurate with his status and to preside over the rearing of their children. Thus, the responsibilities of housekeeping and parenthood shackled Georgia to demanding roles, from which Link, because of his career and gender, could be released. Yet, an entry from Dunbar-Nelson's October 1, 1921, journal reveals that Georgia was not the best domestic engineer, and that while she certainly cared about Link's professional advancement, her own literary output remained crucial:

> From the Y, I went to Lincoln Johnson's house. Georgia seemed glad to see me, and plunged instantly into a stream of poetic talk, mixed with hats, finding mine immensely becoming.... [She] wanted to know how to put on hats, and I began to teach her. She really did not know how, and I made her practise and practise again and again. Link seemed so glad that I was teaching his wife an essential thing that he suggested luncheon:
> "Irish potato salad, and some of my tomatoes from the garden, Georgia, so Miss Alice can see how fine my garden is." "Well fix it," said Georgia, and he did. Two dainty plates of salad, little fine slices of bread, tea, and all. Of course, he had to push away Collection, manuscript, junk from the dining room table to make a place for his tray, for Georgia has her machine, and all her literary stuff in the dining room, but we ate his salad and sliced pineapple, and everything, while Georgia showed me the manuscript of her new book [Hull 1984, 87, 88].

A seeming chauvinist—who only encouraged his wife when she did the conventional "woman things," Link transmitted his views on traditional gender roles to his son Lincoln who—according to people—neither understood nor valued his mother's creative genius. Illustrating a case in point, Johnson's friend, the poet/playwright Owen Dodson recounts how Lincoln, Jr., disposed of his mother's documents after her death:

> I do know that she had a great deal of unpublished material—novels, poems, essays, memoirs, remembrances, all kinds of things. But as the car stopped in front of her house [returning from the funeral], the men were cleaning out the cellar, and I clearly saw manuscripts thrown into the garbage. I said, "A lifetime to the sanitation department!" [James V. Hatch Tapes].

Fortunately, not all of Johnson's canon suffered the same fate. For in her lifetime, she enjoyed the publication of many works, including that of several books. *Bronze: A Book of Verse* (1922)—the manuscript she showed Dunbar-Nelson in the earlier mentioned journal entry—was to be the second of Georgia's published volumes. This book was reluctantly written in response to its predecessor, *The Heart of a Woman* (1918), a book that "was not at all race conscious." With the 1918 publication, Johnson had been accused of having "no feeling for the race," an egregious charge, considering the black political consciousness of the age that demanded Johnson, as a writer of color, to attack racial injustice (Cullen-Jackman Collection). Yet perhaps this accusation was not entirely ill founded and for this reason merits some attention. A review of the tenets of the Genteel School to which Johnson belonged and an excerpt from two of her poems may shed some important light on what basis the accusation may have been made and in specific, explain the reason Johnson avoided racial topics.

The poets of the Genteel School—it may be recalled—penned verses that were devoid of racial subjects in effort to prove to Euro-Americans that they were just like their white counterparts in every matter except the fact of race. Leading poets of this school included Grimké, Alice Dunbar-Nelson, Georgia Douglas Johnson, and Harlem Renaissance co-hostess Anne Spencer. In *Caroling Dusk*, Spencer had made a statement that probably described the attitude of all the "lady poets" whose race, gender, and class compelled them to address the black struggle: "I write about some of the things I love. But have no civilized articulation for the things I hate" (47). Johnson corroborated Spencer's remark and later told Arna Bontemps in a 1941 letter that she really did not enjoy "writing racially": "Whenever I can, I forget my special call to sorrow and live as happily as I may. Perhaps that is why I seldom elect to write racially. It seems to me an art to forget those things that make the heart heavy. If one can soar, he should soar, leaving his chains behind" (Cullen-Jackman Collection). Johnson fulfilled her words and seemingly wrote as much poetry that was devoid of prejudice and injustice as possible. She was only deterred by the castigation of black critics—to whom she responded with the publication of *Bronze: A Book of Verse*.

Further indicating Johnson's racial views are two poems, published early in her career, that intimate her resentment at being "shackled" to the detested African race and at being excluded from her Anglo "family" because of a fraction of black blood. In "Octoroon" she writes: "One drop of midnight in the dawn of life's pulsating stream/ Marks her an alien from her kind, a shade amid its gleam." In "Aliens" Johnson states: "A single drop, a sable strain debars them from their own." These poems, as well as her affiliation with the Genteel School, give substance to the accusation (having no feeling for the race) with which black critics charged her. In fact, this data suggests that Johnson would have identified herself as Caucasian if permitted. In the literary arena, Georgia appears to have found a compromise that allowed her to pen universal literature (i.e., to omit ethnic issues and to sound as though she were white) while being released from the constraints of a race that she resented. Nevertheless, in response to the criticism levied against her by black intellectuals, she published a volume of obligatory race poetry in

Bronze, which scholars judge to be the weakest of her books. Johnson (1922) prefaces her volume with an author's note and writes:

> This book is the child of a bitter earth-wound. I sit on the earth and sing— sing out, and of, my sorrow. Yet, fully conscious of the potent agencies that silently work in their healing ministries, I know that God's sun shall one day shine upon a perfected and unhampered people [3].

W.E.B. Du Bois wrote the one-page forward to this "entirely racial" book— identifying in it the work's crucial theme: what it means to be a colored woman in 1922. In expounding on this topic, Johnson composes sixty-five poems that are divided into nine separate sections: Exhortation, Supplication, Motherhood, Prescience, Exaltation, Martial, Random, and Appreciations. Mention should be made of the section on Motherhood (a theme which only two poems in *The Heart of the Woman* treated), because it addresses the unique problems attending black maternity. One poem, "Black Woman," is particularly noteworthy because it recalls Grimké's *Rachel* in its portrayal of a potential African American mother who refuses to bring her baby into the cruel world of racial violence. It is significant that this same protest recurs in Johnson's anti-lynch play *Safe*, where (in recalling Grimké's short story "The Closing Door"), the young mother commits infanticide to prevent her child from being murdered. Another poem from the Martial section that also bears mentioning is "Homing Braves." In its salutation to valiant black World War I soldiers, whose war effort has supposedly earned for them full citizenship at home, "Homing Braves" anticipates Burrill's *Aftermath*, which shows how the nation violently disenfranchised its defenders.

The general response to Johnson's second book was a positive one, and perhaps some of its success may be explained by an excerpt from Dunbar-Nelson's diary: "Georgia showed me the manuscript of her new book, which Braithwaite is offering to the publishers.... She has done the big thing in letting [Alain] Locke, [W.E.B.] DuBois, and Braithwaite weed out her verses until only the perfect ones remain. What she has left are little gems" (October 1, 1921). Du Bois evaluated *Bronze*, remarking that the book was "simple, sometimes trite, but ... as a revelation of the soul struggle of the women of a race it is invaluable" (foreword to *Bronze*). It appears that although Du Bois granted Johnson's work some praise, he grudgingly and patronizingly bestowed it. What provoked him to be so insulting and condescending is not certain (had Du Bois shared a liaison with Johnson that hostilely ended?); yet the renowned scholar's endorsement was useful, because it validated Johnson's achievement.

With the publication of *Bronze*—through which she exhibited the saving grace of black maternity and the success of *The Heart of a Woman*—which celebrated universal womanhood, Johnson inaugurated her career as a poet. She became the first African American woman to receive national recognition as a poet since Frances Ellen Watkins Harper, the abolitionist writer, whose last poems were published in 1872.

Johnson was more known and more extensively published than any of her "sister" poets. Yet despite her multigenred prolificness, which approaches that of Langston Hughes, her life and responsibilities as a woman precluded any feasibility of Hughes' type of literary entrepreneurship. Compared with Hughes, Mckay, and Cullen, it becomes evident that the gap among the four writers is not as vast as critical opinion might hold. Moreover, Georgia's total canon eclipses that of less stellar poets such as Frank Horne, Fenton Johnson, and Arna Bontemps.

Johnson maintained her niche as a woman poet. However, in the process of doing so, she became the target of critics' attitudes, which viewed her lyric first-person voice as something that was antithetical to femininity. These attitudes manifest themselves in the commentators' praise of her "daring" in exposing a woman's secret self. In "A Paradox" Johnson even intimates at the discomfort that candid expression of passion can produce:

> I know you love me better cold
> Strange as the pyramids of old...
> But I am frail, and spent and weak
> With surging torrents that bespeak
> A living fire.

That she was stereotyped as a female poet in other ways is illustrated by this excerpt from one of social columnist Geraldyn Dismond's *Pittsburgh Courier* articles:

> It so happened that I met Mrs. Johnson before I had read her poems. Consequently, I received a shock. From the place she occupies in the Negro renaissance, I had expected to see a brusque, cold-blooded individual whose efficiency and belief in sex equality would be fairly jumping at one. I imagined she was engrossed in herself and work, sophisticated and self-sufficient.... All of which was wrong.
>
> She is very sensitive, retiring and absolutely feminine ["Through the Lorgnette," *Pittsburgh Courier*, October 29, 1927].

Of course, what is flagrant in Dismond's column is the implication that Douglas Johnson can be accepted and liked despite her "transgression" of writing, providing that she remains a nice, soft woman.

The publications appearing in the late teens and early twenties reflect the bliss that Johnson enjoyed at the beginning of the century. However, her joy was to be disrupted by the imminent tragedy that lurked in the background and arrived on September 10, 1925. On that fateful date, Henry Lincoln's death occurred, and his demise marked a critical turning point for Johnson.

Yet however grieved, Georgia could not have been surprised by her husband's death. She had received two warning signals in 1921 and 1923 when Link suffered from attacks of apoplexy. Fortunately, for the Johnson family, Link rebounded from both strokes and his 1921 recovery was one of the subjects of Dunbar-Nelson's journal entry for Saturday, October 1. In observing Link, the diarist wrote: "Looks well, and says he's feeling all right, in spite of his stroke, save for a stiffness in the muscles of his throat. His speech has the occasional earmarks of the recovered paralytic, carefulness of pronunciation, with an occasional slurring over words with a preponderance of vowels" (Hull 1984, 87). The year 1925, however, proved to be an inauspicious one for the Johnsons, because Henry's large, rotund body did not survive the third stroke that afflicted him, and succumbing to his final bout with apoplexy, Link died of a cerebral hemorrhage caused by a stroke.

Georgia celebrated Henry's life with an "impressive and imposing" funeral that was attended by "many high state officials," including the secretary of labor and the postmaster general. At the service, Link was eulogized as a statesman whose career could be compared to that of Christ, and Georgia received Calvin Coolidge's condolence letter in which the president told her "of my sorrow at his passing and of the sympathy which I feel for you and your sons in your great loss" (*Washington Daily American*, September 14, 1925). Georgia's loss was indeed a great one, for at 48 years of age, Henry's death had left her a widow in a white male-dominated society, had made her the sole parent of two teenage sons (15 and 17), and had compelled her to be the family's economic mainstay. Yet Link's death also gave her an undeniable emancipation from her husband's demands and left Johnson with some freedom to write. The life and the literature that she produced in the years following Link's death now becomes a focal point. Because Georgia lived a long time, her life and literature will be considered within the decades— the twenties, thirties, forties, fifties, and sixties—that comprise her life span.

In the years immediately following Link's death, Georgia returned to the workforce, an arena that she had not frequented since her marriage. The financial burdens of rearing two children and maintaining her home led her to hold a series of public jobs until 1934. The positions which she held during this period included that of substitute teacher and librarian for the Washington, D.C., public schools, file clerk for the Civil Service, and Commissioner of Immigration (immigrant inspector) for the Department of Labor. From 1925 to 1935, she assumed the title Commissioner of Conciliation (labor inspector), Department of Labor, a position that required her to investigate "living conditions among laborers" (Moorland-Spingarn Vertical File).

The demands of employment consumed Johnson's attention and left her with the anxiety of having little time to write. The twin concerns about time and the urgency to earn an income preyed so heavily on Georgia's mind that a reporter was inspired to write in a 1928 newspaper article: "The great fear in Georgia Douglas Johnson's life is that she won't have time to do all the work she has planned to do that she wants to do. Although she works incessantly, her time is too much taken up with making a living to give very much of it to literary work" (*Pittsburgh Courier*, July 1928). Further alluding to Johnson's financial hardships and their challenge to her productivity is a June 21, 1927, letter of recommendation that W.E.B. Du Bois wrote for her: "She has succeeded in writing poetry by the hardest kind of application in the midst of every sort of distraction" (Harmon Foundation Records). Yet, it was Johnson herself, who was the most explicit about her economic plight: "If I might ask of some fairy godmother special favors, one would sure be for a clearing space, elbow room in which to think and write and live beyond the reach of the Wolf's fingers" (*Opportunity*, July 1927, 204).

Despite Johnson's preoccupation with earning a salary, not all of her post–1925 activities were job related. Perhaps her most sensational undertakings of that time were her literary evenings, which were gatherings that she hosted at her Washington, D.C., home for local and out-of-town "literati" of both races. These events both enhanced Johnson's fame and made the nation's capital another locus for the Harlem Renaissance. Fondly recalling the inception of these gatherings Johnson writes:

> Years ago—Jean Toomer said to me "Mrs. J—Why don't you have Weekly Conversations among the writers here in Washington?" It was difficult for me to arrange as home duties had about consumed me before Saturday night, however, I did make an attempt and we began the Saturday evening talks which continued until through about ten years and came to life intermittently now and then to the present [Hull 1987, 165].

The first documentation of this assemblage appears in Gwendolyn Bennett's "Ebony Flute" column, October 1926:

> We who clink our cups over New York fire-places are wont to miss the fact that little knots of literary devotees are in like manner sipping their "cup of warmth" in this or that city of the "provinces." Which reminds me that I have heard Georgia Douglas Johnson say that there is a Saturday Nighters Club in Washington, too ["The Ebony Flute," *Opportunity*, October 1926, 322].

During the decade (1926–36) of its flourishing, numerous black writers—renowned and obscure—frequented Johnson's bay-windowed living room in Washington, D.C. Guests included Jean Toomer, Langston Hughes, Countee Cullen, Marietta Bonner, Bruce Nugent, Angelina Grimké, Lewis Alexander, Jessie Fauset, Wallace Thurman, Arna Bontemps, Effie Lee Newsome, Anne Spencer, James Weldon Johnson, Alain Locke, W.E.B. Du Bois, William Stanley Braithwaite, Mae Miller, Willis Richardson, Mary P. Burrill and her brother-in-law Roscoe Conkling Bruce, E.C. Williams, A. Philip Randolph, Chandler Owens, Professor Kelly Miller, Eric Walrond, Mae Howard Jackson, *Opportunity*'s Charles S. Johnson, Gwendolyn Bennett, Alice Dunbar-Nelson, and Clarissa Scott Delaney. In addition to these Renaissance writers, Vachel Lindsay, Edna St. Vincent Millay, Waldo Frank, and H.G. Wells also came.

One contemporary journalist described these gatherings as "interesting, lively, many-hued":

> If dull ones come, she [Johnson] weeds them out, gently, effectively. The Negro's predicament is such, Mrs. Johnson believes, that only the white people can afford to have dull leaders. It is a remarkable social phenomenon to see this woman, who works eight hours a day in the Department of Labor, wielding by sheer force of personality an important influence ["The Ebony Flute," *Opportunity*, July 1927, 212].

Two accounts from the summer of 1927 attest to the especial brilliance of that year. Gwendolyn Bennett recounts the June 4 meeting where Charles Spurgeon Johnson was guest of honor and Angelina Grimké was "particularly pleasing," and the entire group was "a charming medley":

> E.C. Williams with his genial good-humor; Lewis Alexander with jovial tales of this thing and that as well as a new poem or two which he read; Marieta Bonner with her quiet dignity; Willis Richardson with talk of "lays and things" ... and here and there a new poet or playwright ... and the whole group held together by the dynamic personality of Mrs. Johnson ... some poems by Langston Hughes were read ["The Ebony Flute," *Opportunity*, July 1927, 212].

Dunbar-Nelson records in her July 23, 1927, journal some colorful examples of pre–Salon escapades and the actual literary evening. In the course of the day, she, Douglas Johnson, and another mutual friend are lost and are traipsing over Washington, while the assembled guests are expecting them:

> Georgia looking like the Tragic Muse thinking of the little poets she had invited to meet me and how it was getting on to nine o'clock ... finally reach Georgia's at 9:45. She and I make explanations. A near-high bunch. Willis Richardson and his wife, the most interesting and little John Davis. Much poetry and discussion and salad and wine and tea and Bobbo [Dunbar-Nelson's husband] rescues me at midnight [Hull 1984, 185].

Although Johnson intended to publish a book about her Literary Salon, mentioning in 1942 that she has it "sketched out" and that she has kept "letters and original poems" of "our young writers," which "will make a valuable contribution to the early history of these writers," she never published a book on her Saturday Nighters—much to the loss of American and African American literature (Cullen-Jackman Collection).

"During this splendid period following Link's death," in particular the later 1920s, Johnson became something of a public figure, as evidenced by her travels, speaking engagements and coverage by newspapers. In 1926, she went to Chicago and was "graciously received" by Harriet Monroe of *Poetry* magazine and chatted with Carl Sandburg "of this and that thing about Negroes and their works" ("The Ebony Flute," *Opportunity*, November 1926, 357). In New York City, during the Fall of 1927, she met social columnist Geraldyn Dismond, who was impressed not "by the fact that Mrs. Johnson can create a poem or play, but by the charm of her quiet dignity and tender sympathy" (Dismond, Geraldyn, "Through the Lorgnette," *Pittsburgh Courier*, October 29, 1927). Later that same season, Johnson traveled to Durham, North Carolina, for a Black Fact-Finding and Stock-Taking Conference. At this meeting, she was honored with four other "distinguished ladies"—including Mary McLeod Bethune, Charlotte Hawkins Brown, Alice Dunbar-Nelson, and Mrs. Benjamin Brawley. On her return trip to Washington, she, Dunbar-Nelson, and Du Bois took a taxi to her home, went shopping, and then prepared a "breakfast fit for the gods" before going their separate paths (Hull 1984, 207; entries for December 9 and 10, 1927).

In the spring of 1928, she visited Atlanta, Georgia, where she delivered the dedicatory talk for a new building that was being erected by the Neighborhood Union. Sometime before January 16, 1929, she went to Cleveland, Ohio, and visited author Charles Chesnutt and his family, noting in a letter of that same date to him: "I do not lightly forget the trip I had to Cleveland for standing out most conspicuously is the memory of my talk with you and also my trip to your wonderful home" (Charles Chesnutt Collection, Fisk).

In addition to earning publicity from her travels and speaking engagements, Johnson also gained exposure from favorable newspaper coverage. Especially noteworthy is Floyd J. Calvin's feature on her, which appeared in the *Pittsburgh Courier* July 1928 issue. It is subtitled "Educating Her Splendid Sons, Writing Poems and Plays—Her Days Are Quite Full." At the time that this article was published, Henry, Jr., was one year away from completing law at Howard University, and Peter had finished his first year of medical school at the same institution. As becomes apparent from the attention that this news feature accords her children's education (which ultimately included Bowdoin College and Dartmouth from which they also graduated), Johnson must have sustained extremely heavy financial burdens in educating her splendid sons.

While Calvin's article notes the formal instruction of Henry Lincoln, Jr., and Peter Douglas, it also outlines—in a good deal—the books Johnson has on hand, which "could, on short notice, be prepared for the publishers if she had the time to do it." Summarizing and categorizing these works Calvin writes: (1) "The Torch—inspirational bits written by famous authors, culled from a lifetime of reading; (2) "The Life and Times of Henry Lincoln Johnson," which "will give a detailed account of her husband's life from the time he entered politics down in Georgia at the age of 9" (One of the subjects which Johnson and Carl Sandburg discussed in Chicago was this material, which he told her "should make a corking story."); (3) "Short stories of mixed bloods" called "Rainbow Silhouettes" with plots about a girl passing for white in Salt Lake City, and "a little girl in a colored family, born of a wealthy white woman and her butler"; (4) "The Autumn Love Cycle"; and (5) "Homely Philosophy." The remainder of Calvin's feature considers Johnson as a playwright and gives attention to both her biography and her current civic and literary interests.

In reflecting on the *Courier* article, it may be concluded that, regardless of whatever else Johnson may have been engaged in, her celebrity status accrued to her because of her accomplishments as a writer. During the early to middle 1920s, she began to write plays, remarking in 1927: "Then [after poetry] came drama. I was persuaded to try it and found it a living avenue" ["The Contest Spotlight," *Opportunity*, July 1927, 204]. Critics judge Johnson to have been successful as a dramatist and add that were it not for the peculiarities of the genre and the vagaries of literary fortune, she could just as easily have come down through history known predominantly as a playwright rather than a poet. Moreover, in noting the emphasis that Johnson placed upon this genre in her self-compiled "Catalogue of Writings," a reader might conclude that drama was her major preoccupation as well as her preference (Hull 1987, 168).

Blue Blood, a one-act play that treats miscegenation via the rape of African American women by white men in the post-bellum South was Johnson's first play to win recognition. It won an honorable mention in the 1926 *Opportunity* drama contest. New York City's Krigwa Players produced the play that year, and Appleton Press published it the following year. Yet, however noteworthy this 1926 play was, it was *Plumes*, Johnson's second drama, that won first prize in the 1927 *Opportunity* competition. *Plumes* is a "folk tragedy" that is set in the early twentieth-century rural South. In this work, which is saturated with black folkways, beliefs, and superstitions, the poor mother of a very ill daughter must decide whether to spend $50 on a doubtful operation or on a beautiful funeral.

Critics were very impressed with this play. In fact, a *New York Amsterdam News* review stated that *Plumes* met the three conditions for "real Negro literature," namely "a Negro author, a Negro subject, and a Negro audience ("Book Review," *Amsterdam News*, Nov. 23, 1927). Gloria Hull observes that "in *Plumes* [Johnson] is as 'folk' as she is 'academic' in her poetry, striking an authentic roots level that eluded Grimké and Dunbar-Nelson" (Hull 1987, 170). Johnson included *Plumes* and *Blue Blood* among her four dramas that she designated as "Primitive Life Plays." The other two (both now lost) were *Red Shoes* and *Well-Diggers*. *Red Shoes* was written for the famous African American actress Rose McClendon, and it is a domestic play about a mother who purchased red shoes for her baby's burial, but the shoes were stolen by the child's drunken father for whiskey. In *Well-Diggers*, two Southern black law partners are concerned about whether they should exploit negative racial stereotypes to secure the acquittal of African American clients (Cullen-Jackman Collection).

Another category of drama that Johnson produced is the genre under scrutiny, i.e., the "lynching play." Like Grimké and nearly all African American writers and activists of the period, Johnson was alarmed by the astronomical number of blacks who were being routinely lynched in the nation—a number conservatively estimated at 1,886 persons for 1900–1931 (C. Eric Lincoln's statistics in *The Negro Pilgrimage in America*, 1967). Controversy on the crime of lynching was at its height during the 1920s because of the debate in Congress over the Dyer Anti-Lynching Bill, which ultimately was defeated in 1922. Two of her plays specifically focus on these Congressional "deliberations": "A Bill to be Passed," a one-act play touching Lynching Bill before Congress, outside of Congressional chamber, four character; and "And Still They Paused," concerning the continual delay in passing the bill. As earlier noted, Johnson's *A Sunday Morning in the South*, *Blue-Eyed Black Boy* and *Safe* continue the lynch theme and urge the adoption of federal anti-lynching legislation. In addition to producing lynch drama, Johnson also wrote and published two one-act history plays: *Frederick Douglas* (1935) and *William and Ellen Craft* (1935). These dramas present African American history lessons and are excellent tools of education for all audiences.

In the Johnson Collection, which contains a catalog of 28 plays that Georgia lists and summarizes, is the category of works that she terms "Plays of Average Negro life." Although seven works are listed under this group, only one play, *Starting Point*, is extant in a sixteen-page manuscript at the Yale University Beinecke Library. In this work, Henry and Martha Robinson, conscientious, but aging parents, believe their adored son Tom is "doing so fine up there in the doctor's school in Washington." However, in reality, Tom is writing numbers. Eventually, Tom comes home unannounced and brings with him a surprise wife, Henry's and Martha's "new daughter Belle—

!!" During his visit, Tom gets a telegram from a friend that informs him that his place has been raided and that advises him to stay away. Through Belle's coaxing, Tom is persuaded to "come clean" and confesses to his parents the criminal life that he has been leading. Henry and Martha are traumatized at Tom's revelation, and as scene 2 ends, the shouting between father and son gives way to Henry's slapping Tom, with Martha fainting. At the play's conclusion, father and son reconcile, and Tom agrees to start over as a porter at a bank.

Douglas Johnson provides the following summaries for the other six now nonexistent plays in this average Negro life category: *Holiday*, a Cinderella story about a plain sister who meets love staying at home; *Little Blue Pigeon*, which concerns a "young mulatto mother" who passes for white in order to keep her government job, thus enabling her "to take care of her baby—she being a newcomer in Washington, and a stranger;" *One Cross Enough* about a "light colored girl in Germany" who refuses to add her "cross of color" to her Jewish admirer's "Cross of being a Jew;" and *Sue Bailey*, a "three-act play based upon the stormy life of an unmarried girl who stabs her paramour, and begins to run away from the consequences of her act."

In addition to plays about average Negro life, Johnson wrote what she termed "brotherhood" dramas, which were aimed at annihilating racial intolerance, and a number of similar plays on biracial themes. Perhaps her most notable work on this topic is *Midnight and Dawn*, which is about an African American boy who saves a white boy and loses his eyesight, only to have it restored years later by the white male after he becomes wealthy and prominent. One or two of her plays have war settings and soldiers as characters; and there were a few works on miscellaneous themes to constitute the canon of 28 plays that Johnson lists in her catalog.

In treating her preferential drama topics, Johnson displayed great creative individuality and received the recognition and praise of her colleagues. In his article, "The Importance of Georgia Douglas Johnson," Cedric Dover lauded her as being the champion of visibly mixed-blood blacks:

> She has faced and resolved the psychological and social complications of being a near-white, while retaining enough traces of "tragic mulatto" feeling to stress the merit of her conquest.... She was the mother who nourished a whole generation of Eurasians and other "Mixed breeds" like myself. We found in her the blood and bone we needed to fight... [*The Crisis*, December 1952, 59: 635].

Yet despite her obsession with biracials, Johnson's dramatic canon shows that she wrote extensively about women and evidenced great sensitivity about their lives in diverse environments—e.g., the young government-worker mother and Ellen Craft as concubine-bound slave woman. Regardless of the topic of her play, nearly without exception, the women characters are center stage, as is evidenced in her plays under scrutiny in *Africa American Women Playwrights Confront Violence.*

While she garnered prestige and recognition with her drama, Johnson substantially increased her renown with the publication of her third book of poetry in 1928. It had been an entity since 1921 when it was an intact manuscript called *An Autumn Idyll*, which W.S. Braithwaite was offering to publishers. Appearing under the revised title, *An Autumn Love Cycle*, this volume tells the story of an autumnal woman's love affair, from its inception to its ultimate resolution. It can only be conjectured whether this work is autobiographical or not. One is tempted to wonder if Johnson had an affair during this time which coincided with Link's stroke. Possibly his paralysis served as the impetus for this ardent poetry. Georgia's friend Dunbar-Nelson comments on such a possibility and writes in her diary on Saturday, October 1, 1921:

> Georgia showed me the manuscript of her new book, which Braithwaite is offering to the publishers. She does exquisite verses, and these are wonderfully fine—a story, running like a fine golden thread through them all. "An Autumn Idyll" it is called.... It makes you blush at times, the baring of the inmost secrets of a soul, as it does. I wonder what Link thinks of it? You might call it poetic inspiration, if you will, but it looks suspiciously to me as if Georgia had had an affair, and it had been a source of inspiration to her [Hull 1984].

An Autumn Love Cycle elevated Johnson's status and helped to secure her niche as a recognized woman poet. Crucial to the renown that she achieved with this third publication was the support of the three leading black intellectuals of the age: W.E.B. Du Bois, William Stanley Braithwaite, and Alain Locke. With this particular work, Johnson certainly experienced the benefits of male generosity.

Ann Allen Shockley notes that love, the focal point of Johnson's poems, spilled over into her real world in a contagious way. She wanted everyone to love and to be loved. To this purpose, she sponsored a Lonely Hearts Club for people to meet and correspond throughout the country. Johnson assigned the members categories, according to their education, age, place of residence, marital status, and experience in life. Coinciding with this, she issued a Washington social letter which cost two dollars a year. One Lonely Hearts prospective member called her club a "Godsend to lonesome girls" (Shockley 349).

Johnson also wrote columns entitled "Homely Philosophy," "Wise Sayings," and "Beauty Hints" for twenty-eight black newspapers (Georgia Douglas Johnson Collection). In 1941, she started an interracial column for the *Amsterdam News* to foster a better understanding between the races. She was an ardent proponent of brotherhood. One of her many unpublished works was a book, *Bridge to Brotherhood*, which she wrote to "foster and promote good feeling between the races." It combined eighty poems with songs and music (Shockley 350).

Johnson penned numerous unpublished short stories, some under the pseudonym of Paul Tremain, and others with Gypsy Drago. Seventeen of those written with Drago were culled from his life as a man who did not know he was black until the age of thirty. Her "The Skeleton" won a first prize through the *Washington Tribune*.

Johnson tried in vain to get her book, *The Black Cabinet, Being the Life of Henry Lincoln Johnson*, published. The biography of her husband was to have told "the true story of Republican politics in the South from the Reconstruction to 1924." And almost until her death, she tried to interest publishers in another book, *White Men's Children*, with a theme of the "interplay of bloods" (Shockley 1988, 351).

Despite her creative output in her early years, Johnson was unable to obtain philanthropic aid to finance her writing and to exempt her from employment. She was turned down for grants by the Guggenheim, Whitney, and Rosewald foundations. She wrote to Harold Jackman: "You would be surprised to know how many foundations I have tried, and more surprised to learn that ... each one, said 'no,' but most surprised to learn that I have still high hopes" (Shockley 1988, 351).

Regarding her personality, Johnson was "genuinely nice, optimistic, trustful, self-abnegating and nurturing—sometimes to a degree that became inappropriate or discomfiting, especially when she acted impulsively" (Hull 1987, 186). A case in point appears in a 1929 incident, in which she wrote author Charles Chesnutt a note of appreciation for an award with which he had nothing to do (Hull 186). In general, she was gracious and accommodating, as exemplified by the help she extended Carl Van Vechten in his founding of the James Weldon Johnson Memorial Collection at Yale University in 1942. In this enterprise, she wrote letters to Harold Jackman, in which she gave suggestions about whom to ask for documents. She also supplied addresses and personally contacted authors for their support (Hull 1987, 18).

Biographers remark that for whatever reason, Johnson was especially fond of a large number of lesbians and gays—including Harold Jackman, Glenn Carrington, Angelina Grimké, Alaine Locke, Bruce Nugent, Langston Hughes, Mary P. Burrill, and Wallace Thurman. She called the younger males her "sons"—"Indeed I am rich in sons. Glenn was very lovely to me."—and they addressed her as "mother" (Cullen-Jackman Collection). She was particularly close to Jackman and Carrington, and through their correspondence, glimpses into a larger mixed lesbian-homosexual circle can be seen. For instance, in December 1932, she writes Carrington, "Nina [Angelina] Grimké is back.... Call her up"; and in his 1957 letter to her, he outlines the "several months last year I was occupied with Mr. Locke and his illness." During this time, Carrington notes that he encouraged the weak and dying Locke to dictate his book to him, adding: "I saw more of him and had more heart to heart talks with him during those last sad weeks than anyone else" (Cullen-Jackman Collection).

Crucial to this study is the correspondence, which provides glimpses at the very private Mary Burrill. Its suggestions about her character and her sexuality are priceless. A letter to Jackman dated December 26, 1944, initially introduces Burrill: "Miss B[urrill] was here last week. Came to bury the lady with whom she used to live." Subsequently, Johnson intimates that Burrill has been asking her for poems, which Mary uses as her own: "She asked for another, bearing upon the death of a fr[ie]nd. I did not comply this time. Experience is a hard school but fools will learn in no other." And then addressing her anxiety about Grimké, Georgia writes: "Why is it Nina does not write to me? Please tell her to. I hope she is not sick" (Cullen-Jackman Collection).

Burrill is also the focus of Johnson's letter to Jackman dated January 10, 1945. In this cryptic correspondence, Georgia elaborates on Burrill's plagiarism, enumerates some of Mary's literary accomplishments and intimates that Burrill may be "passing."

> A friend [Burrill?] had me to send her a copy of most of my new poems. Said she wished to send them to a Boston literary friend.... She never sent them and never said why but I continued to send her the poems I read to her over the phone.
> One, "After a Tho[u]sand Years"—she said Oh let me put my name on that as though I wrote it. I said oh no I couldn't do that. She said nothing more did nothing more but took a copy of each ... saying she wished a poem to have read in school. It was not read.
> Now ... Mary Powell Burrill [is] ... very fine in elocution and has done a fine play. Had a poem in a good magazine in the last war.... Some evening will you call to see her—she maybe passing [Cullen-Jackman Collection].

Maintaining Half-Way House—her residence for over fifty years—was one of the predominant forms of Johnson's social life. In explaining the reason for naming 1461 S Street NW, Washington, D.C., as such, she replied: "I'm half way between everybody and everything and I bring them together" (*The Baltimore Afro-American*, May 28, 1966). And indeed she did—including old lame dogs, blind cats, limping animals, and stray people, who were mostly impoverished artists. Zora Neale Hurston was one recipient of Johnson's largess. It was also from Half-Way House that Georgia produced her literature, surrounded by flowers in her yard and window boxes to cheer passersby.

Johnson wrote steadily until her death, remaining until the end in her Half-Way House, which by 1966 had become ruined by urban blight. She stayed on with her books, writing, memories, and dashed hopes, becoming known as "the old woman with the headband and the tablet around her neck." The tablet with pencil was in readiness to write down "an idea, a word, a line for a poem." Even as an octogenarian, she stayed mentally alert, studying journalism at nearby Howard University (Shockley 1988, 351).

Throughout her life, Johnson was active in several literary-social clubs and organizations such as the American Society of African Culture, the (New York City) Civic Club, the National Song Writers Guild, the (D.C.) Matrons, the Poet's Council of the National Women's Party, the Republican party, and the Writers League Against Lynching. She was also a member of the First Congregational Church. In May 1966, she suffered a stroke and was taken to Freedman's Hospital, where with writer May Miller at her bedside, she died quietly on Saturday, May 14. At her demise, she left behind a dozen musical compositions, short stories, plays, and newspaper articles, which may be found in part, at the Georgia Douglas Johnson Collection in Oberlin College, Oberlin, Ohio.

Myrtle Smith Livingston

Born to Lula C. (Hall) and Isaac Samuel Smith in Holly Grove, Arkansas, Myrtle Athleen Smith (May 8, 1902–July 15, 1974) attended Manual High School from 1916 to 1920 and studied pharmacy at Howard University in Washington, D.C., from 1920 to 1922. Much of what is known about her obscure life has been retrieved through the efforts of Dr. Koritha Mitchell, assistant professor, department of English, Ohio State University.

In 1923 she enrolled in Colorado Teacher's College where she earned a teaching certificate in 1924. One year later, she married physician Dr. William McKinley Livingston on June 25, 1925. In 1926, Livingston left Colorado Teacher's College and was hired in 1929 as a physical education teacher by Lincoln University, a historically African American college in Jefferson City, Missouri. As an instructor at Lincoln, she taught every level of physical education and health and established a formal athletic program for female students, enabling young Lincoln women to participate in organized competitive sports for the first time. Livingston was also very active as a dancer and founded the first chapter of the Orchesis Dance Group in 1936. This chapter was the first to be founded at an African American college. The group gave both indoor and outdoor performances in tap and interpretive dance. In addition to these activities, Livingston taught first aid to Jefferson City citizens during World War II and wrote several plays during this period. Livingston was well respected among her students and colleagues. She taught at Lincoln for forty-four years and retired in 1972. In 1974, Livingston died in Hawaii, having moved there with her sister after leaving Lincoln. Her ashes were sprinkled across the Pacific Ocean, and a park, which remains open today, was named in her honor on Lincoln University's campus (Lincoln University Archives).

Livingston's *For Unborn Children* signified her connection to historical movements that helped shape her generation. Coming of age during the Harlem Renaissance, the young writer benefited from endeavors to develop black artists. During her attendance at Howard University, professors Thomas Montgomery Gregory and Alain Locke were laboring to make their institution the nation's training ground for black theater artists. The university's program encouraged playwriting, and by 1924 interracial political organizations began sponsoring literary contests in their magazines.

Gregory, Locke, and Du Bois were promoters, supporters, and judges in these politically sponsored contests. However, they disagreed about what African American drama and theater should accomplish. Gregory and Locke promoted "folk" plays that were devoid of strong political content; they focused on aesthetics because they wanted their students' work to be viewed by the dominant culture as truly artistic. Du Bois, on the other hand, felt that African American artists limited themselves by adhering to any aesthetic that ignored art's inherent political power and that denied the significance of directly protesting racism and injustice. Understandably, Du Bois valued race plays, particularly anti-lynching dramas, because they indicted American racism.

Alice Herndon Childress

Alice Childress (1912–1994)—thespian, director, playwright, novelist, columnist, essayist, lecturer, and theater consultant—was born on October 12, 1912, in Charleston, South Carolina. When she was five, she was taken to Harlem, New York, to be reared by her grandmother, Eliza Campbell, the daughter of a slave, who encouraged her to write. As Childress remarked in an interview in 1987, quoted in *Black Literature Criticism*, her grandmother "used to sit at the window and say, 'There goes a man. What do you think he's thinking?' I'd say 'I don't know. He's going home to his family'.... When we'd get to the end of our game, my grandmother would say to me, 'Now, write that down. That sounds like something we should keep.'" Grandmother Eliza exposed young Alice to museums, libraries, art galleries, theaters, and concert halls. She made a point to expose her granddaughter to Wednesday night testimonials at Salem Church in Harlem. At these meetings, poor people told of their hardships, which Childress mentally stored for future literary use.

Childress attended Public School 81, The Julia Ward Howe Junior High School, and Wadleigh High School for three years before dropping out when both her Grandmother Eliza and mother passed in the late 1930s. An avid reader with an insatiable curiosity, young Alice found a home in the public library where she read two or more books a day. Childress maintained a plethora of jobs during the 1940s to support herself and daughter Jean Rosa, an only child from her first marriage to the late actor Alvin Childress, who was best known for playing the cabdriver Amos Jones in the 1950s television comedy *Amos 'n' Andy*. Childress worked as an assistant machinist, photo retoucher, sales associate, domestic worker, and insurance agent—all jobs that kept her in close contact with working-class people like the characters in her work. The personae in her fiction and drama include seamstresses, domestic workers, washerwomen, the unemployed, as well as dancers, teachers, and artists.

On July 17, 1957, Childress married professional musician and music instructor Nathan Woodard. She revealed that her only child Jean Rosa (Mrs. Richard Lee, born November 1, 1935), from her first marriage died on Mother's Day in 1990 of cancer. A casualty of cancer, herself, Childress passed on August 14, 1994. She was residing in Long Island, New York, with Woodard at the time.

Childress began her writing career in the early 1940s, shortly after she heard a Shakespeare reading and chose acting as a career. In 1943 she began an eleven-year affiliation with the American Negro Theater (ANT), an organization that functioned as a home for numerous African American dramatists, thespians, and producers, such as Sidney Poitier, Ossie Davis, Ruby Dee, and Frank Silvera. Childress involved herself in every facet of the theater, as was the tradition practiced by anyone associated with ANT. Childress is acknowledged as one of the founders of ANT, which institutionalized theater in the black community. As a consequence of her commitment to ANT, in the 1950s, Childress was instrumental in getting advanced guaranteed salaries for union Off Broadway contracts in New York.

Florence (1949), Childress' first drama, was prompted by a bet from her longtime friend Sidney Poitier who insisted that a strong play could not be constructed overnight. Poitier lost his challenge because *Florence*, written overnight is certainly a well-crafted drama that indicts presumptuous whites who believe they know more about African Americans than African

Americans know about themselves. *Florence* also cautions African Americans to reject stereotyped roles. On another level, the play is a tribute to African American parents who encourage their children to achieve the fullest potential by any means necessary. Critics observe that Childress' first play reveals her superb skill at characterization, dialogue, and conflict.

After the ANT production of *Florence*, Childress proceeded to write a myriad of plays and children's books, including *Just a Little Simple* (1950), *Gold through the Trees* (1952), *Trouble in Mind* (1955), *Wedding Band: Love/ Hate Story in Black and White* (1966), *The World on a Hill* (1968), *String* (1969), *The Freedom Drum*, retitled *Young Martin Luther King* (1969), *Wine in the Wilderness* (1969), *Mojo: A Black Love Story* (1970), *When the Rattlesnake Sounds* (1975), *Let's Hear It for the Queen* (1976), *Sea Island Song*, retitled *Gullah* (1984), and *Moms* (1987). Childress's dramas incorporate the liturgy of the black church, traditional music, African mythology, folklore, and fantasy. She has produced sociopolitical, romantic, biographical, historical, and feminist dramas.

Childress' writings have earned several important awards, including writer in residence at the MacDowell Colony; featured author on a BBC panel discussion on "The Negro in the American Theater"; winner of a Rockefeller grant, administered through the New Dramatists and an award from the John Golden Fund for Playwrights; and a Harvard appointment to the Mary Ingraham Bunting Institute, from which she received a graduate medal.

Childress enjoyed a fruitful acting career. In 1940, she appeared as Dolly in John Silvera and Abram Hill's *On Striver's Row*. In 1944, she had a role in the Broadway production of *Anna Lucasta*, for which she earned a Tony nomination. In 1948, she appeared as Sadie Thompson in John Colton and Clemence Randolph's adaptation of Somerset Maugham's *Rain* and as Muriel in Harry Wagstaff's *Gribble's Almost Faithful*. In 1953 she appeared in the Off Broadway production of *The World of Sholom Aleichem* and as Bella in George Tabori's *The Emperor's Clothes*. In 1960 she appeared as Mrs. Thurston in Warren Miller and Robert Rossen's *The Cool World*.

In addition to being a dramatist and a thespian, Childress was also a novelist. Her first novel, *Like One of the Family: Conversations from a Domestic's Life* (1956), illustrates Childress's quick wit as the protagonist, who instructs her white employers to see their own inhumanity. This work consists of sixty-two conversations between Mildred, an African American domestic, and her friend Marge. What emerges from their talks is a rich picture of the life of working African American women in New York City during the 1950s. Childress' second novel, *A Hero Ain't Nothin' But a Sandwich* (1973), was made into a movie in which she served as the screenplay's author. It tells the story of one boy's realistic struggle against drug addiction. *A Short Walk* (1979), Childress' third novel, portrays the brief life of Cora James, who moves from the racist and restrictive early twentieth-century South to the North in search of a better life. This book supplies historical and cultural insights into the black experience from the Harlem Renaissance to the civil rights movement of the 1960s. Childress' fourth novel *Rainbow Jordan* (1981), examines the ramifications of growing up African American and female under the guidance of a myriad of women from the community. While her go-go dancer mother deserts her, Rainbow's substitute mothers nurture and usher her into adulthood. *Those Other People* (1989), Childress' final novel, investigates the issues of homophobia, racism, sexism, and classism. In this work, she focuses on a three-month period in the interconnected lives of five individuals who are viewed as social outcasts: Jonathan Barnett, a seventeen-year-old homosexual; Tyrone and Susan Tate, a brother and sister from a wealthy black family; Rex Hardy, a teacher who has sexually molested a student; and Theodora Lynn, a teenager who is in therapy because she has been sexually assaulted as a child.

Critics observe that Childress' incisive language and skillful manipulation of multiple narrators place her with writers such as William Faulkner and Ernest J. Gaines. Her novels, like her dramas, portray impoverished people who fight to survive in racist and capitalist America. Childress includes black history in her novels to instruct young African Americans about the dauntless individuals who have pioneered the path for them to achieve. Elizabeth Brown-Guillory aptly notes that Alice Childress' principal contribution to African American life and culture was her balanced depiction of black women and men working together to heal their wounds and survive in a splintered universe.

Sandra Cecelia Browne Seaton

Sandra Cecelia Browne Seaton, playwright and librettist, was born on July 10, 1942, in Columbia, Tennessee, to Albert Browne and Hattye Evans, both educators. While her mother taught at school, young Sandra relished listening to her grandmother's stories of bygone days, always narrated with great spirit. Despite the fact that her grandmother's contemporaries condemned the field of entertainment as a career choice, Seaton's grandmother, Emma Louish Evans, frequently performed as an endman in local amateur minstrel shows, demonstrating even as an elderly lady her minstrel routines. Her stories and career are still a significant influence on Seaton's writing. Grandma Evans also fostered great pride in the dramatic contributions of their relative Flournoy Miller, who wrote the book and starred in *Shuffle Along*, a musical that preceded *Show Boat* in integrating songs and story into an artistic whole, and, according to Arna Bontemps, inaugurated the Harlem Renaissance.

Seaton's dramas have been performed in cities throughout the nation, including New York, Chicago, Los Angeles, Cleveland, Ann Arbor and East Lansing, Michigan. Seaton has examined the relationship between Thomas Jefferson and his slave/mistress Sally Hemings in a number of works. The first was her libretto for the song cycle *From the Diary of Sally Hemings*, a collaboration with Pulitzer Prize–winning composer William Bolcom, who set Seaton's text to music. The work, for voice and piano, recreates the thoughts and feelings of Sally Hemings throughout her long relationship with Thomas Jefferson by means of fictional diary entries. Seaton's text presents Sally Hemings as a complex individual who refused to be defined only as Jefferson's mistress. *From the Diary of Sally Hemings*, sung by mezzo-soprano Florence Quivar, premiered at the Coolidge Auditorium of the Library of Congress on March 16, 2001. *From the Diary of Sally Hemings*, was commissioned by Music Accord, Inc., a national consortium of presenters including the Boston Symphony Orchestra at Tanglewood, the Library of Congress in Washington, D.C., San Francisco Performances, the Chamber Music Society of Lincoln Center in New York, the Fortas Chamber Music Series, the Kennedy Center, the Ravinia Festival of Highland Park, Illinois, The Krannert Center at the University of Illinois in Urbana, and the University Musical Society, University of Michigan at Ann Arbor.

The *Washington Post* praised this work for its "subtle, penetrating power." Seaton acknowledges her debt to the internationally acclaimed mezzo-soprano Florence Quivar whose vision was the genesis of this work. In 2008 Alyson Cambridge sang *From the Diary of Sally Hemings* at Oberlin Conservatory and Harkness Chapel at Case Western Reserve University. In Seaton's one-woman play, *Sally*, an aged Sally Hemings recalls her life with Jefferson, reliving and re-evaluating the dilemmas she has faced and the choices she has made. *Sally* debuted at the New York State Writers Institute in 2003 with Zabryna Guevara as Sally Hemings. *Sally* was performed in February 2008 at the University of Colorado, Denver and at Skidmore College in Saratoga Springs, New York, with Mizran Nunes as Sally. Seaton's most recent play, *A Bed Made in Heaven*, which further explores the relationship between Jefferson and Sally Hemings, premiered at Central Michigan University in 2007.

In May 2008, her play *The Will* was produced in Idlewild, Michigan, as part of a weekend event she organized that included a symposium on the connections between African American culture and classical music, youth workshops, and recitals. *The Will* offers both an interpretation of the significance of the importance of Reconstruction for African Americans and an interpretation of African American culture that brings out the place of classical music in African American history and life. The play includes a character based on the life of Elizabeth Taylor Greenfield, known as "The Black Swan," who became one of the most famous opera singers of her time, though she was born a slave.

In August 2008 Seaton's play *The Bridge Party* was performed for the American Bridge Association under the direction of Aaron Todd Douglas. William Bolcom's piano rags provided musical background for *The Bridge Party* at Michigan State University in a 2000 production. A review in *The State News* described *The Bridge Party* as a "careful look at women's wisdom and strength that dissects racial prejudice and its impact on everyday life." Ruby Dee appeared in a 1998 production of *The Bridge Party* directed by Glenda Dickerson at the University of Michigan with a cast that included Adilah Barnes, Michele Shay, Kim Staunton and Lynda Gravatt.

Seaton's play *Martha Stewart Slept Here* was staged in 2008 at the Renegade Theatre festival in Lansing. Her spoken word piece, *King: A Reflection on the Life of Dr. Martin Luther King, Jr.*, premiered at the Black History Month Concert at the Wharton Center in East Lansing, Michigan, in January 2005. Her works in progress include a trilogy of plays about African American students at a Midwestern university during the Civil Rights movement entitled *Room and Board, Do You Like Philip Roth?* and *Reservations*. In May 2009, her one-act drama *A Chance Meeting* featuring George Shirley was performed in Ann Arbor at the Arthur Miller Theater as part of the Ann Arbor Book Festival.

A professor of English at Central Michigan University, Seaton teaches courses in playwriting, fiction writing, and African American literature. Her scholarly work, which has been microfilmed by the Tennessee State archives, focuses on research about African American communities in the South from colonial times through the era of segregation. Seaton received her BA from the University of Illinois (Urbana), where she studied with John Frederick Nims, George Scouffas, and Webster Smalley. She earned her MA in creative writing at Michigan State University where she studied with Robert A. Martin. Seaton has been awarded residencies at Hedgebrook, Ragdale, and Yaddo artists colonies. She is married to James Seaton and is the mother of four children.

Endesha Ida Mae Holland

In 1983, after meeting Dr. Maulana Karenga, the eminent scholar of African history and culture and the creator of Kwanza, Ida Mae Holland (1944–2006) added Endesha to her name, not only to distinguish herself from her mother (with whom she shared the name Ida Mae) but also to symbolize the manner in which she had motivated herself and others to transcend their circumstances. Endesha is a Swahili word that means "Driver—she who drives herself and others forward" (Holland, 1997, 308). This name epitomizes all that Holland stands for and all that her memoir *From the Mississippi Delta* chronicles. She is, indeed, the mighty woman who transcended agony and adversity to achieve her dreams.

Endesha was born on August 29, 1944, in Greenwood, Mississippi, to Ida Mae Holland (Ain't Baby). Although she never knew the identity of her biological father, she experienced the infrequent presence of three daddies "depending on the time of year; a Christmas daddy, Mr. Ethan, who lived in Ohio; an Easter daddy, Mr. Warren, who lived in Chicago; and a birthday daddy, Mr. Goosch who came every August" ("Endesha Ida Mae Holland," http:www.answers.com/topic/endesha-ida-mae-holland). The youngest of four children, Endesha was preceded by Simon Redmond, Jr., who lived in Minneapolis until his death in 1992, her older sister Jean (Holland) Beasely, who currently lives in Minneapolis and "Bud" Nellums. As the baby of the family, Holland was especially attached to her mother, who told Endesha stories as she ironed white people's clothes. In a later interview with *Nation*, Endesha reported that her mother became famous "for pressing so sharp a crease in a pair of trousers that they could stand up by themselves" ("Endesha Ida Mae Holland," http:www.answers.com/topic/endesha-ida-mae-holland).

The Holland family resided in a roach-infested double shotgun house on 114 East Gibbs Street, where Endesha's mother rented rooms out by the hour and retained permanent boarders. Ida Mae exerted a commanding influence on her daughter, who watched her midwife mother battle racism that both barred her from working in hospitals and prevented African Americans from being admitted to them. Endesha witnessed her mother's triumph, for Ida Mae, who was illiterate, became indispensable to the white pregnant community, who demanded her services.

Endesha's trials began early in life. At the age of nine, a white female motorist hit her. While the accident deferred Holland's dream of becoming a majorette, it brought in extra food and money for the family because the motorist felt guilty and provided material resources until she died. When she was eleven, Endesha was babysitting for a white toddler one day, when the mother of young Becky Ann led Holland to her husband's bedroom to be raped. Mr. Lawrence paid Endesha five dollars and then sent her back to watch his daughter. Reflecting upon her sexual assault by Mr. Lawrence, Endesha stated: "It happened to a lot of girls" ("Endesha Ida Mae Holland," http:www.answers.com/topic/endesha-ida-mae-holland). She added, "There was a saying that a white man didn't want to die unless he'd had a black girl" ("Endesha Ida Mae Holland," http:www.answers.com/topic/endesha-ida-mae-holland). At age thirteen, Endesha quit school and earned rent money for her mother and siblings as a prostitute.

One day, in pursuit of a customer, she followed a man into an office of the Student Nonviolent Coordinating Committee (SNCC). It was that day in 1962 that eighteen-year-old Endesha realized the value and power of education. Inside the office she saw African American women working at typewriters and became inspired to join the Freedom Riders Movement for which these black women worked. The Freedom Riders were integral to the Civil Rights movement. This particular branch of the movement focused on voter registration drives in Greenwood, Mississippi. Endesha was immediately taken in by these activists solely on the basis of her literacy. One of her jobs included writing down information for the illiterate townspeople who needed help and who wanted to vote. She traveled extensively across the nation for the civil rights movement, making important speeches and meeting important people who included Dr. Martin Luther King, Rosemary Freeman, Albert Barnett, and John Handy.

In the course of her life, Endesha was jailed more than a dozen times. *New York Times* writer Glenn Collins reported that the other civil rights workers were warned that Holland was a scandalous person; however, "the workers were all inexperienced in going to jail, [and] I was a veteran: I knew how to survive there.... I'd been there so often for stealing and fighting. I felt like a queen in jail. The workers really needed me, and I used to protect them" ("Endesha Ida Mae Holland," http:www.answers.com/topic/endesha-ida-mae-holland). Holland considered being jailed for her civil rights work as a real moment of glory.

Upon her return from a civil rights speaking tour, Endesha's home was firebombed, and she witnessed her mother die in flames at her own front door. Ironically, Holland had been having dreams all her life of her mother getting burned up. She told *People* magazine reporters: "Neighbors saw who did it but were afraid to say.... I think the firebomb was meant for me" ("Endesha Ida Mae Holland," http:www.answers.com/topic/endesha-ida-mae-holland). Endesha believed that the Ku Klux Klan was punishing her for participating in the civil rights movement. She headed north after her mother's murder and shortly thereafter enrolled in the University of Minnesota where she ultimately earned a bachelor's degree in African American Studies (1979); a master's in American Studies (1984) and a doctorate (1985). She invited all the street people she had met in the course of her journey to attend her doctoral graduation, and told *People*: "The whores and pimps and junkies were there.... When they called my name, the entire auditorium rose to its feet" ("Endesha Ida Mae Holland, Mississippi writer and playwright," http://www.mswritersandmusicians.com/writers/endesh-holland). While at the University of Minnesota, Endesha helped to start an African American studies program and initiated Women Helping Offenders (WHO), a prison-aid program that occupied a great portion of her time and that paid her a salary.

In a play-writing class that she took to satisfy degree requirements, Endesha wrote *The Second Doctor Lady*, about her mother. After reading it to the class, "Everyone was weeping" ("Endesha Ida Mae Holland, Mississippi writer and playwright," http://www.mswritersandmusicians.com/writers/endesh-holland). Endesha expanded this play into the celebrated *From the Mississippi Delta*. This three-woman play was performed in the States and in London before opening Off Broadway in late 1991. The play has been widely reviewed and, as *Time* noted, "blends folk tales, childhood memories, salty down-home sociological observations and blues and gospel standards with Holland's unabashed 'confessions.'" Critics generally applauded the drama ("Endesha Ida Mae Holland, Mississippi writer and playwright"). One *Variety* reviewer wrote, "Conceived in straightforward storytelling terms, the play is an extraordinary work of autobiography by someone who struggled against the twin evils of racial bigotry and poverty in the Mississippi delta in the '40s" ("Endesha Ida Mae Holland, Mississippi writer and playwright"). The *Nation*'s Margaret Spillane wrote that Endesha's play "contains two of the most astonishing dramatic moments I have ever seen onstage—the rape of eleven-year old Phelia, and her mother, Aint Baby, presiding over the birth of a couple's thirteenth child." Spillane added: "Ain't Baby regards her midwife's certificate not as an emblem of superiority over her neighbors but as a means to guarantee that their community will carry on.... [And] when Phelia uses her cap-and-gowned moment of glory to name every single person from the Delta and beyond who ever extended love and wisdom to her, she seems to rise atop a pyramid made of their names, their unseen lives unearthed by the act of naming" ("Endesha Ida Mae Holland, Mississippi writer and playwright").

In addition to her highly esteemed memoir, Endesha wrote six plays: *Fanny Lou* (1984); *Miss Ida B. Wells* (1984); *Prairie Women* (1984); *The Reconstruction of Dossie Ree Hemphill* (1980); *Requiem for a Snake* (1980) and *Second Doctor Lady* (1980). The three that have received the most recognition are *From the Mississippi Delta*, *Second Doctor Lady*, and *The Reconstruction of Dossie Ree Hemphill*. The latter two plays are about her mother and her mother's struggle to become a midwife. *From the Mississippi Delta*, as earlier noted, was inspired by her memoir. These plays have garnered many prestigious awards for Endesha, who became the recipient of the Second Place Lorraine Hansberry Award and a Pulitzer Prize nominee. Additionally, the mayor of Greenwood, Mississippi, dedicated a day to her, proclaiming it "Endesha Ida Mae 'Cat' Holland Day" on October 18, 1991.

Dr. Holland taught American studies at State University of New York

(SUNY) at Buffalo from 1985 to 1993 and at the University of Southern California until 2003 when she retired. Dr. Holland passed on January 25, 2003, at a nursing home in Santa Monica, California. The cause of death was from complications of ataxia, a degenerative neurological condition. Dr. Holland's three marriages ended in divorce. She bore one son, Cedric, and is survived by her sister, Jean Beasley; her brother, Charlie Nellums; and her granddaughter.

Michon Boston

Michon Boston, a native of Washington, D.C., was born September 16, 1962, to Theodore W. and Caroline Long Boston. She attended the Duke Ellington School of the Arts and graduated in June of 1980. She went on to earn a BA in English at Oberlin College in Ohio. Encouraged by the many illustrious African American alumnae of Oberlin, including Anna Julia Cooper and Mary Terrell, Boston won a grant from the National Endowment for the Humanities (NEH) for her research on the history of African American female students who attended Oberlin from the nineteenth century to 1979. According to Kathy Perkins, Boston found a voice in dramatic writing while pursuing other creative endeavors, which included music, the visual arts, and media. Her desire to write dramatically was long inspired by watching old black and white movies on television with her mother, observing her sister's activities as a theater major at Howard University, and hearing stories — truth or fiction — from the extended family (Perkins 1989, 367). In addition to *Iola's Letter*, Boston's other plays include *Stained Glass Houses* and *Anthropology*, which premiered at the Source Theatre, Washington, D.C. Boston has served on the board of Women in Film in Washington, D.C., and is a member of Playwrights Forum, Women in Film L.A., and the Dramatists Guild. Boston also designs and makes cloth dolls when she is not writing. Boston resides in Washington, D.C. (Perkins 1989, 367).

CHAPTER 3

The Plays

Lynching Dramas

Rachel (1916)

As earlier noted, the lynching plays had immediate reform as their goal, and they were written to support the National Association for the Advancement of Colored People (NAACP), as it labored to secure federal anti-lynch legislation. The NAACP and its anti-lynching campaign were especially crucial to the production history of *Rachel* and merit cursory attention.

In 1916, Boston philanthropist George Foster Peabody offered the association a $10,000 grant on the condition that it accelerate its approach to stemming racist violence. Responding to its financial incentive, the NAACP established the Committee on Anti-Lynching Programme, which extended the association's role from merely responding to lynchings as they occurred to preparing model anti-lynching bills for enactment by Congress. Grimké's father Archibald, of the association's Washington, D.C., branch spearheaded the new aggressiveness that the NAACP exhibited in its anti-lynch campaign. He quickly and aptly discerned in *Rachel* a means to dramatize and to publicize his organization's platform. The staging of the protest play offered the association the opportunity to present lynch data whose content, itself, advocated anti-lynch legislation.

Thus, using the three-act play to articulate its condemnation of racist violence, the NAACP—under the presidency of Grimké's father Archibald Henry—produced *Rachel* in 1916. The play premiered at the Myrtilla Miner School for girls in Washington, D.C., on March 3 and 4. It was also under the aegis of the NAACP that Archibald secured an additional staging of *Rachel* one year later at the Neighborhood Playhouse in New York City on

April 26. The production materialized after he requested that Dr. Joel Spingarn, chairman of the NAACP board of directors, organize a performance sponsored by the association's New York branch and patronized by most of the local members of the NAACP national board. That same year, Archibald's negotiations culminated in another production of *Rachel* under the auspices of the Sunday School of St. Bartholomew's Church at Brattle Hall, in Cambridge, Massachusetts, on May 24, 1917. In all three performances, the thespians were amateurs or semiprofessionals. However, the 1916 premiere, under the direction of NAACP member Nathaniel Guy, contained the most talent, vaunting actors Zita Dyson and Rachel and Nathaniel Guy.

Grimké benefited from this seeming nepotism. For with the support of the NAACP and the influence of her father, she became one of the first black writers—male or female—to have a serious full-length play produced and performed by African Americans during the second decade of the twentieth century. She also became the only woman dramatist out of the female core of eleven to have a play produced by the male-dominated association during her father's ten-year presidency of the Washington, D.C., branch.

In addition to being significant for articulating the association's condemnation of racist violence, *Rachel* is also important for expressing the NAACP's denunciation of D.W. Griffith's motion picture *The Birth of a Nation* (1915), which preached hatred of African Americans, stirred race riots, and justified the lynching of black citizens. A cursory look at both the association's effort to recall the film and at the obstacles that it met while combating the picture sheds additional light on the significance of *Rachel*'s premiere. Following *The Birth of a Nation*'s Los Angeles debut on February 8, 1915, at J.R. Clune's Auditorium, the NAACP initiated a national campaign to get the picture withdrawn, cut, and re-edited. Opposing their crusade, the film's distributor, Epoch Corporation mounted an unprecedented advertising campaign that magnified the impact of the movie. They employed advance sales, reserved seats, included an orchestral accompaniment, featured monster billboards of night riders in Time Square, scattered posters throughout suburban train stations, and used robed horsemen riding the streets to promote the movie (Cripps 1993, 53).

After the picture's New York premiere on March 3 of the same year, the NAACP intensified its polemics against the film's prejudice. The New York branch filed criminal proceedings against Griffith and demanded the local commissioner of licenses to stop the picture as a public nuisance. The Boston office published *Fighting a Vicious Film*, a 47-page pamphlet, as its contribution to the campaign. The association also sought the production of a motion picture that would portray African Americans positively to counter the deleterious effects of Griffith's work. The dearth of funds prevented such a film from materializing, but *Rachel*, which was staged the following year, answered the NAACP's call for an honest, genteel, and edifying representation of African Americans. Despite the NAACP's crusade to counterattack the film's damage, and despite the association's campaign to rally allies against the motion picture, whites flocked to the theaters to view the film and accepted its murderous logic.

Amid this furor, *Rachel* premiered. Stating the significance of the play, its program announced: "This is the first attempt to use the stage for race propaganda in order to enlighten the American people relative to the lamentable condition of ten million of Colored citizens in this free Republic" (Angelina Weld Grimké Collection). *Rachel* met with mixed reviews, because not everyone approved of its political message. The black artistic-intellectual community objected to the propaganda aspects of the plot and maintained that creative African American writing, including drama, should focus strictly on artistic intent and not become involved in political issues. Within this artistic-intellectual community, ideological differences over the definition of the role of art eventually led to the organization of the Howard Players, a group that chose to perform only noncontroversial, apolitical plays.

Another criticism of *Rachel* focused on Grimké's misrepresentation of her characters' problems. The Iowa *Grinnell Review* wrote: "Exaggeration spoils this play. Had Miss Grimké's negroes been less shabby-genteel, their tragedy would have been more convincing" (*Grinnell*, January 1921). Other critics observed that *Rachel* was "pitched in a highly emotional key" (*Washington [D.C.] Star*, Dec. 5, 1920); that it was "morbid and overstrained;" (*Rochester [NY] Post-Express*, September 14, 1920); and that despite instances to the contrary, it "pictures the negro's life as sad and his efforts to rise as unavailing" (*Utica [NY] Daily Press*, Oct. 8, 1920). The Wilmington, Delaware, *Every Evening* amplified this criticism and wrote: "Many who are familiar with colored people en masse will hardly incline to sympathy with the severely drawn picture presented in this play, as it is too radically at variance with the evidence so largely in view in communities throughout the northern part of the country where the Negro population is numerous"(*Wilmington [DE] Every Evening*, Sept. 4, 1920). Possibly the greatest insult was written by the Washington, D.C., *Star*, which suggested that Grimké should have written a completely different play:

> Perhaps another standpoint on the part of the author would have produced a more helpful drama. For instance, one that would cover the splendid half century of growth made by the colored race since its emancipation in the United States. Or possibly, one based on the progress of the individual, with that progress as his full compensation [*Washington (D.C.) Star*, Dec. 5, 1920].

It appears that some critics found Grimké's subject matter objectionable and preferred that she had not focused attention on the detestable conditions that the drama indicts. The Grinnell critic confessed that "we are made to feel the [black] race's tragedy with sufficient force to be thoroughly uncomfortable" (*Catholic World*, New York, NY, Dec. 1920).

Yet the bulk of the nearly fifty reviews received as of April 1921 were positive. Many of them reiterated *Rachel*'s subtitle, *A Play of Protest*, noted that "all the characters are colored," and praised Grimké for vividly portraying "the black man's burden." *The Catholic World* wrote: "As a protest against white prejudice it makes its mark, and its closing scene rises to the dignity of a masterly (and pathetic) climax. Miss Grimké has sustained her indictment and scored heavily" (*Catholic World*, New York, NY, Dec. 1920).

The *Buffalo (NY) Courier* observed: "There is a terrible tragic note throughout the three acts of this little play, which compels one to think, and if possible to lend aid to try and remove the prejudice against the colored race" (*Buffalo [NY] Courier*, Oct. 3, 1920). The lengthier reviews recounted the plot, and some critics evaluated the artistic merit of the play, noting, "It is a work of real literary value as well, and cannot help but win a place for itself among recent publications along things dramatic" (*Buffalo [NY] Courier*, Oct. 3, 1920). "As a piece of literature, the play is done with vigor and certainty; its dialogue is crisp; its tenderness and its pathos ring true." H.G. Wells, who was given a review copy of the work, yet printed nothing about it, confided to Grimké that her drama was "a most moving one that has stirred me profoundly. I have long felt the intensity of the tragedy of the educated colored people" (letter of H.G. Wells to Grimké, envelope postmarked Dec. 6, 1921). Critic Sterling Brown was unsurprisingly insulting in his review and wrote, "There is no conflict and little characterization: the propaganda depresses rather than stirs" (Brown 1969, 129).

Rachel was originally titled *The Pervert* (Archibald H. Weld Grimké Collection). Grimké later retitled the play *Blessed Are the Barren* and finally *Rachel*. In each revision, except the last, the heroine was named Janet. The change in the protagonist's name seems to have been a last minute decision, for Grimké wrote her father in August 16, 1916, after the play's initial performance in Washington: "You can explain to Helen [the typist] (can't you?) about the change throughout the play of 'Janet' to 'Rachel.' That is the only change" (Archibald H. Weld Grimké Collection). In accordance with the name change, Grimké deleted some phrases at the close of the play that echoed her former title, e.g., "Blessed are the barren!—Blessed are they.—'Then shall they say to the mountains—fall on us;—and to the hills—cover us.'" She also included an epigraph, from Matthew 2:18 that reads: "In Rama was there a voice heard, lamentation, and weeping and great mourning, Rachel weeping for her children, and would not be comforted, because they are not" (*The Holy Bible*).

Rachel is important to American literature because it is one of the earliest American dramas to refute black stereotypes, using characters from the African American middle class to protest racism. *Rachel* epitomizes the way in which the eleven women pioneer dramatists used the stage as a battleground in the struggle for racial equality and as an avenue for expanding the scope of black literature and, in particular, black theater. More particularly, Grimké ventilated her outrage against the violence committed against African Americans who were in many cases more educated and more cultivated than their assailants. Grimké champions this concern in *Rachel* by refuting specific, offensive stereotypes—e.g., mammies, buffoons, "darkies," drunken slaves— and consequently creates black middle and upper-class characters to offset traditional negative images. Published in 1921 by Cornhill Company, *Rachel* represents Grimké's unique contributions to the effacement of the disparaging black images paraded in nineteenth-century American literature and merits serious scrutiny.

Rachel has been analyzed from various perspectives in publications by authors including Jeanne-Marie A. Miller, Nellie Mckay, Gloria T. Hull, Judith Stephens, Kathy Perkins, Udo Hebel, William Storm, David Hirsch, and Robert Fehrenbach.

In one of the most recently published analyses of *Rachel*, Koritha Mitchell, in "Anti-Lynching Plays: Angelina Weld Grimké, Alice Dunbar-Nelson, and the Evolution of African American Drama," brings much needed attention to the important facts of generation removal and generation prevention that occur in the aftermath of racist violence. She correctly notes that with one assault—which claims the life of a father and his son—"the mob destroys an existing home and prevents the construction of a new one" (Mitchell 2006, 217). Further clarifying the devastation Mitchell adds, "Lynching disrupts two generations of marriage and destroys countless generations of children (Mitchell 217). In yet another analysis of the play, Judith Stephens (1992), in "The Anti-Lynch Play: Race, Gender and Social Protest in American Drama," examines *Rachel* as a work written to throw "the image of idealized motherhood back at white women in an attempt to make them see what meaning this so-called revered institution might hold for black women" who had to choose between abjuring motherhood or bearing another potential victim for the lynch mob (333).

An examination of the setting of act 1 shows how Grimké uses a domestic interior to counter the stereotype of "the darkey" exhibited by white American authors of the period. She presents an African American home that is spotless, well-maintained, and the manifestation of taste, refinement, and education. There are "white sash curtains" at a window that is not filthy or broken, and through this window can be seen flourishing trees. "Within the window, below the sill is a shelf upon which are potted plants" that remain intact (139). "Between the window and the door is a bookcase full of books, [especially used by the children during their student years] and above it, hanging on the wall a simply framed, inexpensive copy of Millet's "The Reapers" (139). Additional paintings attest to the gentility of the inhabitants, e.g., imitations of Burne-Jones' "Golden Stairs" and Raphael's "Sistine Madonna." Moreover, a piano with music neatly piled on top occupies a section of the room. At the dining-room table are three chairs that suggest a small, rather than the customary large size of a black family. "Above the table is a chandelier" that provides additional class to the setting; and to furnish employment for the maintenance of the room and the livelihood of its residents, a threaded sewing machine stands.

Thus having established the environment of a family who is culturally equal to many white Americans, Grimké's plea for the stemming of the atrocities committed against blacks—particularly those who were "well educated, cultivated, and cultured " becomes more forceful (Angelina Weld Grimké Collection). Grimké's own privileged class position as a comfortable educated biracial woman qualified her to champion the values and concerns of the early twentieth-century black middle class that she espouses in *Rachel*.

Given her heritage of social activism and class elitism, it is likely that Grimké felt compelled to write the protest play *Rachel* as one means to continue her family's participation in the civil rights campaign. In the process of doing so, she became among the first to use the American stage to denounce social injustice. Yet Grimké's fiction not only reflects the legacy of race consciousness that her distinguished forebears passed down to her, it also reflects her resentment of her mother, which was occasioned by Sarah's rejection of her. Grimké appears to have never forgiven her mother for rejecting her, but in her literature, she assigned all her female characters loving mothers or mother surrogates, attempting, perhaps, to repress her abandonment. The protagonist Rachel (Loving) of the eponymous play under discussion is one example of Grimké's heroines who experiences the affection of a doting mother.

Through *Rachel*, Grimké dramatizes the devastating effects of racism on a refined and sensitive young black woman who abjures marriage and maternity because of prejudice. The heroine's rejection of matrimony and motherhood agitated some members of the African American audience who felt that Grimké advocated genocide as the response to bigotry. Grimké countered this accusation by replying that she aimed *Rachel* "...not primarily to the colored people but to the whites" whom she wished to alert to the black crisis (Grimké [1916] 1974, 51). A quotation from Grimké's handwritten defense of *Rachel* substantiates her intention to specifically appeal to the white female audience:

If anything can make all women sisters underneath their skins, it is motherhood. If then I could make the white women of this country see, feel, under-
stand just what their prejudice and the prejudice of their father, brothers,
husbands, sons were having on the souls of the colored mothers everywhere
and upon the mothers that are to be, a great power to affect public opinion
would be set free and the battle would be half-won [Angelina Weld Grimké
Collection].

William Drake (1987) writes that behind this statement is Grimké's poignant
realization that the rift with her mother, because of race, had deprived her
of shared "sisterhood" and "motherhood" with the one person she most
needed (22). Nevertheless, with women as the focal point, maternity becomes
a major theme in *Rachel* and it is reflected in the protagonist's exclamation,
"I think the loveliest thing of all the lovely things in this world is just being
a mother!" (143). Raphael's *Sistine Madonna*, which overhangs the piano,
underscores the sacredness of the theme and inspires Rachel to reverently
play and sing Nevin's spiritual "Mighty Lak A Rose." The lyrics to this song
could be either the words the Madonna addresses to the Christ Child or
they could be the words that any loving mother might use to describe her
child.

Pending doom, however, threatens the atmosphere that is suffused with
maternal joy and holiness. The complications attending black maternity—
prominent in all three acts—initially surface in Rachel's remarks to her
mother about infants. Rachel expresses first a general anxiety about babies
who grow up to be violent criminals, and later, in a statement that foreshadows her refusal of maternity, she vocalizes a specific alarm for black babies.
"More than the other babies, I feel I must protect them. They're in danger,
but from what?..." (Grimké [1916] 1974, 143). At this point, Rachel intuits
the chief problem of racist murder that attends early twentieth century black
maternity. She senses the unbridled violence that threatens to befall black
offspring and immediately seeks to avert it. Rachel experiences the conflicting
joy and anxiety common to black mothers of the period. Her eager anticipation for babies is marred by the ever-present fear for their potential slaughter.

To further the theme of maternity, several affectionate mothers—including Mrs. Loving, Mrs. Lane, and the heroine Rachel—appear in the play.
Each woman narrates an issue of racism that advances the plot, articulates
one of the principal themes treated by early twentieth-century black playwrights, and sets forth a specific problem accompanying black maternity
(Ellington 1934, 44). Mrs. Loving's lynch narrative articulates the violence
against blacks that pervaded the period and illustrates how it is used to politically repress them. Her narrative also explains the subsequent black migration to the North. Mrs. Loving, as tender as her name suggests, embodies

the bereaved black mother who bears the burden of having a child lynched and who has the responsibility of sharing the circumstances of his murder with her surviving children. On the tenth anniversary of her husband's and son's lynching, she tells Rachel and her brother Tom that their father and seventeen-year-old brother George were killed because Mr. Loving denounced the lynching of an innocent black man in the newspaper he edited. In agony, she relates that white Christian people "broke down the front door and made their way to our bedroom" (Grimké [1916] 1974, 147). As the men dragged her husband down the hall, George tried to rescue him. "It ended in their dragging them both out" (148). Mrs. Loving's narrative inspires pride in Rachel and Tom when she tells them their father daringly and courageously killed four of the mob before he was subdued; and it inspires commiseration with Mrs. Loving when she tells how she fled the South with them in pursuit of freedom in the North.

Rachel's response to her mother's lynch narrative foreshadows the play's climax. She responds with shock upon learning that the South is full of a myriad of little boys who might some day share the fate of her father and half-brother. Rachel bewails the Southern black mothers' plight and acknowledges their constant fear for their children—children whom she states would be better off if strangled at birth: "Why—it would be merciful" she cries out at the end of act 1, "to strangle the little things at birth" (Grimké [1916] 1974, 149). With this statement, Rachel seemingly anticipates the drastic action that Johnson's protagonist, Liza Pettigrew, will take in *Safe*. Later Rachel rages: "And so this white Christian nation has deliberately set its curse upon the most beautiful—the most holy thing in life—motherhood! Why—it makes you doubt—God!" (149). Because of racist violence, Rachel has come to view black maternity as damned. The suggestion arises that her personalized maternity will be equally cursed, for like her biblical namesake, "Rachel weeping for her children and would not be comforted because they are not" (Matthew 2:18), the protagonist is destined to cry for her offspring.

In act 2, which takes place four years later in a room where evident improvements have been made, e.g., green denim portieres and an easy-chair, Grimké delineates the prejudice the North harbored and depicts the moral degeneracy that its racism produces in the character of black children who attend Northern integrated schools. In addition to becoming the adoptive mother of a little boy whose parents died of smallpox, Rachel has during this time become further disillusioned by the realities of prejudice. She becomes fearful for her little son Jimmy when a chance meeting with a black woman and her young daughter brings her face to face with the evils of racial discrimination in the classroom. Rachel learns that the teacher isolated Ethel from the other students, caused her to lose part of her recess, allowed Ethel's classmate to try rubbing the black off her skin, and smiled when they called her a "nigger."

Ethel, who is "naturally sensitive and backward ... not assertive" is pained by the abuse that she suffers the first day of school (Grimké [1916] 1974, 158). In addition to the teacher's psychological harassment, she submits to the physical (and the verbal) harassment of white students, who in viewing her black skin as a filthy surface, try to rub it away. Ethel's face becomes a dirty mask to be assaulted by children, as well as a cover to hide her injured emotions. Ethel's persecution, however, is not limited to secular school. It extends to the white Sunday school where Mrs. Lane sent her. Her mother states that Ethel received the same treatment she did in the day school. In fact, "The superintendent ... asked her if she didn't know of some nice colored Sunday-school. He told her she must feel out of place, and uncomfortable there" (159).

Outraged by this racial incident, Rachel asks Mrs. Lane if she has any other children. Mrs. Lane, completely exhausted by the prejudice to which her daughter has been subjected replies, "Hardly! If I had another—I'd kill it. It's kinder" (Grimké [1916] 1974, 159). Mrs. Lane's response to racism— the refusal of extended maternity—anticipates Rachel's eventual decision not to bear children. Each woman views contraception as an effective method for preventing the practice of further racism. In observing the "thin, nervous, suspicious, [and] frightened" (159) Ethel, Mrs. Lane and Rachel become acutely aware of the destructiveness of prejudice on school children. Mrs. Lane, to ensure that future children are not traumatized by racism as was her daughter, advises Rachel, "Don't marry—that's my advice" (159). Interestingly enough, the protagonist follows Mrs. Lane's suggestion, but only after she scrutinizes the debilitated Ethel and comforts her own son after his experience with prejudice.

Upon observing the child, Rachel pities the withdrawn seven-year-old who is afraid of everyone except her parents. Rachel watches with pain the look of agony on Ethel's face as her mother crosses the room to sit in a chair opposite her daughter and herself; and Rachel grieves when Ethel cowers away from her after she offers the child an apple. Exasperated by the girl's fear and nervousness Rachel states, "It's—it's heartbreaking to see her" (Grimké [1916] 1974, 158). Rachel appears to see in Ethel an image of her own forthcoming self, ravaged by racism. Rachel learns that Ethel believes her ugliness (in the eyes of white America) and blackness have made her unlovable when Ethel expresses happiness at her puppy's blindness. "If he saw me, he might not love me any more" (159). Rachel perceives in the Lanes a family completely unlike hers. The Lanes are subdued by racial prejudice and have come to consider themselves as white America views them: destitute, unsightly, and offensively dark. Mrs. Lane tells Rachel, "My husband

and I are poor, and we're ugly and we're black," and she thus articulates the triple disenfranchisement of many African Americans (158).

An African American herself, Rachel intuits the consequences of this disenfranchisement. She knows that because the Lanes are black, they must be subjected to white America's racism; and she knows that because the Lanes are dark-skinned African Americans, they are subjected to intraracial prejudice as well. Rachel notes that where the Lanes are triply disfranchised, her family is only singly, and their single disfranchisement is that of being black in white America. The Lovings' middle-class status and fair complexions spare them poverty anxieties and intraracial prejudice, but they do not exempt them from America's bigotry as Rachel's adopted son Jimmy learns when he is verbally and physically assaulted at school. He tells his mother, "Some big boys called me ... 'the little nigger!' One of them ... ranned, after me and threw stones; and they all kept calling 'Nigger! Nigger! Nigger!'" (Grimké [1916] 1974, 160).

When Rachel learns that her son has experienced this racial abuse, she is completely distraught. She approaches madness and tears to pieces the rosebuds which her fiancé John Strong has sent her. Jean-Marie A. Miller (1978) offers a convincing interpretation of Rachel's destruction of the rosebuds and sees in their demolition a symbol of infanticide. Miller notes that in decapitating the rosebuds from their stems and grinding their petals underneath her feet, Rachel murders her unborn children whose lives would be marred and ruined by racism if they had been permitted to live (516). Rachel's earlier statement, "Dear little rosebuds—you—make me think—of sleeping, curled up, happy babies" (Grimké [1916] 1974, 160) substantiates Miller's explanation. Rachel, like her counterpart Mrs. Lane, is overwhelmed by the destructive bigotry to which children are subjected. School discrimination is yet another burden that black mothers must confront.

In addition to delineating the moral degeneracy Northern racism produces in the character of African American children attending integrated schools, act 2 discloses the crippling effect of racism on the African American's economic development in the North. Mrs. Loving earlier referred to the inability of John Strong, a young college graduate, to secure dignified work: "You see he had the tremendous handicap of being colored" (Grimké 142). Although the son of a doctor and well-educated, Strong, by act 2, is resigned to "die a headwaiter" (152) to support his mother. He later becomes the character in whom Grimké depicts the resigned attitude of the African American. John and Rachel, who is trained to be a domestic science teacher (i.e., home economics), and Tom, who is trained to be an electrical engineer, are Grimké's intellectual characters. They are young and educated African Americans who are frustrated by the racial restrictions of their social and economic environments. Job discrimination (for themselves and for their children) is still another burden that black mothers must encounter.

Act 3, set a week later, finds Rachel's hold on sanity even more tenuous. She knows that she cannot always protect Jimmy, who relives, even in his sleep, his sad experiences at school where he was taunted and chased because he was a "nigger." She lies awake to listen for his weeping and to offer what comfort she can. When John proposes to her, it is clear that she wants to marry him, but the weeping of Jimmy stiffens her determination as she announces that she cannot marry (Grimké [1916] 1974, 171). Consequently, Rachel rejects her suitor, assumes complete responsibility for her life, and dedicates herself to protecting her adopted son from additional racial violence. Given the play's time frame—which predates the 1960s when trustworthy contraception was not yet developed and marriage inevitably meant motherhood unless the couple was infertile—Rachel's refusal of marriage becomes a choice against maternity. Her decision also becomes a weapon against both early twentieth-century sexism, which required female submission to male rule, and it becomes a weapon against racism. For in refusing to bear children, Rachel deliberately fails to provide additional lynch victims.

Rachel's anti-motherhood and anti-marriage stance can be more fully appreciated when her creator's private life is considered. Grimké's life as a single, motherless woman must be placed within the context of the late nineteenth- and early twentieth-century homosocial subculture to which she belonged. She was one of many professional women who were deeply committed to politics and social welfare who chose not to marry and have children because they were comfortable with other women. Grimké lived a life that embraced singlehood, feminism, independence, and homosociality, and she created women characters that reflected her lifestyle. Rachel deserves especial consideration because she mirrors her author's attitude toward marriage and political activism as expressed in Grimké's diaries and collection. She also experiences similar racial and gender conflicts that many other black women of Grimké's time and background encountered.

Moreover, within the context of black culture, Grimké was not alone among women writers and women activists who disagreed with black men's brutality to black women and with their patriarchal attitudes toward politically and socially active women and with black men's go-carefully attitudes toward racist white men. Grimké evidences this viewpoint in her decision to keep Rachel unmarried and consequently allows her heroine to conduct her anti-lynching campaign unhampered by the demands of a husband who could be violent in exerting his dominance. Grimké averts the restrictions and the criticism (by black males) for Rachel that numerous married activists and club women were unable to escape.

Grimké's senior—Ida B. Wells, whose anti-lynching campaign Endesha

Ida Mae Holland and Michon Boston chronicle—is one example of a high profile activist/journalist who became the object of black males' castigation for politically exerting herself. Resentful of the clubwoman's activism, African American men applied pressure to "keep her in her place" (Giddings 1984, 110). Upon Wells' election as the financial secretary of the Afro-American Council, the *Colored American* newspaper issued this response:

> [Wells] is a woman of unusual mental powers but the proprieties would have been observed by giving her an assignment more in keeping with the popular idea of women's work and which would not interfere so disastrously with her domestic duties [Giddings 1984, 111].

The newspaper suggested that Wells be made head of a women's auxiliary instead. This insult was one of many, for Wells was to suffer additional criticism by black males when she took the initiative to visit the scene of a lynching in 1909. The journalist/activist wrote, "I had been accused by some of our men of jumping ahead of them and doing work without giving them a chance" (Giddings 1984, 117). Thus, having viewed the opposition by black males that an actual black woman activist (with numerous counterparts) encountered—opposition that the protagonist Rachel Loving might have also experienced had she been married—Grimké's decision to keep Rachel single and free of additional children can be more fully appreciated.

In considering the play, one notes many parallels between the character and her creator. Most obvious is the single marital status which they both choose. Under varying contexts, Rachel and Grimké foreswear men, marriage, and motherhood. Following Jimmy's encounter with racist hostility, Rachel banishes her fiancé from sight and vows never to have children. "I swear that no child of mine shall ever lie upon my breast, for I will not ... know the loveliest thing in all the world, the feel of a little head, the touch of little hands, the beautiful utter dependence of a little child" (Grimké [1916] 1974, 161). Upon this vow, she commits herself to taking care of little black children—to loving them, and to protecting them from the hurt of prejudice. Rachel's decision to remain unwed and motherless is consequently motivated by her desires to safeguard the lives of unborn children and to protect those who already live. In doing so, it is likely that Rachel protests God's creation of a racist world that blights the lives of innocent people. Her statement, "Oh God! You who I have been taught to believe are so good, so beautiful how could you permit—these—things [racial indignities]?" (160) substantiate this suggestion.

Where basic altruism largely influenced Rachel's decision, scholars examining Grimké's 1903 diary and manuscript poems suggest that her lesbian relationship influenced her decision not to marry. Hull remarks that

Grimké's vow, "I shall never know what it means to be a mother, for I shall never marry. I am through with love and the like forever," was made after her love affair with an unnamed woman had disastrously ended (Angelina Weld Grimké Collection). Grimké adhered to this resolution and never married or bore children. Perhaps her sexual orientation enabled her to keep her resolve. Rather than with marriage and children, Grimké chose to occupy her life with her father and her writing. She, like the character Rachel, seemingly sublimates her sex drive and assumes responsibility for the welfare of another.

In addition to paralleling each other in marital status, Rachel and Grimké parallel each other in social, professional, and emotional background. Creator and character are both from the black genteel class, as evidenced by their education, their employment qualifications, and their cultivated tastes. Each was educated to be a teacher (Grimké, physical ed, English, and history teacher; Rachel, a teacher of domestic science) and to appreciate refinement, i.e., the aesthetic achievements of African Americans as well as those of Europeans and Euro-Americans. That Rachel and Angelina are mentally undermined by external pressures is evidenced by the mental breakdowns that they both suffer.

A "sensitive and delicate spirit," Rachel is destroyed by the racial hostility leveled at blacks by the outside world. Grimké is seemingly devastated by a disastrous love affair and by her father's death. Gloria Hull, in commenting on Grimké's decline, writes: "In her later years she went a little crazy. (She couldn't be sane; and she wasn't.) It may be recalled that during her father's illness and death, the strains of neurosis and paranoia in her personality became more pronounced—to the extent that she was threatening to exhume and rebury him" (Hull 1979, 24).

But Grimké is not to be remembered for her ruination that was incurred by the blighting effects of unmitigated grief, American racism, and the possible thwarting of a lesbian relationship. She is to be noted for the radical anti-lynching campaign that she waged in *Rachel*. Using black middle-class characters, Grimké protested the subjugation of African Americans that occurred at the beginning of the twentieth century. In the use of the stage, Grimké rendered an immediacy to the problem of racist violence that blacks suffered and offered resolutions to African American problems (i.e., lynching, discrimination) that provided a woman-centered analysis of oppression. Grimké set forth the problematics of black maternity and illustrated one female African American writer's response to the brutality and the inhumanity of the terrorism inflicted upon black people and black women.

Safe (c. 1929)

Georgia Douglas Johnson's *Safe* also demonstrates the important connection between racist violence and African American women's reproduction.

In exploring this link, *Safe* brings attention to the desperation to which some black women were driven in their effort to protect their offspring from racist murder in the absence of just laws and anti-lynching legislation.

Safe, which has received very little attention, was never acted or printed during Johnson's lifetime; nor was it readily available until Elizabeth Brown-Guillory published it in her *Wines in the Wilderness* (1990). It was among Johnson's anti-lynching dramas that included *A Sunday Morning in the South* (1925) and *Blue-Eyed Black Boy* (c. 1930), which were submitted to the Federal Theatre Project.

It may be noteworthy that *Safe* is set in 1893, a turbulent time in the history of American race relations. That Johnson places her drama in a post–Reconstruction setting, despite its authorship date of 1929 suggests that she may have wanted to emphasize the persistency of racial violence, which continued up to (and beyond) the date of her play writing. Decrying this political climate, with its unchecked lynchings, Johnson—like Grimké before her—dramatizes the devastating effect of racism on a sensitive young woman.

Liza Pettigrew is the principal figure in the play. From her position at center stage, she exudes the conflicting joy and anxiety common to black mothers of the period and reveals the gravity that has historically engulfed black maternity. A survey of the young married protagonist shows that she is expecting her first baby. Ignoring her neighbor's injunction to stay away from the window, Liza watches the abduction of Sam Hosea, an innocent young black boy, who screeches for his mother to avert his imminent lynching. Distraught by the terror that she witnesses from her window, Liza shortly murders her newly born son to prevent him from growing up to experience a similar tragedy. The fictionalized Liza had numerous real-life counterparts—including black slave women and "free" nineteenth and early twentieth-century African American women who also employed this extreme "safety" mechanism to protect their children. In considering the conditions under which one African American mother committed infanticide, *Safe* highlights the fact that black boys are generally not allowed to develop into men. For when they mature and take a stance to do right or to defend themselves against racisms, they are—as the play illustrates—routinely lynched. Liza Pettigrew embodies the maternal unrest that this victimization of African American males caused in black women. Underscoring the fact that black women could not (and did not) enter motherhood lightly, she experiences a pregnancy that is fraught with contending bliss and apprehension. Her eager anticipation for her baby is marred by her gripping fear for its potential lynching as she considers the unbridled violence that threatens to afflict her offspring. A look at Liza's disposition in the play's opening scene both establishes her emotional vacillation and illuminates the jeopardy surrounding her son.

As the curtain rises, Liza is eagerly preparing for the arrival of her child—i.e., making baby nightgowns and other outfits. After jubilantly announcing that she has completed her baby's wardrobe and that her due date is near, she hears from her husband John that the life of an upstanding neighborhood youth is in danger. Lowering his newspaper, John tells her, "I see they done caught Sam Hosea and put him in jail." Ushering in the complications accompanying black maternity, he adds that Sam's mother must be crazy with fear, if she is aware that he has been seized. At John's disclosure, Liza's joy at maternal expectancy immediately gives way to the dread of another slain black life in their community. She struggles, however, to dispel her fear and her gloom by concentrating on the positive characters of Mrs. Hosea and her son. Asserting that she knows Mrs. Hosea, who is a thin brown-skinned woman, Liza adds that Mrs. Hosea belongs to her church and that she used to regularly bring Sam with her. Liza then describes Sam as a nice motherly sort of boy, who is not more than seventeen.

In acknowledging and affirming Hosea's characters, Liza both attests to the conscientiousness with which Mrs. Hosea has reared Sam and notes the exemplary character of the youth. Liza also draws attention to the important fact that Mrs. Hosea has carefully exposed Sam to the church and to its reinforcement of the local mores that obligate African Americans to obey their prejudiced and prescriptive code of conduct. Seeking to reassure herself that Sam's imprisonment is not due to his violation of any portion of the code's special restrictions for African American men—especially those governing their behavior toward Caucasian females—she asks whether a white woman was involved in Sam's trouble. John replies no and then specifies Sam's infraction: In a dispute over wages with his white boss, Sam returned a slap that his employer gave him. He hit a white man back.

Liza's mother, Mandy Grimes, pronounces judgment against this fatal transgression and specifies that Sam must flee far away from home. As Liza concurs with Mandy, her conversation comes to a halt when Hannah Wiggins, the town gossiper, bursts into her home. Blurting out the news about the latest community tragedy, Hannah announces that a mob has formed downtown and that it might be "hell to pay tonight!" (Johnson 28). The predictable plot unfolds as Liza worries whether a mob will take Sam out of the jail, and John goes outside to search for additional information about Sam. Musing on his victimization and on the futility of his effort to assume adult responsibility, she laments the fact that for all his laborious struggle to support his widowed mother, Sam only gets a slap in his face when he stands up for himself in the pursuit of justice. In a comment foreshadowing the drastic action that she will take to safeguard her child's life, Liza bewails the fate of African American boys and declares, "I don't want to ever have no boy chile!" (Johnson 28).

Gently reproving Liza, Mandy tells her that the selection of her child's gender is not hers to make, for God makes that decision. Ironically, if gender selection were a viable option, then Liza and her many counterparts would probably exercise it and thereby achieve the same goal for which the lynch mob strives—i.e., the decimation of black males and the ultimate extermination of the black race. While being admonished by her mother, Liza hears a gunshot that signals trouble for the black community. She learns from Hannah who looks through the cracked door that an enormous crowd is headed their way. Liza is frightened by this report and by the increasing noise that the advancing mob makes. Incredulously and apprehensively, she asks if the crowd would burst in upon them. With some uncertainty, Mandy replies no, but she tells her daughter that they will keep the lights out, nevertheless. Mandy's decision is a wise one, for shortly, additional gunshots ring out. Terrified, the women jump and look at each other. Liza is tormented by two fears—that of the actual gunshot—and that of her husband's prolonged absence.

Articulating her daughter's fright, Mandy, who also wonders about John's welfare, declares that her son-in-law should have been home by now. In search of John, Mandy, Liza, and Hannah go to the window and peep cautiously behind the shade. Uncertain of what atrocity might be beheld, Hannah warns Liza to stay back and not to witness any horrors in her delicate state. Liza retreats, but she is instantly alarmed when the confusion of many footsteps and the hooves of tramping horses is heard. Worried that Sam's fate may be associated with these noises, she demands to know if the mob has apprehended him and if they will hang him. All too suddenly, Liza's question is violently answered. She hears Sam's screech for mercy and help and knows at once, the mob has seized him. Instantly running to the door to look out, she is dragged back by Mandy and Hannah who know that the mob will shoot Liza. While her own life is spared, Liza is devastated by the murder of Sam, who she knows to be a decent and hardworking young man. Crumbling up on a chair and shivering as her teeth chatter, Liza wails: "Did you hear that poor boy crying for his mother? He's jest a boy—jest a boy—jest a little boy!" (Johnson 29).

Liza's repetition of the word "boy" forebodes a mysterious evil, and as the outdoor roar continues—mirroring that which churns inside Liza, Hannah verbalizes the effects of Sam's murder on Liza, noting that the youth's killing is very bad for her. Mandy looks critically at her daughter and then asks Hannah to go and get the doctor. Hannah obliges, and in her absence, Liza continues to shiver and shake and to vacillate between worrying about John and about the young lynched Sam Hosea. The exterior mirthful atmosphere, which the lynching has occasioned, now presents an especial stark contrast to the agonizing interior where Liza broods and begins to suffer labor pangs. At the sound of additional hoarse laughter heard from without, she "begins walking up and down the floor all doubled over as if in pain. She goes to the window occasionally and looks out from behind the shade.... She trembles slightly every time she looks and begins pacing up and down again" (Johnson 32). Liza's erratic behavior invites her vigilant mother to beckon her to lay down and to await the physician who will arrive shortly.

Unsurprisingly, Liza has been traumatized by the evening's violence that she has witnessed. Therefore, despite the fact that she is in labor, she is unable to mute the screams of the innocent lynch victim in her ears. She recalls his shriek for Mrs. Hosea with a piercing clarity. It should be noted that not only is Sam's squeal imprinted in Liza's mind, but his mother's inability to protect him is also therein inscribed. Fearful that Sam's murder will affect Liza's delivery, Mandy commands her daughter to concentrate on delivering her own baby safely. Perhaps at this juncture—in her agitated mind—Liza resolves to follow Mandy's advice far too carefully. Stage directions indicate that she is "wild-eyed" and that "she turns her head from side to side as she stands half stooped in the doorway [and] hysterically disappears into the next room" (Johnson 30). Portending disaster, Liza's exit is frightening. Her repetition of "Born him safe!... Safe" intimates that she may be going to prepare a questionable and possibly heinous method to ensure her child's well-being (Johnson 30).

In Liza's absence, John enters and explains his tardiness. He tells the women that he had to avoid the advancing mob, as it passed by his house. More anxious about Liza than about the danger he has just survived, he checks on her and then goes to the door to admit Doctor Jenkins, who has come to deliver the baby. While the physician examines Liza, John chats with Mandy and learns that the lynching may produce wretched effects on Liza's childbirth. Amid their discussion, the sound of a baby's cry is heard from the next room. Responding to the sound, they jump up and look toward the closed door. Nervously, John asks Mandy if Liza is all right. Mandy anxiously replies that she hopes so. She adds, however, that she has never seen her poor child look the wretched way that she looked tonight. Fully justified in her alarm for Liza, Mandy, and John, learns from Doctor Jenkins who presently enters that Liza is fine and that she delivered a healthy baby, who they heard cry. Upon her delivery, Liza demanded to know whether the child was female. Jenkins replied that she bore a fine male. He added that he turned his back to wash his hands in the basin, but that when he looked around again, Liza had her hands about the baby's throat choking it. Jenkins noted that he tried to stop her, but his effort was in vain, because the deceased baby's little tongue was already hanging from its mouth. Dr, Jenkins concludes that upon murdering the baby Liza repeated: "Now he's safe—safe from the lyncher! Safe!" (Johnson 32).

Determined to protect her son from the racist violence that claimed Sam Hosea's life, Liza accomplishes her goal at a dreadful expense. Her "preventive" act of infanticide wreaks destruction on the souls of her family members, as a cursory glance illustrates. Her husband John, in particular, collapses upon a chair sobbing, with his face in his hands. Weeping for the termination of his offspring's life with its thwarted potential, John is inconsolable and despondent. Her mother, Mandy, is equally devastated by Liza's "ultimate solution," which deprives her of her much anticipated grandchild. The final scene shows that: "MANDY stooped with misery, drags her feet heavily toward [Liza's] closed [bedroom] door. She opens it, softly and goes in" (Johnson 32). That the Pettigrews are mired in a relentless gloom is ultimately suggested by the posture of the attending physician Dr. Jenkins, who "stands, a picture of helplessness as he looks at them in their grief" (Johnson 32).

As *Safe* ends, it is clear that Liza Pettigrew suffers the bane that threatened early black maternity. Unwilling to subject her newborn son to the period's unchecked racist violence, she extinguishes his life and practices the ultimate contraceptive act. Her extreme method of confronting the era's terrorism—with its peculiar ramifications for the lives of black men—illustrates the desperation to which some early black women were driven. Deprived of trustworthy contraception, they committed infanticide to "safeguard" the lives of potential lynch targets. *Safe* captures the black mother's powerlessness to protect her children from brutality and illustrates one way in which racial violence impinged upon African American life and upon black women's reproduction. *Safe* also, like Grimké's *Rachel*, illustrates a tragically singular truth about lynching, depicting in particular how African American families were diminished—emotionally, psychologically, and numerically by a single act of murder.

In critiquing Johnson's drama, scholar Elizabeth Brown-Guillory aptly observes that *Safe* "is a significant play because it captures the ordinary lives of black folks of the period" (Brown-Guillory 1990, 14). Infused with commonplace characters such as Hannah, the town's gossiper, *Safe* depicts with an arresting clarity the strong sense of community togetherness, which early African Americans cherished. This cohesiveness is especially evident when John goes to the assembly of black men in search of news about Sam Hosea's fate. That this group is ineffective is rightly discerned by Brown-Guillory who writes, "Though the black townspeople band together, they remain powerless and at the whim of an angry white mob" determined to kill an African American *that* night (14).

Another feature of ordinary early twentieth-century black life is reflected in the deep piety of the African American community. When, for example, Sam Hosea is being lynched, Mandy repeatedly calls on God and tells Him that the black population is in His hand. However, when God does not seem to provide the necessary protection, Mandy and Liza take matters into their hands. Liza best represents their autonomy when she suffocates her newborn baby and thus protects him the only way she knows. In this particular case of infanticide, Johnson seemingly suggests that when there are no viable alternatives for protecting her child, the black mother will sometimes sacrifice her offspring (Brown-Guillory, *Wines in the Wilderness* 14).

A summary review of *Rachel* and *Safe* underscores the devastating effects of lynching on African American families. The disintegration and misery that the Lovings and Pettigrews sustain document the mob's ability to terrorize long after the original grisly torture occurs. Neither Johnson nor Grimké needed to portray the actual physical violence of lynching in their plays. For when the mob targets a black man—as with Mr. Loving and Sam Hosea—his family deteriorates along with his maimed body. The ruination of the Loving, the Hosea, and the Pettigrew households all substantiate this statement. As Koritha Mitchell cogently notes, making reference to a hanging corpse is not essential, because the victim's home is a lynched body. When a father, brother, or son is torn from the family, the household is castrated and its head removed (Mitchell 1992, 222).

Trouble in Mind (1955)

Like Georgia Douglas Johnson before her, Alice Childress bypasses the gentry and uses poor and uneducated African Americans to denounce racist violence and social injustice. In *Trouble in Mind* (1955), the two-act comedy-drama under scrutiny, she principally addresses the issue of racial stereotyping and labors to dismantle the negative and erroneous images of black people. Striving to have African Americans viewed both authentically and objectively by society, Childress strips away the white-imposed facades on the black characters in *Trouble in Mind*. Perhaps the most notable object of her demolition is the play's ignorant and passive mother who surrenders her child to the lynch mob. Unaware of the recourses to take in aiding her son, she idly watches as he is lynched after personally accusing and condemning him for committing a "crime." Childress corrects the myth of the unmaternal, indifferent black mother. She clearly illustrates that no African American woman would both blame and refuse to help her endangered child, as an examination of Willeta Mayer, protagonist, veteran thespian, and Alice Childress' mouthpiece in the play will indicate. In stripping away negative black stereotypes and myths, she single-handedly challenges the damaging and offensive portraits of black mothers pervasive in white minds.

Childress recalls Angelina Grimké who champions the identical goals in *Rachel* and *Mara*, which represent her contribution to the effacement of the degrading black images paraded in American literature and culture. *Trouble in Mind* premiered at Greenwich Mews Theatre in New York City on November 5, 1955, under Childress' direction and ran for ninety-one performances. It garnered an Obie award for the best original Off Broadway play of the 1955-1956 season and made Alice Childress the first female African American to win such an award. When Broadway offered to stage the play, Childress refused the proposal, because the producer insisted that she radically revise her script. Elucidating her rejection of Broadway's offer, she stated: "Most of our problems have not seen the light of day in our works, and much has been pruned from our manuscripts before the public has been allowed a glimpse of a finished work. It is ironical that those who oppose us are in a position to dictate the quality of our contributions" (Brown-Guillory 1988, 31).

Trouble in Mind required "pruning" because it is a satiric work about Caucasian writers, producers, and directors who in their ignorance of African Americans perpetuate and support harmful and incorrect depictions of blacks. Protesting the perpetuity of such negative and inaccurate portrayals, Childress uses this play as a vehicle to demand that African American actors both maintain their personal identity and integrity in the workplace, while rejecting all demeaning roles, regardless of financial losses.

Trouble in Mind was originally a production consisting of three acts. It had basically a happy ending, while the published version contains only two acts and a somewhat ambiguous and depressing conclusion. Critics note that Childress was not pleased with either ending. The play's initial production was plagued with problems, including a clash between the original director and cast that prompted Childress to assume his role. The conflict appears to be a somewhat ironic one, because *Trouble in Mind* is also about a troubled production. More specifically, it concerns a turbulent production of a fictional anti-lynching Broadway play, *Chaos in Belleville*. Like their actual counterparts, the fictional black characters are compelled to deal with their prejudiced white director and with his bigoted and condescending attitude. In the course of the play the real-life Wiletta confronts Al, her tyrannical director, and exposes his racism and suffers the consequences.

Trouble in Mind was produced twice in 1964 by the BBC in London. It was Childress' first professionally produced drama outside of Harlem and received excellent reviews. In particular, Loften Mitchell in *Black Drama* stated, "Now the professional theatre saw her outside of her native Harlem, writing with swift stabs of humor, her perception and her consummate dramatic gifts (Mitchell 169). Continuing the praise, in "The Literary Genius of Alice Childress" John O. Killens wrote: "In this play Childress demonstrated a talent and ability to write humor that had social impact. Even though one laughed through out the entire presentation, there was inescapably, the understanding that although one was having an undeniably emotional and profoundly intellectual experience, it was also political" (Killens 1974, 45).

Employing the play-within-a-play, *Trouble in Mind* takes place on a Broadway stage where a racially mixed cast and a Caucasian director are in rehearsal for the white-authored anti-lynching play *Chaos in Belleville*. While the outer drama is a comedy, the inner play is a drama that focuses on black voting rights. The cast members in the outer play live in the year 1957 and are compelled throughout the rehearsals to deal with a parallel in their personal lives to the lives of the characters of the inner play. "This play within a play" states Childress, is a "private symbol" and represents African Americans as the stepchildren of American society (Minot 1965, 307). It becomes the vehicle by which Childress comments on the various ways blacks survive in racist America. Two such ways of survival include the practice of "Uncle Tomming" and the "Wearing [of] the Mask"—important coping mechanisms that warrant immediate attention for the illumination that they shed upon the actions of Wiletta Mayer and fellow black cast members.

Referencing the eponymous character in Harriet Beecher Stowe's 1852 novel, "Uncle Tom" is a pejorative term for a black person perceived as behaving in a subservient manner to white authority figures. In conjunction with her black colleagues, Wiletta Mayer "toms" for her white director until the moment of her epiphany when she can no longer be humiliatingly deferential to the white authority figure.

Wiletta's "tomming" performance begins at the start of act 1 where she gives a mini-course on the fundamentals of "tomming" to the ingenue actor John Nevins, who brags that he has done some Off Broadway and that he has taken acting classes. Willeta responds to his boast by sharing with him the success formula, i.e., how to "tom" and how to keep his job. She cautions the ingenue not to inform "the man" of his formal training, because whites want African Americans to be born with the gift of acting. Blacks, she tells him, are expected to be naturals. When John asks whether it is imperative for him to lie, Wiletta answers affirmatively and orders him to also cater to the white authorities. She instructs John to laugh at all their statements to make them feel superior. Explaining the reason to laugh, Wiletta specifies that whites do not like, trust, or accept unhappy African Americans, so blacks must laugh when nothing is funny. To this dissembling and obnoxious behavior John responds, "Sounds kind of Uncle ... Tommish" (Childress [1955] 1971, 297), to which Wiletta replies it is. She further tells him that if he wants to remain employed, then he must behave accordingly.

Wiletta quickly follows up the tomming lesson with instruction for wearing the mask—the historic concealer of the sadness, misery, pain, and grief that African Americans sustain at the hands of prejudiced individuals. The subject of one of Paul Laurence Dunbar's most famous poems ("We Wear the Mask"), the false deceptive role playing that constituted the mask functioned as a strategy for survival for blacks who endured a harsh reality. Under the mask that enables blacks to survive their ill treatment and to hide their hurts, Wiletta advises John to mute his actual opinion of their play when it is requested. She encourages the young actor not only to withhold his truthful thoughts, but to also butter up the director—to feign enthusiasm about his play. Wiletta can pass on this particular lesson because as an actress and as an African American, she has been wearing one for years—masking everything from her feelings about her professional mistreatment to that of her personal ill-treatment. Earlier in the text it is noted that Wiletta is touched by the rare star recognition and the gentle treatment that she receives from Henry, the doorman. Her mask enables her to accept the denial of respect and celebrity that she deserves with a cultivated indifference. The stereotypic "colored show," *Brownskin Melody*, in which she has starred, suggests that her career has consisted of participation in the racially demoralizing musical comedies of the 1930s that restricted her to "clowning," i.e., singing, dancing, and laughing incessantly on the stage.

Undeterred by such negative limitation, Wiletta perseveres in show business. However, she demands from the aspiring John Nevins his reasons for acting. Irritated that he has chosen to become a thespian, she also demands to know why he has not selected an elite profession. At this point, Wiletta intimates that acting is not good enough for black people with education and opportunities—resources that she lacks. Yet it is her statement, "You don't have to take what I've been through ... don't have to take it off 'em" (Childress [1955] 1971, 298) that exposes the false deceptive role-playing that she has been practicing to conceal her pains and disappointments. In later scenes, Wiletta both articulates her anger about the scarcity of meaningful acting roles she has played and expresses her deep desire to be a legitimate actor.

At Millie Davis' entrance, current racial tensions from the outside world—i.e., the Montgomery, Alabama, bus boycott and housing segregation—are brought on to the rehearsal stage for the first of many times. Commenting on the newspaper headlines that reference the Little Rock 9 incident, Millie complains about the racists who throw stones at the young black children who are trying to attend school. She is highly irate that the militia must be summoned to safely escort the children into the school building. Millie is thirty-five years old and wears her wealth on her body—a mink coat, pastel wool dress and hat, suede shoes and a purse. She wears stylish clothes offstage because her stereotypic roles confine her to wearing bandannas and loose dresses. Protesting this dress code, she expresses her wish to wear some decent clothes, because the only chance she gets to dress up and to be beautiful is offstage. Millie agrees to continue wearing the baggy cotton dresses, but she refuses to wear another bandanna on her head. In another comment alluding to her "wealth," she claims that her husband, who is a railroad dining car waiter, does not want her to work. Millie's husband has an elite, but stereotypic job for male African Americans of the period. It is among the highest paid positions and is greatly prized.

Judy Sears and elderly, self-effacing Sheldon Forrester, the last two actors in the play *Chaos in Belleville*, arrive on stage, and cast introductions are made. Judy is a young white actress and plays the stereotypic role, Miss Renard, the Southerner's daughter, who sympathizes with the mistreated blacks. Alluding to racially restricted roles of the period, Millie quips that she wants a chance to fight the white southern father. Dubious of that opportunity, Wiletta reminds her that that opportunity will never come.

Childress continues to articulate her resentment at racial stereotyping in a humorous dialogue that further ridicules the clothes, roles, and names accorded black actors. A cursory look at the important conversation indicates that these actors wore strong impregnable masks to conceal their humiliation by the debasing roles that they were forced to play. Millie recalls a recent embarrassing part and complains: "Last show I was in, I wouldn't even tell my relatives. All I did was shout 'Lord, have mercy!' for almost two hours every night" (Childress [1955] 1971, 300). Wiletta then teases Millie about having played every garden flower, including the gardenia, magnolia and chrysanthemum. Returning the barb, Millie laughingly tells Wiletta that she has played the jewels: opal, crystal, pearl. Interestingly enough, in the play within the play, the ladies will once again have stereotypic names (Ruby and Petunia) and will once again play stereotypic roles (cleaning maids and personal servants to Miss Renard).

Shortly, Al Manners, the play's white director arrives, accompanied by his assistant Eddie Fenton and Henry, the doorman. Al, who is making his directorial debut, and the Caucasian actors and writers are convinced that *Chaos* will relate a message of racial tolerance to its white audience. Moreover, they believe their play will advance the case for civil rights for African Americans. However, most of the black cast members disagree, because they know that they are playing the same stereotypical domestic roles that they have always played. The African American actors assumed these demeaning parts exclusively for economics, not for promoting the white director's idea of brotherhood. Childress initiates the image dismantling process in act 1, page 15 at the rehearsal of *Chaos*. Here, she also begins the establishment of parallels between the lives of the cast members to those of the characters in the inner play.

In the opening scene, Carrie/Judy asks her father Renard/Eddie (who temporarily reads the part) if the servants can celebrate Petunia's/Millie's birthday with a barn dance. Renard objects because of the pending election. When Renard "consults" Ruby/Wiletta about the matter, she replies with stereotypic ignorance, "I don't know nothin" (Childress [1955] 1971, 300). Carrie ultimately prevails upon her father, who grudgingly allows the servants to have their dance. She shares the good news with the women servants and then prepares to lay out her organdy dress. However, Ruby intercepts and performs the service for her. At Judy's departure to take a nap, Petunia blesses her.

This scene bears vivid parallels to *Trouble in Mind*. For just as Renard controls his servants' lives, Al dominates and menaces his cast. Neither "director" receives straight answers from his black servants/cast because they do not truly want to hear what the "underlings" have to say. Each man is convinced of his superiority and behaves accordingly—despite the fact that he is deluded about the realities of the servants/cast. The African American characters warrant especial attention in this scene as they struggle to conceal their professional and personal disgruntlements behind their masks.

Millie, for example, despises the domestic role that she is forced to play and consequently insults Judy throughout the reading. As Petunia, she sarcastically tells Judy she's one of God's angels. To the white-imposed term "stomp," Millie demands, "What the hell is a stomp ... why didn't they call it a barn dance?" (Childress [1955] 1971, 308) Earlier, Sheldon questioned the term "iffen" that his character was required to speak. Totally perplexed as to the word's meaning, he reiterates the foreign term and reflects upon its possible definition. The parallel between Wiletta and Ruby becomes pronounced at this point. For when Renard asks Ruby about her opinion on using the barn, she gives him the same response ("I don't know nothin'")— that she gives Manners when he asks her about using the term "darkies" in the script. Wiletta is instantly alarmed by her involuntary and repetitive answer. But her feigned ignorance and lack of opinion become ironic, since it will be her desire to express an opinion that will provide the principal source of dramatic action in act 2. It is noteworthy that in addition to retaining the word "darky" in the script, Manners also keeps the word "nigger," despite the cast's objection to the offensive term. Al, the tyrant, as are his white counterparts in *Chaos* and *Trouble*, is arrogant and insensitive to the feelings of the African Americans. He lacks insight into how reading and staging such a play make the black thespians feel.

Following this scene, Manners returns to the beginning of *Chaos* in act 1, page 3. Numerous stereotypical roles, attitudes, and themes of the preceding scene are reinforced. As the section opens, Ruby is shelling beans on the back porch with her husband Sam/Sheldon sitting beside her. Their son Job/John enters and announces that he plans to vote. Attempting to dissuade him from this dangerous course of action, Sam reminds Job that Mr. Renard forbids his blacks to get involved with the voting issue. Job responds that he has received a draft notice and that a friend has told him that when a man is drafted, he is supposed to vote. Job follows his friend's advice and goes out to vote. Hearing Job's parents' protestation, Carrie and Renard come out to investigate. Renard calls African Americans worthless ("None of 'em is worth their weight in salt") to which Carrie replies that if whites are superior, then they should prove it by their actions (Childress [1955] 1971, 310).

Unlike the players in *Chaos* who blindly obey "Massa" Renard, the actors in *Trouble in Mind* express—however subtly—their discontent. Millie picks on Judy and drives her to tears in this section, while Sheldon continues to employ humor to mask the indignities and the lack of manhood that he suffers. Wiletta even tries to unteach her tomming lessons to John, in which she advocated exchanging dignity for success. When Eddie praises his newly decorated apartment, Shedon asks if any blacks live in the building. At Eddie's expression of uncertainty, Sheldon rightly concludes that African Americans do not reside there. The poor living conditions of Sheldon, who hates rooming with others, parallel those of the *Chaos* sharecroppers who work and live on "Massa" Renard's land. They also reflect Childress' concern with the issue of segregated housing that dominated the period.

The next discussion of *Chaos* presents an enlarged view of the story. Some of the local black citizens will vote for the first time in the upcoming election. Both whites and blacks oppose this resolution, and strong hostilities pervade the community. Renard does not want to hold the dance in this volatile environment, and he believes along with Ruby and Sam that Job is doomed. As Ruby becomes the center of attention, she relieves her anxieties about her son in a popular protest song. She gives an exquisitely soulful rendition that does not impress Al because he wants to know what Wiletta was thinking while she was singing the song. To achieve his purpose, Al humiliates Wiletta by playing a word association game. The game is significant in that it both references a contemporary political event (the Rev. Dr. Martin Luther King is speaking in Montgomery, Alabama on Sunday night) and it enables Wiletta to verbalize her thoughts on lynching (Killin'! Killin'!) as well as her aversion to playing the requisite menial roles. After repeating the song at Manners' request, she makes a slight improvement, for which he takes credit. Like Renard, Al wants to control everything, and his superior, insensitive attitude incenses Wiletta.

This section is also important for the noteworthy discussion on "tomming" that it presents. Sheldon tells Wiletta: "Man says somethin' to me, I say ... 'Yes, sure, certainly.' You 'n' me know how to do. That ain't tommin,' ... we don't mind takin' low because we tryin' to accomplish somethin'" (Childress [1955] 1971, 317). However Wiletta is tired of abasing herself and emphatically tells Sheldon "I mind ... I do mind ... I *mind*" (317). At Sheldon's departure, Wiletta confides to Henry some information about herself. In particular, she shares that she does not like to reflect on the past because doing so enrages her. Foreshadowing her next outburst, she warns about the negative consequences of testing her mounting temper. She discloses that she wants to be an actress and that she has always wanted to be an actress. Moreover, she resolves to *be* an actress. After commenting on the violent resistance to school integration, she laments her lack of place in the universe, because everyone is trying to push her off the face of the earth.

A thundering speech from Renard/O'Wray opens act 2. In his monologue, which is directed to whites, he advocates a surface "moderation" and "tolerance" of African Americans. In his opinion, such superficial behavior will relax tensions over voting and will demonstrate the superior nature of whites. Within the context of this speech promoting moderation and tolerance, it becomes significant that Al fails to pay attention to Willetta's issues with the play. For example, when Wiletta attempts to tell him that she thinks the third act of *Chaos* is not the natural outcome of the first, he waves her into silence and tells her to promise him that she will not start thinking. Another case in point is when Al resolves to take up with the white writer the portrayal of Arabs in his script but refuses to confront him about the offensive terms "darky" and "nigger" that the black actors detest using. These instances further illustrate Manners' insensitivity and intolerance as well as portray the way he invalidates African Americans.

The beginning of act 3 is the next section of *Chaos* to be rehearsed. It opens with the performance of menial tasks (e.g., Ruby is ironing clothes) amid a tense atmosphere. Petunia peers anxiously through a window, wondering with everyone else if the lynchers have apprehended Job, while Job's father sits in a corner whittling a stick and Carrie cries. Everyone hears an angry lynch mob and wonders if Job is dead or alive. Fearing for her welfare, Ruby attempts to send Carrie to Renard's. But Carrie, the concerned liberal, replies that she does not want to leave Ruby alone. Sheldon immediately corrects Carrie's mistake, retorting that Ruby cannot be alone since he and Millie are with her. In this instance, Judy reveals her racism as she indicates that she does not want to leave an African American woman alone without the protective presence of a white person. Her comment suggests that Caucasians do not consider African Americans as people or as equals. Yet Carrie resolves to save Job's life with the intervention of her father and a judge. Sam prays an emotional prayer in which Carrie participates. When she emphatically adds yes to his divine petition, she receives disapproving looks from Al and Bill that rebuke her for an "undignified" prayer style that is restricted to blacks. As Ruby sings, Job enters. Uttering the only maternal support that she will make for the rest of the play, Ruby cries, "I'm the one to talk to my boy!" after Petunia blurts out that the mob is seeking Job.

From this point on, Ruby behaves as an atypical mother of a doomed child. The conflict between how Ruby acts and how Wiletta feels (and would behave as an actual black mother amid the turbulent circumstances) precipitates the play's crisis and Wiletta's epiphany. This process warrants examination, for in it, the play's major themes of racism and racial stereotyping are dramatized. In a most unnatural and unmaternal way, Ruby/Willeta tells her son that he should have left town before he started all of this misery when he asks her to help him escape. Blaming Job for demanding his civil rights, she savagely assures him that he has none. Ruby commands him to apologize for doing wrong, i.e., voting, and then orders him to surrender himself to the lynch mob. During this chastisement, Job evidences great incredulity at the mob's wrath when he states that he was not voting for a black man, but rather for a white man like themselves. When Carrie adds that her father will have Job placed in the county jail for safekeeping, Ruby and Sam tell Job to accept Renard's help. Ruby is naive in thinking her son's innocence will prevent the mob from killing Job, since history illustrates that the law is impotent before the lynch mob and that many times, the law is the lynch mob.

The character Ruby continues to alienate Wiletta's motherly sensibilities as she reinforces the negative image of the unmaternal black woman. Ruby condemns, berates, accuses, and turns against her son. She does not try to help him, but rather commands him to turn himself in. The scripted mother in this play is a foil to the black mothers in other works who stand up for their sons, who seek help for them, and who try to aid in their escaping. Pauline Waters in Johnson's *Blue-Eyed Black Boy* becomes defiant when she learns that the mob plans to lynch her son. She takes action and sends to the judge to save their child. Sue Jones in *A Sunday Morning in the South* argues with the police officer about the innocence of her grandson Tom and tells the policeman that he cannot arrest Tom. As a rule, the black mother works hard to save the life of the child she has born. She exhausts every possibility and even endangers her own life to spare that of her offspring. In *Trouble in Mind*, the African American mother is not proactive and/or anxious about her son's fate in the way that Rachel Loving, Liza Pettigrew, Sue Jones, Pauline Waters, Mrs. Marston, and Mrs. Loving are.

A return to the stage shows that Manners is dissatisfied with Wiletta's performance, because she continues to be unable to divorce herself from the role of the unrealistic mother she must portray. Perplexed, Wiletta tells Manners that she fails to see why Job could not get away. Ignoring Wiletta's statement, Manners insists that since none of the cast has witnessed a lynching, each member must imagine one as did the dramatist. Sheldon, however, has seen one, and at his description of the horror, the world of the play within the play is connected to both the world of the primary play and the actual world. He narrates a horrific event that contradicts the falsified lynching account that was submitted by the author of *Chaos*. Sheldon recalls that as a nine-year-old boy, he stood at the window and heard "The screamin' comin' closer and ... and the screamin' was laughin'.... Horse just pullin' along ... and then I saw it! Chained to the back of the wagon, draggin' and bumpin' along.... The arms of it stretched out ... a burnt, naked thing that once was a man" (Childress [1955] 1971, 335). Sheldon states that he started to scream but that no scream came forth. He identified the victim as Mr. Morris, a revered and generous man of the African American community, who talked back to whites and who was quick to tell them what was on his mind. Mentally immersed in the violent South from which he fled at seventeen, Sheldon momentarily drops his mask and flinches when Bill rests his hand on his shoulder. Sheldon's lynch narrative provokes Manners to say that he feels guilty when he hears about barbarism. Al is not, however, provoked to ask the playwright to make script changes—i.e., to avert Ruby's son's lynching or to remove racial slurs from the dialogue. He simply tells the ensemble to take a lunch break.

Following the meal break, the cast returns to act 3 in *Chaos*. Job is still resolved to vote, and Ruby plans to take Carrie's suggestion to have Job placed in jail for protection. Ruby orders Job to get down on his knees so that she can pray for him, but seeing Job/John on his knees infuriates Wiletta, who has undergone a transformation that has infused her with dignity, pride, assertion, and truth. Overtaken by her change, Wiletta commands John, "Get up off the floor wallowin' around like that" (Childress [1955], 1971, 339). Her maternal nerves frayed, she observes that the playwright wants the white man to be the play's hero, but he wants her to be the drama's villain. In mounting rage, she takes a parental approach and asks Al if he would send his son to his death. When he replies that Job is in the protective custody of Judge Willis, Willeta states that the black mother knows that the lynch mob is impervious to the law and therefore would not surrender her child. As generations of (fictional and nonfictional) black mothers preceding her, Wiletta wants to safeguard her son's life and cannot comprehend why Manners and the playwright have not scripted Ruby to actively do so. Unlike Grimké's Rachel who abjures marriage to stem the number of black lives claimed by the lynch noose or Johnson's Liza Pettigrew who murders her own son to keep him safe from the mob, Ruby does nothing to assist her child. She becomes an accomplice to the lynch mob and helps to achieve their purpose.

In demanding a script change wherein the supporting mother and family try to avert the son's murder, Willeta challenges whites to portray the African

American mother realistically—that is, as an actively concerned parent who will do everything possible to help her child. Exasperated, she cries that the story should develop in a different direction. She declares, "I'm sick of people signifying' we got no sense" and implicitly explains why she can no longer "tom" or wear her mask (Childress [1955], 1971, 343). Resolving to no longer conceal her true self, her true opinions, or her true feelings, Wiletta calls Al a prejudiced man and rebukes herself for telling John to laugh and grin at everything he says. She also directs some anger toward Sheldon for his tommism, because he echoes every word Al says and constantly ingratiates himself with whites. Wiletta becomes the sole character to undergo a metamorphosis that results in a positive change of action. Initially behaving as the tomming and mask-wearing Ruby, she exits from the play—probably unemployed—as the diva who dared to confront her racist director and his willful misrepresentation of African Americans. She responds to the lie about black maternity, dispelling the myth that it is characterized by indifference, ignorance, and fear. Free of her mask and "tomming" behavior, Wiletta resolves to fight for legitimate acting roles and for accurate portrayals of African Americans.

Miscegenation Dramas

As stated earlier, several of the anti-lynching plays—i.e., Grimké's *Mara* (unpublished), Livingston's *For Unborn Children* (1926) and Johnson's *Blue-Eyed Black Boy* (c. 1930) address the issues of miscegenation and the sexual violation of African American women by white men. The issue of miscegenation has commanded great interest since the days of slavery. The products of biracial unions, mulattoes were misfits on the plantations. Often used as house servants, they were separated from the masses of African Americans who were field hands. This physical separation and the advantages of being employed in "the big house" created a cultural and caste barrier, which contributed to intraracial prejudice. Yet despite their mixed ancestry, mulattoes could not have social intercourse with whites, and after the cessation of slavery they found themselves in a no man's land. Numerous writers of both races have addressed the problem of the mulattoes in concert with the present dramatists under consideration.

Mara (unpublished)

The first analysis is devoted to an examination of *Mara*, a work that has not been extensively analyzed. In particular, this study focuses on

Grimké's use of the play as a vehicle to dismantle the stereotype of the African American woman as licentious and untutored. In addressing this issue, the play highlights a significant analogy between the heroine's white rapist and Satan, the seducer of the biblical Eve, who then figures as the protagonist's sister in temptation. The comparison underscores the innocence of the heroine Mara Marston and that of her numerous historic counterparts who were the victims of uninvited sexual acts that included rape.

The second of Grimké's protest dramas, *Mara* is still in manuscript form. The holograph text consists of numerous drafts and revisions and one final complete hand-written version of about 190 pages. Gloria T. Hull estimates that *Mara* was written sometime in the early to middle 1920s after the success of *Rachel* and before the latter part of that decade (Hull 1987, 124). No evidence suggests that Grimké ever attempted to produce or publish *Mara*.

Yet had she sought to bring *Mara* before the public, the text of the play intimates that Grimké would have targeted an audience similar to the one for which she designated *Rachel*. It should be recalled that the dramatist aimed *Rachel* not to the African American audience but rather to the white, specifically to the female constituents whom she wished to alert to the black crisis.

With women as the focal point, Grimké's plea for the stemming of the violation of African American women—particularly those who are "well-educated, cultivated, and cultured"—might have gathered considerable force among the female viewers, who in observing the defilement of Mara Marston could have seen potential images of themselves, ravished by unscrupulous men (Angelina Weld Grimké Collection). Examined from this perspective, *Mara*, like its predecessor *Rachel*, becomes an instrument to raise the consciousness of white women who could agitate for equality and justice on behalf of African Americans, specifically African American women.

Mara also becomes a means of dismantling the white female audience's stereotypes of the black woman as a temptress and her mulatto offspring as degenerate. The play examines the circumstances of the heroine's rape and shows that neither she nor her actual counterparts were to be blamed for an unsolicited violation that frequently resulted in illegitimate mulatto offspring. Moreover, Mara and Ellen Marston, women of biracial extraction, provide virtuous images of black womanhood that counter the negative view of the black woman in general and the "tragic mulatto" in particular, who was believed by some to have "combined the worst elements of two races" (Shockley 1988, 300).

Caught between the animosity of blacks and the contempt of whites, the mulatto was a character to whose plight leading nineteenth and early twentieth-century writers such as William Wells Brown, Pauline Hopkins, Frances Harper, and Charles Chesnutt turned their attention. As a three-quarters white woman, Grimké knew the problems of being the scorned product of two bloods, and she may have written *Mara* as a cathartic exercise to address her own dilemma as a cultured, educated mulatto in a country that devalues blacks, black women, and biracials. That "there is no indication that Grimké ever attempted to stage or to publish ... [*Mara*] (not even a typed copy)" substantiates this suggestion (Hull 125). It is both unfortunate and regrettable that *Mara* did not appear before the public. For in addition to its moral and political appeals to the white female audience, Mara had the potential to appeal to the emotions of the biracial female audience who needed to see the problematics of their existence reflected on the stage.

An analysis of Grimké's two protest plays decrying the subjugation of African Americans during the early twentieth century shows that both dramas were written to counterattack white literary distortions of black character. However, where *Rachel* was written to efface the disparaging images of blacks in general, *Mara* was written to erase a specific black stereotype—that of the morally lax African American woman, who consciously solicited sexual acts, including rape.

Like *Rachel, Mara* focuses on a sensitive young African American woman who is destroyed by racial bigotry. The play is set in the South at the beginning of the twentieth century and addresses the Southern black woman's powerlessness in protecting herself against the white man's lust. Grimké uses the image of the black woman ravaged by a white man to refute the allegation that sexual immorality is exclusive to the behavior of African Americans (Angelina Weld Grimké Collection). In portraying the victimized black woman, Grimké recalls the socio-political systems—structures that merit attention in order to comprehend Mara's violation—that European Americans have used since the seventeenth century to explain the degradation of African Americans and to justify the defilement of black women. Erlene Stetson in *But Some of Us Are Brave* (1982) encapsulates three principal systems that were instrumental in validating the subjugation of black people and the sexual abuse of black women (72, 73). One such system originated in 1662 with the Virginia colony's passage of nine laws that determined the status of newborn babies. One law specifically mandated that all children born within Virginia would follow the condition of the mother. This law was significant in two ways. It was a change from English common law, which declared that a child's status was determined by the father's condition. And it implicitly condoned sexual intercourse between white men and black slave women, in effect allowing white men more legal, social, and psychological freedom by not holding them responsible for any offspring resulting from sexual relations with female slaves. It is noteworthy that more than two hundred years later, the laws passed after Emancipation also guaranteed the same freedom from responsibility to white men who had fathered children by slave women.[1]

Mara's rape by the wicked Carewe may be viewed as a personal tragedy that mirrored the widespread sexual violation that many black women experienced at the hands of white men. Grimké would have been aware of the slanderous myth about African American women. And she may have had it in mind when she made Mara and Mrs. Ellen Marston paragons of righteous women who conformed to strict morality. Possibly in reaction to the stereotype of the depraved, untutored black female, Grimké created Mara as an innocent young genteel woman who for eighteen years has been cloistered within the walls of her family's estate, and who, until Carewe's assault, remained chaste. And perhaps to further debunk the myth of the black woman's dissoluteness, Grimké fashioned Mrs. Marston as a conscientious and loving mother whose solicitude for her daughter's welfare underscores her rich maternal skills in nurturing. Moreover, while being the consummate mother—teaching Mara about propriety, femininity, and evil—Ellen extends her affection and care to her husband Dr. Richard Marston, for whom she is the perfect wife.

The Marstons reside in The Cedars, an isolated family estate, which is enclosed by a ten-foot-high wall, ostensibly built to keep evil out. All the action of *Mara* occurs on the family premises in July. In act 1, Ellen Marston recalls the reasons her family has relocated in the South to live in semi-seclusion. She tells her retired physician husband:

> Your health broke down—and you had to give up your practice.... Since you had to live in the South—we had to protect Mara in some way—She was too beautiful. Not a single law in the state would protect her—So you built the walls. Outside are all the white brutes—and they can't get in. They can't know she is here [Grimké, *Mara*, n.d.].

The focal point of Mrs. Marston's conversation is clearly the protection of her attractive daughter, who, as a black woman, is open prey to lustful, unrestrained white men. To safeguard their own, the Marstons erect a wall to provide the security that the law denies. Ellen Marston's concern for her daughter's chastity is one that black mothers have shared since the African race was first transported to the New World where writers of both fiction and nonfiction have addressed the sexual abuse that the "peculiar institution" visited upon the "daughters" of Ellen.[2]

That Mrs. Marston has inherited the historic burden of anxiety for her daughter's virtue becomes increasingly apparent in a conversation with the doctor, who announces that a male member of the Carewe family has moved within fifteen miles of The Cedars. When Mrs. Marston demands, "But Richard, how can this possibly affect us?" she receives an unsettling answer. Dr. Marston replies, "Do you know what kind of men all the Carewe men are?... My father was no worse a scoundrel than the rest. That doesn't make me hate him any the less. The brute virtually killed my mother. I'm thinking ... about Mara." The doctor intimates that his mother was raped by a Carewe—whose male members are infamous for despoiling black women. Richard indirectly states that he is the issue of the miscegenation, and he hints that Mara may experience a tragedy similar to that which afflicted his mother. Dr. Marston further alarms Mrs. Marston when he tells her "I met [Carewe] ... within five miles of us.... There is no cross road at all between the place where I met him and here.... He must have passed by this place."

Suspecting that Carewe has spied her daughter, Ellen agitatedly responds with a volley of questions: "Why was he *here* so far from home? ... was he in an automobile ... was this man young—beautiful?" To her interrogation, Dr. Marston supplies noteworthy answers that initiate the comparison between the predatory wiles of Carewe and the deceptive stratagems of Satan. Richard's information about Carewe's tactics is significant because it proves that Mara (and her myriad counterparts) was an innocent victim who did not orchestrate or invite rape.

Dr. Marston remarks that Carewe was on horseback when he "passed by this place," and this comment generates the initial image of Satan stalking his prey in the Garden of Eden. That Carewe was on horseback rather than in an automobile suggests, too, that like his evil prototype, Carewe wanted proximity to his quarry—possibly for the purpose of surveying the environment through which she moves. Dr. Marston's response that Carewe is young and beautiful further associates the villain with Lucifer and recalls the scriptures' statement, "Satan himself masquerades as an angel of light" (II Corinthians 11:14), appearing attractive at whim.

Richard's delineation of Carewe troubles Ellen, because she knows that a young handsome white man would be especially captivated by her beautiful young daughter.[3] Recalling an earlier conversation with the lovely Mara— Ellen, in futile hopes of allaying her mounting fears—persists in questioning the doctor about Carewe. And as she speaks, a nervous tension envelops her conversation with Richard.

MRS. MARSTON. Could you tell, do you think, about what time it was when he passed—here?

DR. MARSTON. Judging by the way he was riding—He was walking the horse—I should say before sun down.

MRS. MARSTON. An hour or two before, perhaps?

DR. MARSTON. Very likely.

MRS. MARSTON. (*nervously*) Then it *was he*—the child—heard.... She says ... a man just as [you] described him passed here ... walking his horse.... And she said Richard that she feared this man ... and this wasn't the only time ... that he has passed here [Grimké, *Mara*, n.d.].

Ellen realizes that Mara is indeed being stalked and reaches the pinnacle of fright. While her husband "turns abruptly without a word and begins to walk up and down again[,] Mrs. Marston looks at the dark wall and at the gate ... [she] shivers a little." Ellen knows that evil has infiltrated their interior but asks Richard, "Are we—safe here?" Although the doctor replies, "Why not?" Mrs. Marston's anxiety is not assuaged. For following a silence, she inquires, "You don't think it is possible—do you—for any one to get over the walls?" Her husband pauses for a fraction of a second and answers:

Certainly not.... I'm not going to worry about it any more tonight. He was headed toward home. He wouldn't be likely to prowl around here at night in the dark [Grimké, *Mara*, n.d.].

But Richard Marston is wrong, for subsequent scenes illustrate that Carewe will again prowl around The Cedars at night in pursuit of Mara.

In act 2 as Dr. and Mrs. Marston plant Mara's annual birthday bush, they inform her for the first time that she is not their only child. Richard says, "You have always thought ... you are our only child.... Well Mara, you aren't ... you are our seventh." The doctor adds that their other children "died all of them—between the ages of 13 and 18 for reasons God ... only ... can answer." He then explains the meaning of Mara's name—"bitterness"—which recalls her suffering biblical namesake, whom Grimké mentions in a reference under the manuscript's title: "And she said unto them, Call me not Naomi, call me Mara; for the Almighty has dealt very bitterly with me" (Ruth 1:20).

Dr. Marston recounts, "We had not named you when our sixth child died.... Neither life nor God had been kind to us when we named you Mara. We had you then, but we were prepared ... to lose you." However, because Mara did not die, the doctor talks about the family custom of planting a birthday bush whose growth corresponded to that of Mara. He confides, "When you were 13 we thought we'd try an experiment. So we planted the first bush there. And we believed ... that if it flourished and grew all right—so-so." "Would I," rejoins Mara. The doctor states that now that Mara is 18, this bush will be the final one. He then gives Mara an opal ring as a birthday present. But Mrs. Marston objects to the gift and whisks Richard away where she privately tells him, "Opals bring bad luck ... unless they're birthstones."

The doctor, the embodiment of rationalism, dismisses his wife's superstitiousness. And Ellen sends Mara upstairs to dress for the evening's festivities in special clothes that include a dress sewn from silk and cobwebs, which Mrs. Marston has made for her daughter. The cobweb fabric is interesting and seemingly pregnant with meaning. The material suggests the entrapment of some unsuspecting quarry. And the irony, of course, is that while Mara adorns herself in "predator-like" clothing, she will in fact, become the prey. A message appears to surface in this instance. For as the author points out the clothes that elicited a fatal attraction for Mara Marston, Grimké intimates that women ought to be alert to what they wear if they want to be safe from assault. Furthermore, in anticipation of the isolation in which Mara's encounter with evil and her eventual destruction occur, Grimké also implies that women should be aware of situations (as well as clothes) that place themselves at risk.

With attention given to apparel, Mara, "dressed in filmy white ... radiantly beautiful and happy" enters shortly, reprimanding her father for his inappropriate attire. To her query, "Daddy, you aren't going to wear those horrid riding-clothes ... to my birthday party?" the doctor replies, "Not by a long shot," and goes indoors to change. Mrs. Marston, who is busy with Mara's special birthday dinner enters the house to complete meal preparations. She forbids her daughter to come inside until all is ready and leaves Mara by herself in the enclosed yard.

In her solitude, Mara parallels the biblical Eve who singly strolled Eden just before her fall. Mara's solo presence recalls that of the numerous mulatto heroines, e.g., Clotel, Althesa, whose aloneness also facilitated their rape by lascivious white men. In particular, Mara's isolation enables the fiendish Carewe to seduce her, unimpeded by her parents' interference. Like Eve before the fall, Mara is jubilant and blissfully exclaims, "God! God! Can you hear me? I'm happy. Mara is happy." Eager to express her gratitude to God for her happiness, Mara asks "Are you far away, God.... Because I'm going to dance for You ... just a little 'Thank you Dance'—for You." She then "dances, delicately, lightly, gracefully ... humming to herself the while."

Pending doom, however, threatens this atmosphere that is suffused with ecstasy. For while she continues to dance, the archfiend, Carewe "noiselessly appears ... looks about [and] spies Mara." His "bold black eyes" behold her with an amazement that gives way to admiration—possibly because he is in the territory of goodness—foreign soil to him. And Mara, engulfed in purity, as suggested by her white dress, is a curiosity that inspires wonder and approval. When Mara sees him, "She stands quite still and looks at Carewe.... For several minutes they look at each other and then slowly, as if drawn by some irresistible force, she goes toward him." Perhaps the innocent girl is attracted to the agent of her fall because his "almost unblinking piercing black eyes" function as evil magnets that cast a spell on her. But it is a fatal spell, whose power could have been thwarted had Mara recognized and avoided evil when she saw it. Possibly at this juncture where innocence endangers one particular woman's life, Grimké implies that all women—for the purpose of ensuring their own safety—are obligated to know villainy when they see it in order to escape its harm.

Nevertheless, prompted by naivete and inquisitiveness, Mara asks, "Who—are you?" And Carewe, for whom stage directions specify that there always be a slight hesitation before he speaks replies, "That depends ... on circumstances." During their conversation, Mara is unconsciously flirtatious and disarmingly frank. She even tells Carewe: "I think you're beautiful ... [but] ... being beautiful isn't necessarily in your favor.... You may be evil.... Mother says that things may be beautiful ... and yet evil." In light of the catastrophe that befalls Mara, Mother Marston would have done well to also have warned Mara about the ramifications of being friendly and open with strange men—a principle that was perhaps uppermost in Grimké's mind as she delineated Mara's behavior toward Carewe.

In his conduct with Mara, Carewe is the incarnation of the beguiling serpent who gleans sufficient information to destroy Mara and the Marston household. Through cunning, he learns the structure of the family unit residing within the walls, ("Who else inhabits this Eden besides you?") and he learns to whom the gate keys are entrusted. Carewe discovers and exploits Mara's Achilles' heel—her desire to see him again—and he succeeds in getting Mara to lie ("I can only come upon conditions. You're to promise to tell nobody you've seen me or that I'm coming back.").

It may be significant that Carewe, like his fiendish counterpart, wastes no time in seeking to corrupt Mara and, therefore, asks her to unlock the gate at their first encounter ("Supposing I should say to you, open the gate and let me in. Would you?") Although Carewe is unsuccessful and is denied admission through the gate, he gains a foothold with Mara, and the mournful hoot of the owl that she notes foreshadows imminent tragedy for the Marston household. Moreover, when Carewe rides off, Mara recognizes him as the man she earlier heard and feared.

In act 3 which takes place the following week at night, Mara adorns herself in her birthday finery and goes into the yard where she teases her parents about a secret she has. The effects of Mara's seduction by Carewe are quickly becoming evident. Dr. Marston who has observed his daughter's nervousness remarks, "Mara, you seem unusually restless even for you tonight.... What is the matter?" Mara smiles and responds, "It's a beautiful secret Daddy, I'm going to tell you in a few days...." Mara's withholding of information is novel to her father, and he comments, "I never knew you not to share a secret with me before." However, Mara assures him, "It's the first one ... and the last. I promise you that." Another sign of Mara's secretiveness appears in the conventional form of a "bird call." And in response to the "song," Mrs. Marston states, "I've heard it several times lately: at night. It must be some new kind of night bird." When Mara laughingly replies, "It is," and intimates that she knows the identity of the new bird, both of her parents look at her, and Dr. Marston demands, "Mara do you know what it is?" Evasively, Mara replies, "You two funny, funny old dears—a bird that sings at night must be a night bird. Mustn't it?" Still nervous and restless, Mara adds, "Daddy, I—I haven't been outdoors today." Dr. Marston comprehendingly says, "I suppose you wish to go out now;" and Mara replies, "Just for a little while." She exits to rendezvous with Carewe—never to return chaste and sane.

In her absence, a thunderstorm that heralds and mirrors the havoc that is to be wreaked on Mara arises. Amid the tumult and the lightning of this conveniently contrived storm, Mrs. Marston and the servants close the windows and fortify the house. Martha (who is named Joanna Jessups in a different version of the play) speaks in the quasi-comic dialect of uneducated African Americans and says, "It am guine tu rain lik de Debbil. Miss Ellen Ise gwine up tu close de winders." It is interesting to note that the family takes precautions to safeguard their home when, unbeknownst to them, it is Mara who most needs protection at the time. Concerned for Mara's welfare, Mrs. Marston calls her daughter and sends Jasper to search for her—but in vain. When he returns without Mara, Jasper tells her parents, "I ain't gib up. I jis' wanted tu see wedder sheil come in."

Jasper Jessups and his wife are loyal servants, and they take care of the Marston family the way black domestics have traditionally cared for white families in plays written by European Americans. Their presence recalls that of minstrel characters who were employed by black and white writers of the nineteenth and early twentieth centuries to provide humor within a work. But underneath the minstrel mask—as applied by black authors—is a satirical treatment of color and caste prejudice and practice within the African American race (Bell 1987, 35). The fact that Jasper is "a small black man" and his wife Martha/Joanna is a "huge elderly woman" who wears an apron and a "knotted bandanna handkerchief," recalling the image of the traditional black mammy, substantiates the issue of color bias. And that the Jessups are servants to the affluent Marstons validates the matter of caste predilection.

As Jasper resolves to continue his search for Mara and Ellen cries over her daughter's dropped handkerchief, the door opens, and Mara, "wide-eyed, staring, haggard, bedraggled, wet, [and] dirty," enters. She has been raped (although the violation comes out exclusively by inference) and evidences through her insanity the suffering, sorrow, and grief that follow in the wake of her sexual assault.

Mara neither knows her name nor her parents' identity and asks, "Why do you call me Mara? Mara! Mara! ... Tell me who are you two?" She asks for God in his house and brokenly speaks of someone (herself) who died outdoors ("Mara is dead ... I saw her die. I was there"), possibly meaning that the ravaged victim has witnessed the death of the virgin Mara. Her father, a pale-skinned man, frightens her. And each time he reaches out to comfort Mara, she recoils from him, probably because he reminds her of the white scoundrel Carewe. It is possible at this juncture that every man will now appear to be a rapist. Mara's aversion to men is most clearly seen in her hostile response to Dr. Marston when he tries to prevent her from returning to the storm. Shrieking as her father touches her hand to avert her exit, Mara yells:

> No! No! No! I hate you. You touched me once before—like this. (*Fights with her father*) I tell you I hate you! I hate you! Let me go. I'll tear you! (*Tries to tear him with her teeth*) You're nothing but a lying rascal.... You're the foulest thing ... in Hell (*Screams*) yes Hell! Hell! Hell!... You fiend.... (*Suddenly with a great effort throws him off. In a terrible voice*) God saw what you did to Mara.... May you know hunger and thirst always. May you want and get and lose.... May your enemies hate you as I do. May you know nothing but bitterness ... and may you die as you have lived [Grimké, *Mara*, n.d.].

It is noteworthy that amid the denunciation and the curses Mara intimates that she was raped, and she ventilates her outrage against all men who, in her agitated mind, lie and defile women. Mrs. Marston, who has heretofore played a secondary role in the life of her daughter (who favored her father) now assumes center stage in the wake of Mara's hostility to men. As the legions of black mothers before and after her, Ellen becomes the support of a despoiled and distraught daughter. The voice of sanity and reality for Mara, she explains to her child why her dress is wet ("You have been out in the rain, don't you remember?") and she functions as Mara's great protector. Ellen's guardianship is demonstrated when her sole command impels Mara to cooperate with Dr. Marston and to answer his questions about the "dead" Mara and the frequency of Carewe's visits. Before Ellen's prompting, Mara is belligerent to her imploring father and expresses an "attitude full of hatred for him" and "retreats slowly until she is behind her mother." But Mara becomes docile and compliant after Ellen demands, "You must answer the questions. I'll not let him hurt you." Ellen has become a human fortress for Mara and displaces the ten-foot wall that proved useless in safeguarding Mara's chastity. Ellen's deepest maternal fear, the rape of her daughter, has materialized. And in some way, because Mara is of her mother's flesh, Ellen also experiences a violation for which there is no legal redress. She knows that because Mara is damaged psychologically as well as physically that she will probably renounce men and bear no children of her own to continue the family bloodline. Consequently, Ellen will see neither herself nor her daughter replicated in succeeding generations. A type of genocide seems to be at work in the Marston family, for Ellen has lost six children in the past and now stands to lose her seventh, the Marston's final chance for posterity. Ellen's motherly heart is crushed by pain at the destruction of her last child, and in an effort to avert further damage to Mara, "Mrs. Marston blocks the way" when Mara again tries to return to the storm.

Ellen and the rest of the household finally get Mara to bed after she faints from repeated attempts to escape. Jasper who has discovered a rope ladder hidden against the wall, tells Dr. Marston that he has just seen Carewe ride away. Mrs. Marston and the doctor then discuss their lack of legal recourse in the South for the rape of their daughter. Dr. Marston intimates that he will avenge Mara's violation, and when Ellen reminds him of God, Richard renounces Him and forbids God's name to be spoken in The Cedars again.

The doctor's rage is comprehensible, for it is based on his perception of a God who permits a legal system to deny its African American citizens justice and protection. Moreover, his anger is also understandable because Richard knows that in seeking vengeance for Mara's rape he assures his death and the probable murder of his loved ones—since African Americans during the early twentieth century did not have the right to retaliate against the unchecked violence that European Americans perpetrated against them. Thus the entire Marston family, as was the case with many of their racial counterparts, is affected by the rape of a single member.

In act 4, set in the hall living room of The Cedars, Dr. Marston is seen waiting for Carewe. Richard appears completely drained of energy and is oblivious to everything around him, including Mrs. Marston, who equally exhausted by Mara's tragedy, now looks "very pale, old, and tense." Mara is still distracted and walks about the house, not knowing herself or anyone else. Intermittently, she warns that "he" is coming, and when the sound of two horses' hooves is heard, Dr. Marston goes outside, fires two gunshots, and returns stating, "He—will—not—return—again." The doctor has killed Carewe and a companion who have come to The Cedars in search of Mara.

In the second scene, a white lynch mob composed of "men, boys, and even women" crashes into the Marston home. Mrs. Marston, again becomes the protector and confronts the throng. She "makes one final superhuman effort and stands in front of Dr. Marston. She faces the mob.... She stands there, her head thrown back her nostrils dilate ... [and] As well as she may, Mrs. Marston places her body between them and her husband. The Mother ... protecting its young." Nevertheless, "several men spring upon the doctor" and strike him forcibly on the head. He crumples up and the attackers pick up his inert body and carry it outside—presumably to be lynched. In the meantime, Ellen, who has also been assailed by blows is lifted up by several men. "When she fully realizes she is overpowered and is being carried out ... she begins to scream. The cries are terrible." At the same time, a "man who has been licking his lips" and a "man who has been testing his hands [for strength]" rivet their eyes on Mara and furtively steal upon her. Mara, who is singing a song that foreshadows her death ("I needs must follow death, who calls for me, call and I follow") is interrupted by these two men who spring upon her. "One man strikes her forcibly in the face [and] she crumples up as her father did." The assailants then bear her out and no one is left inside. "Outside, the screams of Mrs. Marston can be heard ... suddenly there is silence." And thus, in one evening, an entire family, two generations, and all potential generations are lynched by a mob that will go unprosecuted.

Grimké uses the slaughter of the refined and upright Marstons to protest the atrocities that were perpetrated against African Americans—particularly those who were "well-educated, cultivated, and cultured" (Angelina Weld Grimké Collection). Perhaps this classicism, which suggests that educated blacks are regarded as of more intrinsic value than noneducated ones, becomes more obviously ideological when viewed against Grimké's aristocratic background outlined at the beginning of this study. Grimké's household influenced her decision to focus her literary attention on the "talented tenth," i.e., upper-class conservative blacks. Yet while she campaigned for the civil rights of all African Americans in her protest works, Grimké articulated and advanced the interests of the social stratum she knew best.

Grimké's black gentry is the focus of Jean-Marie A. Miller's evaluation of the protest drama. Professor Miller (1978) notes, "The most outstanding characteristic of *Mara* is its use of black genteel characters, whose refinement is in glaring contrast to the cruelties waged against them solely because of their race" (518). The facts that the Marstons are wealthy and black (Richard is a physician, Ellen is a leisured housewife, and Mara is a "privileged" daughter) and that they are lynched by a white vandalizing mob substantiates Miller's observation, as does Carewe's destruction of the young, innocent Mara.

In viewing *Mara* from an autobiographical perspective, critic Gloria T. Hull remarks, "The drama reflects Grimké's ... close relationship with her father in the love that exists between Mara and Dr. Marston" (Hull 1987, 127). For example, when the doctor enters in act 2, "His eyes go dark with a certain fierceness and tenderness toward Mara. They exchange a long look of welcome." Mara then runs to him, throws her arms about her dad and kisses his shoulder. "With his free hand he pats her head and then puts his arm about her." Having been abandoned by her mother at seven and being reared by her father from then on, Grimké was more familiar with paternal, rather than with maternal affection. And possibly for this reason, Grimké's protagonist cleaves to her father, rather than to her mother, prior to Mara's rape and her alienation against men.

For Unborn Children (1926)

In *For Unborn Children* (1926), another lynching play addressing the miscegenation theme, Myrtle Smith Livingston reverses the traditional pairing of a southern Caucasian man and African American woman. Such a pairing may be related to the fact of Livingston's gender, but through it, she expresses the black female perspective on the African American man's preference for white women. Marion, the lynch victim's sister, ventilates her anger with the black man's spousal choice: "What is to become of us when our own men throw us down?"—as does Livingston when she has Leroy embrace his "punishment" for interracial mixing. (Livingston 184). It is useful to recall that black and white dramatists have historically agreed that biracial mixing is bad, although some believed that African Americans might benefit from such a union. Nevertheless, on stage, the mulatto had to die—even if he or she possessed only one drop of African blood. Dion Boucicault's *The Octoroon* (1859) is perhaps the best known work among the tragic mulatto literary tradition, which was continued in white-authored plays such as Edward Shelton's *The Nigger* (1909), Eugene O'Neill's *All God's Chillun Got Wings* (1924), and Howard Sackler's *Great White Hope* (1967). African American dramatists extended this theme in works including Langston Hughes' *Mulatto* (1935), Adrienne Kennedy's *Funnyhouse of a Negro* (1964), and *The Owl Answers* (1965), and Alice Childress's *Wedding Band* (1966).

Livingston's one-act play *For Unborn Children* was initially published in the July 1926 issue of *The Crisis*. In the journal's literary competition in 1925, Livingston's work was the recipient of the third-place prize of ten dollars. *For Unborn Children* has been anthologized in books since the late 1920s.

Grandma Carlson is the principle figure in the drama, even though her grandson Leroy occupies a pivotal role in the work as the lynch target. From her position at center stage, she radiates the anxiety, anger, and pain common to black mothers of the period whose sons have chosen white women and have consequently imperiled the lives of both the immediate family and the general black community. A survey of this matron, shows that she is a "gentle, well-bred, old lady," that like Grimké's Ellen Marston, presides over a refined middle-class family, who inhabits a tastefully furnished house: "There is a sofa to one side, a table in the center, and a leather comfort chair in the corner; another leather chair sits in the upper part of the room: A window [clean and unbroken] is in the rear" (Livingston [1926] 1974, 185). At the beginning of the play, Grandma Carlson and her granddaughter Marion anxiously await the arrival of her grandson Leroy who is three hours late. Justifiably alarmed by this young lawyer's tardiness, his sister cries, "Oh! If he would only let her [his white fiancée] alone! He knows what it will mean if they find out" (186). The play's 1926 Southern setting substantiates the fear of Leroy's murder, which Marion and Grandma Carlson share. For it is a certainty that African American men were lynched for dating white women during that era.

Expressing an historic response to miscegenation, Grandma Carlson replies, "I'd almost rather that he should die now than to marry a white woman" (Livingston [1926] 1974, 185). Grandma Carlson experiences excruciating pain when Leroy arrives and announces that on the following night he plans to take his fiancée Selma North where he can legally marry her. Leroy's statement generates both a discussion in which Grandma Carlson articulates the anguish the black mother suffers when her fated son chooses the forbidden woman and a lament from Marion who sheds important light on the scorn black women, not good enough for some African American males, suffer. Feeling rejected and abandoned by the child she has nurtured since birth, Grandma Carlson cries: "Don't you love us at all anymore since she came into your life?" (186). She and Marion greatly feel the sting of being sacrificed for Selma, and Marion passionately cries: "His family and his career ... mean nothing to him now; ... his whole heart and soul are wrapped up in his girl" (186).

Marion then upbraids the biracial couple, "There must be something terribly wrong with her.... You poor fool" (Livingston [1926] 1974, 186). Ever the racial separatist, Marion allows for Leroy's preference for fair-skinned women ("If it's color you want"), but demands that he stay within his race and choose among the white-skinned African American women (186). Despairing because she knows that she cannot dissuade Leroy from marrying Selma, or prevent other eligible black men from rejecting and devaluing their own women, Marion laments, "What is to become of us when our own men throw us down?" (186). She exits from the room sobbing, vowing never to breathe Leroy's name again if he marries his fiancée. Grandma Carlson, who is equally devastated by Leroy's decision, remains in the room with her grandson. When Leroy asserts that he has the right to be happy with non–African American women, Grandma Carlson gently responds: "We have the right to be happy, child, only when our happiness doesn't hurt anybody else; and when a colored man marries a white woman, he hurts every member of the Negro race!" (186). She further explains to the bewildered Leroy that before African Americans can seize their just freedom, they must prove to their white oppressors who would deny it that blacks are equal to them. However, African Americans are unable to do so when black men place white women over their own. At Leroy's declaration that he loves Selma too much to give her up, Grandma Carlson replies that sometimes we demonstrate our love by sacrificing the object of it. She then tells Leroy he cannot make Selma happy because she will long for her own race, her own kind, and he will not be enough her.

At her final attempt to abort Leroy's marriage, Grandma Carlson tells him to consider the unborn children whom he sins against by marrying Selma. Children, remarks Grandma Carlson, deserve a mother who loves them, and a white woman cannot be the committed, loyal, and self-less mother that an African American baby needs. To substantiate her point, she divulges the family secret that she has long withheld. She reveals to Leroy that his mother was a white woman, who could never stand the sight of him and Marion and that she hated her two biracial children because they were not white. Totally repulsed by this information, Leroy resolves to not risk giving his children such a racist mother, who chose not to be a part of her black children's lives. Shortly, Selma arrives, warning him that the mob is coming, to which Leroy replies "(*in amazement*) A mob!—after me?" Upon being summoned outside by the mob, Leroy exits fearlessly and victoriously to be lynched as were many African Americans before him. Elizabeth Brown-Guillory notes, "Unlike anything to appear in any play during these decades, Leroy offers himself up to the mob with great restraint and dignity" (1988). The critic adds that Livingston shapes Leroy into a Christ figure as he goes to the mob, arms outstretched, with these final words: "Don't grieve so; just think of it as a sacrifice for unborn children" (11).

In illuminating the violent and inhumane repercussions of interracial mixing, *For Unborn Children* levied a strong indictment against American racism. It very particularly underscored the vulnerability of contemporary African American males to white women and illustrated the fact that cautionary commentary from African American women was just as imperative in the 1920s as it was in the 1890s. Investigations by Ida B. Wells disclosed the well-known fact that black men frequently and willingly ruined their lives by choosing white women for wives and lovers. Influenced by the activist/journalist, Livingston renders a scathing critique of Leroy's forbidden love relationship. Employing Marion as her mouthpiece, she explains the source of miscegenation statutes: Laws would never have been passed against it if states could have believed white women would turn Negro men down, but they knew they wouldn't; they can make fools out of them too easily (Hatch and Shine 1974, 186). Considering the fate of Leroy Carlson, it may be fruitful to recall that Wells's investigations expose the fact that rape was not alleged in most lynch cases. Rather, she proved that when mobs claimed to be motivated by an African American male's rape of a white woman, "rape" actually referred to a consensual relationship, often initiated by the woman: "White men lynch the offending Afro-American, not because he is a despoiler of virtue but because he succumbs to the smiles of white women" (Wells 1969, 54). Both Livingston and Well seemingly intimate that during intimacy the African American male was neither violent nor aggressive with his white lover.

Blue-Eyed Black Boy (c. 1930)

In *Blue-Eyed Black Boy* Georgia Douglas Johnson continues the miscegenation theme, this time employing the traditional pairing of the victimized white girl and the demonized black man as her assailant. Incensed by the legal system that denied African Americans protection from the period's racist violence and black women protection from rape by white men, Johnson protested these injustices in her anti-lynching drama. In the present play, she ventilates her especial outrage at the laws that exempted white men who fathered black children from supporting and defending them. *Blue-Eyed Black Boy* draws upon the black female's history of sexual abuse as it features a black mother, who for the sake of averting her son's lynching, reveals that she was raped by a white man. The play recalls this painful personal subject in order to politicize it—i.e., to insist that the forbidden topic of the sexual exploitation of the black woman by white men be included in the public debate for anti-lynch legislation. With this dual argument at the core of *Blue-Eyed Black Boy*, Douglas Johnson centers its plot around a violated black woman, whose mulatto son becomes the target of a lynch mob.

Blue-Eyed Black Boy has only "recently" been recovered. No evidence suggests that Johnson ever attempted to produce or publish this play, although it may have been among her many unpublished works, which were performed in the schools, church halls, and lofts in the Washington, D.C. area. The text of the play intimates that had she sought to bring *Blue-Eyed Black Boy* before the public, she might also have targeted a white female audience for whom her plea for the stemming of the violation of black women might have gathered considerable force. For possibly in discovering the defilement of the heroine, such an audience would have seen potential images of themselves, ravished by lascivious men. Examined from this perspective, *Blue-Eyed Black Boy* becomes another instrument to raise the consciousness of white women who could agitate for equality and justice on behalf of African Americans—particularly African American women Moreover, *Blue-Eyed Black Boy*, like Grimké's *Mara*, becomes a means of dismantling the white female audience's stereotypes of the black woman as a seductress and her mulatto issue as degenerate. In its allusion to the circumstances of the protagonist's rape, *Blue-Eyed Black Boy*, as did *Mara* before it, shows that neither the black protagonist, nor her actual counterparts were to be blamed for an unsolicited rape that often resulted in illegitimate biracial children.

Pauline Waters is the central character in the play. From her center stage location, she emanates the conflicting bliss and disquietude common to black mothers of the period, while revealing the gravity that has historically engulfed black maternity. A survey of this matron, whose fictional calamity mirrors that of her numerous real-life peers shows that she is a proud woman who enjoys a privileged-class standing in her community. Having benefited from her late husband's prominence and from bearing two children who sport Caucasian features, she revels in her social status and in her children's "superior" beauty. Unlike the Marstons, who are genteel and of a superior social class, Pauline and Rebecca derive their superior social standing from the vestiges—i.e., hair texture, skin color—of their white ancestry. These attributes account for much of the family's prominence in the town.

Pauline's opening dialogue with her daughter Rebecca, as she submits her wedding dress to Pauline for inspection, reveals that Pauline erroneously believes that their family's eminence will exempt them from racist violence. The women note that everyone in the Baptist church looks up to them and that they are deserving of the high pinnacle upon which Pauline's proud husband has placed them.

That Pauline has influenced her daughter's internalization of her values and morals becomes apparent when Rebecca vaunts that she has tried to walk straight all her life. Pauline is gratified by the social and economic rewards that her tutelage has reaped and duly responds that she is proud, especially since Rebecca is presently engaged to a young doctor. Pauline awaits this physician and prospective son-in-law, who will come and change the dressing on her injured foot. During the interval preceding his arrival, she has a significant conversation with Rebecca that establishes the sterling character of her son, Jack. Their important dialogue constructs an African American masculinity that distances him from the conventional image of the savage black rapist whom he subsequently finds himself accused of being. Attesting to Pauline's production of an intelligent and hardworking young man—suitable husband material—Jack emerges from their discourse as an exemplary youth who has foregrounded his relationship to his mother and sister.

He becomes the object of attention when Rebecca looks at the kitchen stove containing an uneaten meal and expresses her wish that Jack would come home, eat his dinner, and thereby allow her to wash the dishes. She complains that he should have been home an hour ago, and entertaining reasons for her brother's absence, Rebecca makes a statement that both underscores Jack's moral rectitude and that foreshadows the falsity of the rape charge that the white girl will shortly levy against him: "Well, there's one thing sure and certain. He's not running after girls" (Johnson [c. 1930] 1990b, 34). Pauline corroborates Rebecca's assertion and then notes Jack's scholarly penchant and industriousness: "Just give him a book and he's happy. Says he going to quit running that crane and learn engineering soons you get married. He's been mighty tied down since your father died taking care of us" (34).

Pauline's sympathy toward Jack for subordinating his career goals to his family obligations soon gives way to her praise of his celebrated good looks — his distinguished eyes in particular. Observing that Jack is hailed the smartest and the best looking African American boy in the whole town she brags: "Yes, he is good looking even if he is mine" (Johnson [c. 1930] 1990b, 34). She then targets his distinguishing features — his eyes. Stage directions indicate that Pauline "looks far off thoughtfully" after mentioning her son's eyes and that Rebecca emphasizes the uniqueness of their hue. She states that Jack is the only one in the family with blue eyes, everyone else's — dad's, Pauline's and hers are black, inviting speculation about the origins of Jack's singular eyes. The possibility/probability arises that Pauline was sexually violated by a white man, whose genes produced Jack's blue eyes. However she refuses to entertain this idea and evidences severe discomfort. In her anxiety to terminate the subject of Jack's peculiar eye color, with its allusion to her shameful rape, Pauline directs her attention to the sound of an approaching vehicle. She commands Rebecca to hush and to go and let the doctor in.

Dr. Thomas Grey enters, and in his treatment of Pauline's injured foot, he is the consummate physician. Yet, it is interesting to note, that while he takes meticulous pains to safeguard Pauline's life, it is her son who — unbeknownst to all — needs protection at that very moment. Presaging Jack's need for imminent rescue, Grey tells Pauline that he saw some rough looking hoodlums assembling on the streets as he came in. Dr. Grey adds that it looks like there could be some trouble somewhere. To this timely warning, Pauline — who fails to perceive danger in the assembly of white men — replies that there is always some type of daily commotion stirring. She tells Dr. Grey to ignore the hoodlums, to pay them no mind. Yet as Pauline dismisses Grey's admonition, the conveniently contrived knock at the door occurs — signaling a revelation that will convince Pauline of the error of her indifference. When the door is opened, Hester Grant, the bearer of bad tidings "comes panting in" (Johnson [c. 1930] 1990b, 35). Blurting out the news about the latest community tragedy and its relevance to her friend, she tells Pauline that Jack has been arrested and put in jail. At this point, the chief complication attending black maternity surfaces. For with Hester's announcement, Pauline's worst fear — and that of most early twentieth-century black mothers is realized. She knows instantly that Jack has been accused by whites of violating one of the many racist local mores and that he will be imminently lynched.

Seeking to hear her son's precise infraction, Pauline listens to Hester, who recounts Jack's alleged assault of a Caucasian female: "They say he done brushed against a white woman on the street. They had er argument and she hollowed out he's attacking her" (Johnson [c. 1930] 1990b, 35). Since Jack has reportedly disobeyed one of the code's special restrictions for African American men in his conduct toward a white woman, he has ensured his punishment. Yet a cursory reflection on the historical relations between white women and black men in America shows that the white girl's accusatory scream—like those of her many factual counterparts—could have been a retaliatory act against this especially good-looking black man, who resisted her possible sexual advances. Evidence of Jack's noble character and upbringing indicate that he counters the stereotype of the black brute rapist. Nevertheless, that the white girl has deliberately set in motion those forces that will orchestrate the murder of yet another innocent African American becomes painfully apparent. The predictable plot unfolds as Hester, rehearsing a familiar and historic scenario adds: "A crew of white men come up and started beating on him and the policeman, when he was coming home from work, dragged him to the jailhouse. They, they say there's gointer to be a lynching tonight. They gointer break open the jail and string him up!" (35).

Unlike Ruby in Childress' *Trouble in Mind*, Pauline is resistant and unable to accept the inevitable lynching, which whites claim is the only justifiable punishment for black males who assault white females. When she incredulously and vehemently protests: "String him up? They can't do that ... to my son," she discloses a mistaken trust that her family prominence and her son's upright character will transcend the lynch mob (Johnson [c. 1930] 1990b, 35). Struggling to avert pending tragedy, she—at great risk to herself—exercises the only option that can potentially save Jack. She deliberately violates the white paternal code of silence that mandated black women to conceal the white identities of men who fathered their biracial children. Cryptically revealing the identity of Jack's white father in front of Rebecca, Hester, and Dr. Grey, Pauline exclaims, "I know what I'll do. I don't care what it costs" (36). To this purpose, she removes a small gold ring from her jewelry box and commands Dr. Grey to speed over to Governor Tinkham's house and to give him this ring. She mandates Grey to tell the governor that Pauline sent this ring and that they are going to lynch her son, who was born 21 years ago. She further tells Grey, "Mind you say 21 years ago. Then say, listen close. 'Look in his eyes and you'll save him'" (36).

To this revelation of forbidden knowledge, Dr. Grey listens in great astonishment. He then grasps the small ring in his hand and hurries toward the door. Assuring Pauline that he will accomplish her errand for her, he promises to put the ring in the governor's hands and to deliver her message as quickly as possible. At Grey's departure, Hester who is equally uncomfortable with this prohibited information, expresses her hope that Pauline knows what she is doing. Because Pauline is certain that she has seized the only measure that can potentially save her child, she reassures Hester that she is aware of her actions. At this juncture, where Pauline applies to Tinkham's fatherly sensibilities, she evidences her belief that if she informs the governor that it is his son who is being lynched, that he will call out the state troops to avert Jack's murder.

The interim during which she awaits her son's hoped-for deliverance proves to be an especially tense time. For myriads of white men armed with guns and piled in wagons begin assembling to murder Pauline's innocent son. When Rebecca is alarmed by the congregation of the lynch mob and the implications for Jack, she screams—wondering what to do. Pauline commands her to trust God, and heeding her own advice, Pauline makes a significant prayer that expresses her self-ascribed guilt for her participation in her own rape. She indicates that her forced submission to the governor was her sin as well as his, and she remorsefully cries: "Lord, Jesus, I know I've sinned against your holy law, but you did forgive me and let me hold up my head again.... Help me to save my innocent child.... Save him, Lord" (Johnson [c. 1930] 1990b, 36). It is noteworthy that this personal prayer could also articulate the sentiment of her numerous historical peers, who also internalized their guilt of being raped and of giving birth to illegitimate biracial children.

A survey of the play's final scene shows the confirmation of Pauline's intuition. Her theory that the governor would probably deploy state troops to avert his son's lynching is rewarded. For just as Jack is about to be hanged, the state troops and the guards come and rescue him, and Pauline's blue-eyed black boy is spared a lynching—this time. In considering the governor's timely rescue of Jack, scholar Elizabeth Brown-Guillory provides important elucidation. She writes that through his intervention, "Douglas Johnson ... suggests ... that some white men who fathered black children offered some kind of protection" (15). And for Pauline Waters, who depended upon the goodness of Tinkham's paternal compassion, it was fortunate that they did.

As *Blue-Eyed Black Boy* ends, it is clear Johnson's drama is distinguished by its surprise ending with its abortion of a lynching and its portrayal of an assertive black femininity. Pauline Waters ushers in a new kind of African American woman and motherhood. Proactive in her resistance to her son's lynching, she successfully appeals to Governor Tinkham for help by disclosing Jack's true identity as his child. As Saschaw Krause notes in *The Anatomy of Resistance: The Rhetoric of Anti-Lynching in American Literature and Culture, 1892–1936*, *Blue-Eyed Black Boy* displaces traditional patterns for racial harmonization based on female observation of Victorian gender norms. Instead, the play seeks alternative forms for racial survival without relinquishing black female respectability (e.g., Pauline never leaves home, but sends a messenger—Dr. Grey—to the governor). With this work, Johnson officially declares active intervention as the only feasible means to prevent lynching and to preserve African American family life (Krause 240).

As in her other plays, Johnson in *Blue-Eyed Black Boy* represents lynching as a terror to the black family—to black marriage and to black motherhood. However, in this particular drama, she substitutes distress and despair with active and positive maternal intervention. Yet Pauline's appeal to Tinkham, the white American male, recalls the traditional action plan that mandates a biracial collaboration to abolish lynching as an assault upon black maternity. It could be argued, however, that instead of making the endangerment of maternity the foundation for constructing biracial sameness, *Blue-Eyed Black Boy* alludes to the history of biracial relationships as a preexisting yet denied and muted connection between blacks and whites.

The intervention of Jack's white father seemingly serves two crucial purposes. First, it substantiates Elizabeth Brown-Guillory's statement—that some white men provided some protection for their white children and thus revokes the notions about undivided white support for lynching. Mention should be made that the governor's opposition to lynching renders such terrorism a sadistic hobby of "poor white trash" or white hoodlums. Expanding on this notion, Krause notes that "*Blue-Eyed Black Boy* represents lynching as improper and deplorable behavior and depicts it as a means of widening, not reconciling, interest- and economic-base diversifications within the white race (Krause 240).

The intervention of Jack's white father also revokes the notions of the African American woman's alleged immorality and depravity by employing "the white pro-lynching outline of gender, foregrounding that white women are worthy of protection only because of their purity, chastity, and piety; in short because they are 'true women'" (Krause 240). Johnson thus repudiates the debasement of black womanhood through her presentation of Pauline as a female of sterling character and as a self-sacrificing mother. Moreover, in her presentation of the governor's assistance to Pauline, Johnson uses Tinkham to help equate African American and white femininity. Lynching is consequently robbed of its crux, i.e., the white woman by prevention (241).

In further critiquing *Blue-Eyed Black Boy*, Elizabeth Brown-Guillory astutely observes that Johnson mirrors a society that sets double standards for the lives of its African American citizens. On the one hand Jack faces a lynch mob because he allegedly brushed up against a white woman; while on the other hand, Pauline is raped by the (unpunished) governor and gives birth to his son without repercussions. Johnson, herein, suggests that black women are devalued in American society and that they are not accorded the same respect given to white females. The playwright also makes the point that African American men are unable to defend their women and consequently must often silently bear the burden of rearing mulatto children. Mr. Waters' support of "his" blue-eyed black boy is a glaring case in point. Johnson further hints at the double standards under which African Americans must live when she describes a white mob that threatens to murder and white troops who come to save a white man's black son. Brown-Guillory correctly concludes: "The message is clear: the play is about the powerlessness of black people" (Brown-Guillory 1988, 15).

Wedding Band: A Love/Hate Story in Black and White (1966)

Alice Childress' *Wedding Band: A Love/Hate Story in Black and White* further expands the theme of miscegenation and its treatment of forbidden liaisons. It focuses on an interracial love affair, which is destroyed by white and black prejudice. *Wedding Band*, for the most part, was greatly ignored by critics and producers when it was written. Mid-twentieth-century producers eschewed controversial subject matters such as biracial marriage and the then current miscegenation laws observed in many southern states. There was one rehearsed reading of the work in 1963, and while it was optioned for Broadway by producers, the play was not produced because Childress refused to make script changes that would alter her intent. The first production took place at the University of Michigan in 1966 and received favorable reviews. However, it was not until late 1972 that *Wedding Band* was finally produced in New York before a large audience at the Public Theatre. In 1973, ABC finally produced a television version of the play, but several southern ABC affiliates banned the showing.

At *Wedding Band*'s initial New York production in 1972, Alice Childress was designated to direct. However, as the play approached its premier night, problems occurred, and Childress was dismissed and replaced by Joseph Papp, the director of the New York Shakespeare Festival. He retained much of Childress' direction, and the play received good reviews.

Wedding Band debuted Off Broadway to a rather mixed reception. While the critics were primarily enthusiastic and praised it as a drama about Afro-America that is not a "black play," it was also described as a story that could have been excerpted from a women's journal. Catherine Wiley, in an essay in *Modern American Drama: The Female Canon*, observed that denying that the play is a "black play" reassures a potential audience that the play will not be of interest to only an African American audience and assumes that white audiences would not be interested in seeing a play about African Americans. Various reactions to *Wedding Band* came from additional white and black critics. In an insulting review, Clive Barnes of the *New York Times* wrote, "Indeed its strength lies very much in the poignancy of its star-cross'd lovers, but whereas Shakespeare's lovers had a fighting chance, there is no way that Julia and Herman are going to beat the system. Niggers and crackers are more irreconcilable than any Montagues and Capulets," (Brown-Guillory 1988, 32). Loften Mitchell wrote more compassionately and more astutely, "Miss Childress writes with a sharp, satiric touch.... Characterizations are piercing, her observations devastating.... The play reaches a rousing climax when the Negro woman defines for a white woman exactly what the Negro has meant in terms of Southern lives" (32).

Wedding Band examines how legal authority and social custom serve as a force to maintain racism within society. It centers around a racially mixed love affair that is destroyed by white and black bigotry. The play's action occurs over a three-day period in South Carolina during 1918 at the close of World War I. Thirty-five-year-old Julia Augustine and forty-year-old Herman are the primary characters who have been secretly meeting for one decade because the state laws forbid both interracial marriage and interracial cohabitation. Like Leroy and Selma in Livingston's *For Unborn Children*, the couple wants to escape the South and move to the North where they can marry. However, Herman is obligated to remain in South Carolina until he reimburses his mother $3,000 for the loan she has granted him to purchase a bakery business.

As the play opens in act 1, the couple is celebrating the tenth anniversary of their common-law marriage. Upon complaining about his mother, who is "a poor ignorant woman ... mad because she was born a sharecropper ... outta her mind 'cause she ain't high class society," Herman gives Julia a petite, but florid wedding cake (Childress 679). It has a bride and a groom on top and ten pink candles commemorating their years together. To further delight Julia, Herman gives her a wide, gold wedding band, which is mounted on a chain to allow Julia to wear it in public. Act 1 ends with Herman promising to buy Julia a Clyde Line boat ticket to New York, where he will join her debt-free a year later. Seized by influenza, Herman falls and is helped into Julia's bed as the act ends. The fact that only one neighbor assists Julia with Herman—and only does so at her request—underscores the danger and the illicitness of the biracial relationship. For no one wants to risk lynching, imprisonment, fines, and beatings for harboring criminals, as are the racially mixed lovers. Moreover, the backyard apartments—the last in a series of "out-of-the-way" residences where Julia rendezvous with her white lover—also highlight the clandestine nature of her relationship.

At the beginning of act 2, Herman remains in Julia's bed with influenza. Fanny, the African American landlady who elevates herself above her race, looks at Julia's collapsed lover and cries: "It's against the damn law for him to be layin' up in a black woman's bed" (Childress [1966] 1994, 672). She refuses to call a doctor. Yet resolving to avoid legal action directed against sheltering this mixed-race couple and social disdain from the whites who hold her in high regard (Fanny boasts that she has overheard whites whisper that she represents her race in an approved manner), she sends for Herman's mother and sister Annabelle to care for him. At their arrival, a vicious expression of racist hatred that accounts for the entrenchment of hurtful miscegenation law ensues.

When Herman's mother Frieda, alias Miss Thelma, arrives with horse and buggy to pick up her ailing son, she initially pretends that Julia is not there. Described as a "'poor white' about fifty-seven years old" in clothes that are "'well-kept-shabby,'" Thelma commands her daughter Annabel to go through Julia's dresser drawers to find Herman's possessions, boasting that she will burn them. While continuing to ignore Julia's presence, Thelma asks Herman where his money is and accuses Julia of stealing it. Understandably insulted, Julia states that she will not match words with Thelma because, "I'm too much of a lady," to which Thelma retorts, "A lady oughta learn how to keep her dress down" (Childress [1966] 1994, 680). Thoroughly incensed by this monster who dares to invade her home and to call her a slut, Julia begins to defang the viper, shouting to Thelma: "I'm your damn daughter-in-law, you old bitch! ... The black thing who bought a hot water bottle to put on your sick white self when rheumatism threw you flat on your back ... who bought flannel gowns to warm your pale, mean body. I bought what he took home to you" (682).

Unable to accept or believe Julia's selfless unrequited acts of kindness Thelma yells: "Lies ... tear outcha lyin' tongue" (Childress [1966] 1994, 682). However Julia counters: "The lace curtains in your parlor ... the shirt-waist you wearin—I made them" (682). When Fanny urges Miss Thelma to leave, Julia quickly reveals Herman's mother's real name. "Miss Thelma my ass! Her first name is Frieda. The Germans are here ... in purple paint" (683). Frieda screams back, "Nigger whore ... he used you for a garbage pail" (683). Furious with Frieda, Julia shouts to this mother who has refused to move her son without the protection of darkness: "Out! Out! Out! ... keep him home" (683). She then dashes into her home and returns with an armful of clothing, resolving to "Clean!... Clean the whiteness outta my house" (683).

The last scene opens with Julia dressed in her wedding gown. She appears artificially excited (I'm so happy! I never been this happy in all my life!). Perhaps the wine in the glass that she carries is the source of some of her joy. However, as she talks with her neighbors who surround her, she learns that one of them, Mattie, is not legally married because South Carolina forbids divorce. Even though her first husband abused and deserted her,

Mattie cannot legally discard him so that she can marry her child's father with whom she lived eleven years. While this information is being disclosed, Herman enters, bearing two tickets to New York. The memory of the previous day's exchange of rancor and racial insults, however, pervades Julia's mind, so she gives the tickets and her wedding band to Mattie and her daughter Teeta.

When Julia and Herman begin to talk, they recall the years of love and intimacy that they shared. At this point, they resolve the strains placed on their relationship. Herman, however, is dying, even as the couple talks. Aware that his family have come for her lover, Julia locks out Herman's mother who, formerly was more interested in maintaining appearances than in saving her son's life. Unsurprisingly, the promised escape to New York never occurs, and Herman dies in Julia's arms.

In observing the critical themes in *Wedding Band*, prejudice and tolerance surface as glaring issues. More particularly, it is the community's intolerance and society's racism that prevent Julia and Herman from marrying and from seeking a doctor for Julia's lover. Miss Thelma, alias, Frieda, is perhaps the best expression of racial bigotry. She embraces a racist ideology and is a devotee of the Ku Klux Klan, which terrorizes African Americans. Frieda so despises the African American woman whom her son loves and is so nauseated by their relationship that *she* refuses to call a physician for him. At one point, she tells her daughter, "Annabelle, you've got a brother who makes pies and loves a nigger" (Childress [1966] 1994, 683). Moreover, Julia's isolation from the community is the outcome of prejudice and intolerance. She lives alone, moves often, and has no friends because of the southern states miscegenation laws. The law that prohibits their marriage serves to illustrate the depth of social intolerance and bigotry that permeated the south in the early to middle twentieth century.

Wedding Band also features a social-class prejudice that is found within both white and African American society. Fanny, Julia's entrepreneur landlady, feels socially superior to her tenants because she owns property. Ever the classicist, she confides to Julia that "Some people are ice cream.... I try to be ice cream." She later tells Julia, "I can't afford to mess that [white people's high opinion of her] up on a count-a you or any-a the rest-a these hard-luck, better-off dead, triflin' niggers (Childress [1966] 1994, 653). Frieda is opposed to Annabelle's marriage to a "common sailor" despite her sharecropper origins. Frieda and Fanny both demonstrate that subtle nuances of bigotry can be just as oppressive and hurtful as the more obvious racial prejudices that create tension in this work. Citing the dominant theme, Elizabeth Brown-Guillory writes, "blacks and whites must learn to judge each other on individual merit, instead of blaming an entire race each time a white–black relationship, intimate or casual, terminates" (Brown-Guillory 1988, 32).

Judicial System Dramas

A Sunday Morning in the South (1925)

In *A Sunday Morning in the South,* Johnson ventilates her outrage at the lack of federal anti-lynch legislation to secure the well-being of African Americans and illustrates how black males in particular were regularly lynched for crimes they did not commit. *A Sunday Morning in the South* was never acted or printed during Johnson's lifetime, nor was it readily available until Hatch and Shine published it in their *Black Theater USA: Forty-Five Plays By Black Americans 1847–1974* (1974) collection under the "Black Folk Plays of the 1920s" section.

Sue Jones is the principal figure in the drama, even though her grandson occupies a pivotal role in the work as the lynch victim. From her position at center stage, she exudes the conflicting joy and anxiety common to black mothers of the period and reveals the gravity that has historically engulfed black maternity. A survey of this grand matriarch, whose fictional tragedy mirrors that of her myriad real-life counterparts, shows that she is a familiar character type, whose delineation invokes the image of the mammy. Having rendered years of service to both her white and black charges, seventy-year-old Sue Jones is seen, as the curtain rises,

> putting the breakfast on the kitchen table. She wears a red bandanna hand-kerchief on her grey head, a big blue gingham apron tied around her waist and big wide old lady comfort shoes. She uses a stick as she has a sore leg, and moves about with a stoop and a limp as she goes back and forth from the stove to the table (Johnson [1925] 1974, 213).

Apparently sick and fatigued by extensive maternal responsibilities, Sue Jones spends her waning years attending to the needs of her own immediate family. Significantly, it is within this familial context that she becomes the prime instrument for exploring the play's "theme of the theory versus the reality of justice for black people"—a leading discrepancy that contributes to the perilous state of black maternity (Hull 1987, 171).

Her function begins early in the play's exposition where the exemplary character of her grandson, Tom Griggs, attests to her production of a responsible young man who is groomed to assume the rights and privileges of citizenship. That Sue has inculcated spiritual values and has indoctrinated the work ethic in Tom is evident in the announcement that he makes at the beginning of the play, "There's the church bell. I sho meant to git out to meeting this morning but my back still hurts me. Remember I told you last night how I sprained it lifting them heavy boxes for Mr. John?" (Johnson [1925] 1974, 213). Sue remembers. And after scolding him for needlessly

working like a horse, she makes a comment that reveals her grandson's innocence and actual whereabouts the hour that he will have allegedly raped a
white girl: "Twant no moren eight when I called you to go to the store and
you was sleeping like a log of wood; I had to send [your little brother] Bossie"
(213).

That Sue has also fostered a strong sense of justice and ambition in
Tom becomes apparent in the remark that he makes during the family's discussion about the recklessness with which whites have been lynching blacks
in their community. Corroborating Sue's appeal for the legal protection of
black citizens he states his intention to attend night school where he will
obtain the formal education to help "change the laws ... make 'em strong"
(Johnson [1925] 1974, 214). Sue's wise tutelage and Tom's submission to it
keeps him alive for nineteen years in the hostile South, where they lynch
African Americans for anything. She is understandably proud of Tom and
justified in her conviction that he will remain a productive and law-abiding
citizen. Yet (like Pauline Waters before her) she evidences an erroneous confidence in *her* belief that Tom is exempt from racial violence when she answers
his question, "I wonder whut would I do if they ever tried to put something
on me" (214) . Misplacing her assurance and relaxing her guard—as no black
mother of *any* period should do—she replies, "Sonnie, you won't never hafter
worry bout sich like that" (214). So mistaken is Sue in her trust that Tom's
behavior will transcend the lynch mob that even the lyrics to the spiritual
sung by the congregation in the adjacent church ("Let the light from the
lighthouse shine on me") contradict her and forebode her imminent need for
someone to avert Tom's murder.

During this significant discussion—as Sue promises Tom that he will
never be framed for sexual assault—"A quick rap is heard at the door and it
is almost immediately pushed open and an officer enters as the four at table
look up at him in open mouthed amazement" (Johnson [1925] 1974, 214).
At this point, the chief complication attending black maternity surfaces. For
with the officer's break-in, Sue's worst fear—and that of most early twentieth-
century black mothers—is realized. She knows instantly that Tom has been
labeled a rapist and that he will be lynched momentarily. Gripped in terror,
Sue awaits the officer's impending attack, and the predictable plot unfolds
as the policeman demands whether Tom Griggs resides there. Making every
effort to protect her grandson while cooperating with the prejudiced law
enforcer, who disrespects her, Sue stammers, "Yes Sir," to the inquiry (214).
At her answer, the officer perfunctorily questions Tom about his whereabouts
and then rudely discredits Sue and Bossie who vouch for him. The dialogue
between the characters merits attention because it provides an example of
the historical abuse that African Americans have sustained at the hands of
white policemen:

SUE. (*answering quickly for Tom*) Right here sir, he was right here at home. Whut you want to know fer?

FIRST OFFICER. (*roughly*) Where were you last night at ten o'clock?

FIRST OFFICER. (*to Sue*) You keep quiet, old woman.

TOM. (*uneasily*) Gramma told you. I was right here at home—in bed at eight o'clock.

FIRST OFFICER. That sounds fishy to me—in bed at eight o'clock! And who else knows you were here?

SUE. Say Mr. Officer, whut you trying to do to my granson. Shore as God Almighty is up in them heabens he was right here in bed. I seed him and his little brother Bossie there saw him, didn't you Bossie?

BOSSIE. (*in a frightened whisper*) Yessum, I seed him and I heered him!

FIRST OFFICER. (*to Bossie*) Shut up. Your word's nothing. (*looking at Sue*) Nor yours either (Johnson [1925] 1974, 215).

The dialogue also reflects the insignificance, the mistreatment, and the legal powerlessness of contemporary African Americans in general and that of African American mothers in particular. Moreover, it very specifically illustrates the details of Sue's futile (but gallant) attempt to defend Tom against this white authority who demeans and disrespects her.

Following this exchange, the officer checks his paper, which contains a physical description of the alleged rapist ("age around twenty, five feet five or six, brown skin..."). He immediately decides that Tom *must* be the culprit—even though the description could apply to many black males and only vaguely applies to Tom. It bears mentioning that the officer's verdict both underscores the especial victimization of African American men and that it further delineates the peculiar plight of the black mother, who at any moment, stands to "lose" her child because of racist allegations. Sue protests the officer's prejudiced decision and verifies Tom's innocence a second time. She fails, however, to alter the policeman's judgment. Instead, she is compelled to helplessly watch as a second policeman immediately forces his way into her home, supporting the "raped" white damsel on his arm. To her horror, Sue hears the first policeman command the girl: "Take a good look, Miss. He fits your description perfect. Color, size, age, everything. Pine Street Market ain't no where from here, and he surely did pass that way last night. He was there all right.... We got it figgered all out" (Johnson [1925] 1974, 215).

When the officer asks the girl (who is not even certain that Tom *is* her assailant), "You say he looks like him?" She shakily replies, "Y-e-s (*slowly and undecidedly*) I think so. I ... I...." Her affirmative response suggests that she is eager to appease the policemen and the lynch mob in their demand for black blood as the atonement for the collective "injury" that whites claim they have sustained (Johnson [1925] 1974, 215). The girl's answer ensures Tom's death, and, realizing her contribution to the murder of another African American, she "covers her face with her arm and turns quickly and moves away from the door" (215). Elizabeth Brown-Guillory speculates on the impact the girl's acquiescence will have on black subjugation. She writes that when this "weak and confused Southern belle, at the insistence of the mob, participates in the ruination of a young black life, the victim becomes a symbol of black oppression" (Brown-Guillory 7). Tom certainly does, for in suffering for a crime that is imputed to him, he both recalls and anticipates the many African Americans who lost their lives because of the groundless accusations made by whites.

After the policemen and white girl agree that he is guilty, the first officer "makes a step toward Tom and slips handcuffs on him before any one is aware what is happening" (Johnson [1925] 1974, 215). Sue objects to this injustice and tells the policeman that he cannot arrest her grandson, because he has not done anything, Her protestation, however, only elicits an insult: "Be quiet, old woman ... keep cool Grannie" (215). When the officer adds, "He'll be right back if he's innocent," Sue receives this tacit assurance that Tom *will* be lynched (since it was an anomaly for African Americans to be judged innocent of *any* charge that early twentieth-century Euro-Americans would bring against them) in great alarm (215).

Struggling to avert the inevitable after being told by a friend that a lynch mob has abducted Tom from the police, Sue makes a frantic but futile effort to save Tom. She appeals to her "good white folks," that is, to her former employer, the judge, and to his daughter, Violet, whom she nursed as a baby. Because her crippled leg prevents her from running to her human sanctuaries, Sue asks her friend, Matilda Brown, to personally "tell Miss Vilet her ole nuse Sue is callin' on her ... tell her they done took Tom and he is perfect innercent ... ax her to ax her pa the Jedge to go git Tom and save him" (Johnson [1925] 1974, 216). However, Sue's appeal to her prominent employers goes unanswered. For all too soon, Matilda returns from her mission, announcing: "They—they done lynched him" (217). With a biased legal system that fails to serve and to protect African Americans, Tom's dispatch is not amazing. Neither is it astonishing that his death may have occasioned that of his doting grandmother. Stage directions indicate that at Matilda's disclosure, Sue

> (*screams*) Jesus! (*gasps and falls limp in her chair*) [Her friend] Liza puts the camphor bottle to [Sue's] nose again as Matilda feels her heart; they work over her a few minutes, shake their heads and with drooping shoulders, wring their hands (Johnson [1925] 1974, 217).

As *A Sunday Morning in the South* ends, it is clear that Sue Jones suffers the bane that threatened early twentieth-century black maternity as she loses her grandson to the unchecked racial violence of the age. Her collapse and the murder, itself, again illustrate the devastating effects of lynching. This single act of terrorism simultaneously destroys an individual, a family unit, and the security of an entire community—which is subject to loose another black life at the next charge of rape made by a Caucasian. *A Sunday Morning in the South* captures both the black mother's powerlessness to protect her children from such fatal accusations and reveals her inability to prevent her offspring from being lynched for crimes that they did not commit. Moreover, it clarifies how racial hostility impinged upon African American maternity and how it contributed to the tenuousness of the black mother's hold on her progeny at the beginning of the twentieth century.

It is worth recalling that the black woman's sons were the cherished targets of lynch mobs. Georgia Douglas Johnson, who bore two male children during this turbulent period was personally familiar with the peculiar woe of black maternity. Bearing testimony to the especial victimization of the black mother's son, she based the plot of *A Sunday Morning in the South* around Tom Griggs, who was arrested and lynched because he loosely "fits" the description of a black man who allegedly raped a white girl. The fictionalized Tom Grigg had legions of contemporary real-life counterparts whose murders occasioned inconsolable maternal grief. Included among the victims during the time that Johnson constructed her play were: "Shap" Curry, Moses Jones, and John Cornish, whose bodies were mutilated and burned on May 6, 1922, in Kirvin, Texas, for a murder they reportedly committed; Samuel Carter, who was lynched in 1923 for aiding his son's escape from a mob in Bronson, Florida; and Len Hart, who was lynched in August of that same year for allegedly peeping into the window of a white woman's home near Jacksonville, Florida (Hatch and Shine 1974, 211).

In the wake of the resurgence of racial violence, as expressed in the burning of more than forty southern black churches within eighteen months by white supremacists; the chaining of a black man (James Byrd, Jr.) to a truck and dragging him three miles to his death by Aryan Brotherhood member John King; and the racially motivated shooting spree of outspoken racist Benjamin Smith, which claimed the lives of Asians and blacks (including former Northwestern University basketball coach Ricky Byrdsong—to cite only a few examples of the rampant ethnic terrorism plaguing the late twentieth and early twenty-first centuries—*A Sunday Morning in the South* acquires an especial timeliness. It renders an analysis of racial violence, which in addition to illustrating the particular risks of black maternity, sheds important light upon the justifications (for ferocity) that many modern perpetrators of racist violence employ in bereaving contemporary black mothers of their children. More particularly, the play suggests that present-day transgressors apply a rationale similar, if not identical, to that of their predecessors for committing their heinous acts. A cursory glance at some historical infamies help to substantiate this point.

Writer Jerry Adler (1994) notes that the notorious case of Susan Smith, who drowned her two young sons and then "told police a [black] gunman stole her 1990 Mazda and sped off with her sons in the backseat," is only one event that illustrates the continuity of a racial strife that derives from the same prejudice against African Americans (African American men in particular) that vitiated human minds in Johnson's day ("Innocents Lost," *Newsweek*, November 14: 27). Smith's "tale of a gun wielding black man who ordered her out of her car and drove off, inexplicably, with her two sons in back" set off a "statewide, later nationwide search" for the accused (28). However, because of the discovery of Smith's racist hoax, few blacks were singled out and arrested by the police—as they were in the second incident involving the 1989 murder of pregnant Caroll Stuart—whose husband shot her to death in their car and then blamed her murder on a black stick up man. In this instance, Mr. Stuart's accusation led to the pursuit of numerous African American men and to the erroneous arrest of one, who was eventually released.

That the lynching of African Americans continues to be problematic, even at the onset of the twenty-first century, is evident in the infamous James Byrd murder. For while his killing was a "heinous crime against a man and his family, it was also something larger" (Cohen 1999, 28). Explaining the ramifications of this homicide, Adam Cohen writes: "Lynching is the iconic Old South crime, used to punish slave insurrections. Lynch mobs traditionally hanged their victim from a rope tossed over a tree limb. But dragging deaths were not uncommon, first from horses, later from cars and trucks. Lynching was at once a brutal act of vigilante injustice and a larger statement—a warning to blacks to remain subservient" (28). Byrd's manslaughter, which issued a stark foreboding, became the model for two copycat crimes occurring *days* later in Slidell, Louisiana, and in Belleville, Illinois, which also warned contemporary blacks to remain subservient. In both cases, whites in moving cars seized black men and dragged them. While the two attacks resulted in physical injuries rather than in death, the episodes served as an unsettling reminder of the malice that persists against African Americans and as a notice of the violent efforts being used to monitor and to regulate their behavior (Fields-Meyer 1998, 3). The tragedy of Paul Garnett Johnson, who was decapitated and burned by white men Louis J. Ceprano and Emmitt Cressell, Jr., who invited him to their house party, further illustrates the especial hatred continuing against African American men (Benning 1997, 5).

In reviewing the issue of police brutality against African American men *and* African American women, the Rev. Al Sharpton observes that this abuse has reached a crisis that should be regarded as a national emergency requiring federal action (Sharpton 1999, 162). Sustained by their historic belief in the insignificance of black life and by the negative stereotypes of African Americans ensconced in their minds and paraded in the media, the white majority—including politicians and their mostly white core political supporters—tolerate "heavy handed police tactics [against blacks] as long as they don't have to see them" (White 1999, 63). Euro-Americans seemingly reckon that most non-whites, especially young black men are "considered suspect, and that wholesale violations of their civil liberties are an acceptable price to pay for a drop in the crime rate" (White 63). Jack White explains, "That is why police brutality is an explosive issue from New York to Los Angeles" (White 63). An infinity of examples—all of which attest to the cheapness with which black life is regarded in the nation—can substantiate White's statement. Yet perhaps the classic notorious barbarisms involving New York City's Abner Louima, a lawbiding black man; California's innocent Tyisha Miller; New York City's Amado Diallo; and Margaret L. Mitchell best exemplify some modern savageries that policemen have committed against black people.

Investigation shows that in August 1997, New York City police officer Charles Schwartz held Louima down while another officer, Justin Volpe tortured him with a broken wooden broomstick. As a result of the sodomy, Louima suffered a ruptured bladder and rectal lacerations. A year later, in Riverside, California, on December 28, 1998, 19-year-old Tyisha Miller was killed as she sat in her car at a gas station, hit by 12 of 24 bullets fired by four police officers who said they felt threatened by a gun in her lap. It should be noted that no shots had been fired from a gun found in the car with a flat tire (Sharpton 1999, 162). About six weeks later, in New York City, Amado Diallo, a hardworking African immigrant, died on his Bronx doorstep after police looking for a rape suspect fired 41times at the unarmed man. Police brutality also claimed the life of Margaret L. Mitchell, a college-educated black woman who had been homeless since developing a mental illness. Officers alleged they feared the 5-foot-1, 102-pound woman because she lunged at them with a screwdriver. Not confined to the gunning down of African Americans, police brutality extends to racial profiling—a practice in which officers stop and frisk African Americans solely because of their race. Even before the terrorist attacks of 9/11, which resulted in increased security measures, black women were consistently targeted for strip-searches at airports, while black men were designated for searches at traffic stops. (A police report in New Jersey admitted to employing racial profiling—accusing, arresting, and imprisoning persons because of their race.)

Modern African Americans—like their predecessors who protested the rampant lynchings occurring during the first two decades of the twentieth century—are confronting this issue of police brutality. The uproar over the Diallo shooting resulted in daily protests led by the Rev. Al Sharpton and the arrest of more than 1,000 people, including entertainers and politicians. Actress Ruby Dee, who was arrested when she and her late husband Ossie Davis participated in the protests, made a timely statement in reference to racial violence: "The seizing and shooting and beating reminds me of when there were lynchings all over the country. We've got to start saying, No further. This must stop" (Flanagan 1999, 9). *A Sunday Morning in the South* is Georgia Douglas Johnson's way of communicating the same message. In her drama, she denounced the subjugation of African Americans that occurred at the beginning of the century and she illustrated, very specifically, how violence impinged upon early black maternity.

In critiquing this work, the late scholar James V. Hatch keenly observes that despite the fact that "*A Sunday Morning in the South* is not Johnson's most tightly structured drama [because] the plot is predictable and the conclusion inevitable, the play's emotional impact is nevertheless very powerful" (Hatch and Shine 1974, 232). *A Sunday Morning in the South* succeeds in rendering a forceful immediacy to the problem of racist violence, and it succeeds in challenging readers to address it. In the wake of the present racial divide—exacerbated by racist shooting sprees, the passage of Proposition 209 in California (which abolished Affirmative Action) and the hostile behavior directed at America's first black president, Barack Obama—the lynch drama of Georgia Douglas Johnson is as relevant at the beginning of the twenty-first century as it was at the beginning of the twentieth century when she wrote it. An examination of this work illustrates how she confronted racism when it first vitiated modern American society and invites the present generation to adopt practical (and preferably nonviolent) methods to correct social ills.

The Bridge Party (1989)

In *The Bridge Party* (1989), which also addresses the inefficacy of turning to the law for protection against lynching, Sandra Seaton presents a segment of the African American experience that has been long ignored. She examines the lifestyle of Southern middle-class blacks living before the modern civil rights era. Seaton used for the basis of her maiden play the stories that family members told to her when she was a child growing up in Tennessee. More particularly, she incorporated two actual events—i.e., lynching and the succeeding house to house search of the black community—in her drama, which is set in the fictional Delphi, Tennessee. Seaton adamantly states that *The Bridge Party* is not a docudrama. In a 1993 interview with Kathy Perkins, she remarked that to one extent, the drama is an answer to the presentation in contemporary television and films of African American women as either sex objects or as earth mothers. Seaton explicitly stated:

> I'm frustrated by the one-dimensional portrayal of black people by the media today. Over and over again black people are seen only in relation to whites, as though the whole identity of individual African Americans can be reduced to their reactions to racism. White people can be presented as complex human beings with unique personal identities, but all too often, sometimes with the best of intentions, black people are portrayed as though they had no private lives, no past, no inner depth—rootless in the strongest sense, not geographically but spiritually [Interview with Sandra Seaton by Kathy Perkins, Lansing, Michigan, April 12, 1993].

The first of the three contemporary lynching plays, *The Bridge Party*, like its earlier predecessors, combats the mythology of the black male rapist. It very specifically indicates that African American men did not provoke lynching by raping white women, as an examination of the lynch victim's circumstances will illustrate. Moreover, it continues to parallel pioneer lynching plays in not featuring African American men on the stage. The Edwards men are away—either in the army or at work. Seaton states that the presence of African American men would have created an extremely different dramatic logic. She was determined to address lynching and segregation without depending on violence and melodrama, which the presence of black men could have facilitated (Sandra Seaton, "How I Came to Write *The Bridge Party*," presented at the Association for Theatre in Higher Education [ATHE] Conference, New York City, August 7, 1996).

Seaton first began work on *The Bridge Party* in the 1960s in a playwrighting course at the University of Illinois (Urbana) taught by Webster Smalley. She resumed work on it again in 1988 as a graduate student with Robert A. Martin of Michigan State University. *The Bridge Party* received stage readings at Columbia College in Chicago (March 23, 1990, directed by Paul Carter Harrison) and at the Complex Theater in Hollywood (May 11, 1993, directed by Adilah Barnes). Additionally, the drama won the Theodore Ward Playwrighting Prize for New Works by African American Playwrights, awarded by Columbia College. William Bolcon, the Pulitzer Prize–winning composer supplied music for stage productions of *The Bridge Party* (Perkins 1989, 318).

The Bridge Party is set in the sitting room in the home of retired educator Emma Edwards in the summer of 1942. The play's action occurs amid the weekly bridge party organized by the African American women's club, the "Bridgettes"—one of the many social organizations, which the enforcement of segregation laws in public venues compelled black Americans of the pre–civil rights era to create for themselves. It must be emphasized that the members of this exclusive social club were "affluent," refined, and privileged

African Americans. Most of the women in the "sorority" were teachers as
are the Edwards sisters. Others, as are their guests, were physician's wives
and morticians. In *The Bridge Party*, Pett Mae is an educator and the wife
of a prominent black doctor, while Ruth and Agnes are undertakers who
have continued the family business after the deaths of their husbands.

Act 1 opens with the bridge party in progress, co-hosted by sisters
Leona, Marietta, and Theodora Edwards. Each of the sisters is "nervous and
jittery underneath," but covers up her anxiety with discussions about club
dances, clothes, skin color, and hair (Seaton 323). At the sound of a passing
car, the conversation turns to the state of the accused molester, fourteen-
year-old Cordie Cheek—the central concern of everyone. Initiating the dialogue, Leona remarks that she heard that Cordie Cheek was returning today.
She makes his return conditional, adding, "If he is ... I heard his trial was
over" (323). Having said that, she glances nervously at the door. Marietta,
who has acquired some information discloses that Cordie Cheek did not
have a trial, because the all white Nashville Grand jury let him go. An incredulous Pett Mae, Ruth, and Samuella cry: "A colored child. Saved." Samuella
adds that his case was dismissed for lack of evidence. The jury deliberated
and refused to indict the innocent boy.

Leona, who has taught Cordie Cheek, who last saw him in the spring,
and who keeps the paper with its announcement of his rape charge and trial
under her bed, refuses to be encouraged by the atypical justice awarded
Cordie's case. She states that she cannot and will not be calm until the boy
returns to town. Making his return even more conditional and even more
uncertain, she adds that *if* Cordie Cheek comes back, that everyone will be
out to see him.

In act 2, Marietta announces Cordie's actual and unsurprising fate:
"They didn't bring that boy Cordie Cheek back from Nashville" or protect
him from the mob's hands (Seaton 345). The predictable and tragic murder
precipitates a memorial of the youth. Grieved, Leona rehearses how Cordie
told her his family was relocating to town where he would attend Macedonia
Hill where she taught. Ruth observes how well kempt Cordie was: hair always
combed, shoes all shined. Unable to accept the lynching of the innocent
Cheek youth, Pett Mae cries, "The paper said they freed him on that charge
of messing with a white girl" (345). Marietta recalls an additional cruelty
that Cordie has sustained and tells the ladies that he was lynched because
of the same thankless girl for whom his mother toiled. Marietta reminds the
Bridgettes that after the girl's mother's death, Cordie's mother cooked, cleaned,
and nurtured the "raped" girl and her siblings.

A review of act 2 shows that while the women were enjoying their bridge
party in the Edwards' sitting room, the mob was reveling in its own "bridge
party" down by the Duck River. Marietta provides details of the atrocity:

"After the grand jury freed the boy, the same ones that took him down for the trial, they picked him up again, turned off the road ... the Cheek boy tried to run off. The brother, the whole gang, they went right after him, grabbed the boy, held him down.... They kept him out there two hours, wanted the boy to write a confession—but his hands ... were burned so bad— he couldn't even move ... they shot him close up ... then they hung him before he died" (Seaton 346).

Amid this revelation, two hastily deputized white men burst in upon the women. Fearing the African American community's reaction to the racist lynching of Cordie Cheek, the "deputies" are in search of guns in the neighborhood homes. Their interaction with the African American citizens warrants attention because it illustrates the law's abuse, rather than its protection of black people, whom it actually hates. As in Georgia Douglas Johnson's *A Sunday Morning in the South*, the intruding "officers" disdain African Americans and distrust their word. Townsend is the more offensive of the hastily deputized men. For in addition to being prejudiced, rude, disrespectful, accusatory, and jealous, he is venomous. His partner, Frank Byrd, who knows the Edwards family upon whom they have intruded, is more respectful. At Townsend's initial entry, he accuses the women of concealing something (guns), of gambling, and of prostitution. Pointing to Pett Mae he says, "This darkie been playin' poker for money" (Seaton 347). Byrd informs Townsend that Pett is the wife of an African American physician to which Townsend replies, "He ain't no real doctor, is he?" (Seaton 348). Throughout his harassment, Townsend bangs on the Edwards' piano, exclaiming at one point "Lord, if I told my pa bout this" (Seaton 347). When Townsend calls the African American doctor "a nigger," Frank Byrd rebukes him, reminding him that he is in the revered Will Edwards' house (Seaton 348). Townsend announces that they secured all the guns in neighboring black communities and then crashes at the bridge table of Pett Mae and Ruth. Irritated by Pett's nervous chatter, he shouts to her: "Shut your mouth. I said shut your mouth! Damn it, I said shut up" (Seaton 350). Shortly, the men exit to the local tavern in pursuit of the proprietor's guns. However, they promise to return to collect Will Edwards' sporting guns.

During the police interrogation and harassment, Emma Edwards, Will's wife, has managed the situation, maintained order, and kept everyone alive. Feigning respect and accommodation, she has treated Townsend with kindness and has rekindled bonds with Byrd, who joyfully tells her, "Been knowing you since I was a little boy" (Seaton 349). When Townsend returns to her home to collect her husband's sporting guns, she continues to manage him and the potentially volatile situation.

Staggering drunk into Emma's home, Townsend makes a lewd pass at her beautiful daughter Theodora. After he is duly ignored and rejected, he demands the guns, but Emma reassures him, "Will has taken all of his guns and has gone hunting with the Meharry College black physicians and with President Hale" (Seaton). Emma's question about Frank Byrd's whereabouts leads Townsend to brag that he is now the law around here, a most unfortunate reality for all the women present. As the embodiment of the corrupt law that militates against the welfare of African Americans, he demands satisfaction from the women he believes to be prostitutes. He tells the ladies, "Ain't you never heard of hospitality" (Seaton 360). He then "grabs Pett Mae and shoves her toward the door" (Seaton 360). At a defiant statement made by the visiting Mary Jane, he accosts her, exclaiming "What's wrong with this darkie? She crazy or somethin'?" (Seaton 360). Clearly, in all his dealings with the Edwards women and with their women friends, this embodiment of the law is consistently abusive—physically and verbally. Emma, however, placates him and requests the visiting Mary Jane to thank the officer for all his "protection." Feeding his ego, she persuades him to go and extend his protection to the young Frank Byrd, who is down at the bar drinking amid criminals.

Through Emma Edwards' wit, charm, and deft management of the conflict, Sandra Seaton achieved her goal of addressing lynching and segregation without relying on melodrama and violence. She dramatized in *The Bridge Party* the manners in which middle-class African American women respond to racial crisis in the absence of black males. They counter their fear and emotionalism with reason, tranquility, and the application of deft interpersonal communication skills. It is both interesting and noteworthy that Seaton disclosed that she constructed the drama as "an act of faith and an experiment." Moreover, she indicated that she was unsure whether other people would be interested in a play that deals with a lynching through the prism of a group of middle-class African American women playing bridge" (Seaton interview). The attention accorded this worthy play indicates with certainty that *The Bridge Party* garnered much interest and that it enriches as well as extends the tradition of anti-lynching dramas written by contemporary black females.

Ida B. Wells Dramas

The Ida B. Wells plays explore the life and the times of activist/journalist Ida Bell Wells-Barnett (1862–1931). They examine pivotal events in the genesis of her civil rights career and highlight the lynchings of her three friends, whose murders impacted her analysis of lynching and propelled her to launch her own anti-lynching campaign. Ultimately, the dramas present acts of resistance committed by a woman whose very life is an argument for justice, equality, and anti-lynching legislation.

Miss Ida B. Wells (1983)

In the dramatic biography *Miss Ida B. Wells*, which continues to address the inefficacy of turning to the law for protection against lynching, Endesha Ida Mae Holland presents the life story of journalist/activist Ida Bell Wells-Barnett. Employing an experimental dramatic technique wherein bifurcated characters and a series of monologues are used, Holland ushers the reader through some seminal events in the activists's life, including her Mississippi childhood, in which she was orphaned, and her career as a crusader and organizer of the anti-lynching movement. The personae "Wells One" and "Wells Two," who are combinations of historical fact and creative imagination, highlight the achievements of Wells who endangered and devoted her life for and to the pursuit of the abolition of lynching. These characters, in the dramatization of the journalist's life, invite African Americans to assume risks and to participate in the campaign to become first-class citizens who are supported and protected by the law.

Miss Ida B. Wells, was first produced in 1982 by At the Foot of the Mountain Theatre in Minneapolis. It was subsequently produced at other Minnesota theaters and in the Buffalo, New York, area where Holland later lived. The drama was part of the touring repertory of New WORLD Theater, located at the University of Massachusetts (Amherst) and was directed by New WORLD artistic director Roberta Uno. In addition to *Miss Ida B. Wells*, which was written in partial fulfillment of her thesis for the master's degree in American Studies at the University of Minnesota, Holland has written the plays *Second Doctor Lady*, *Requiem for a Snake*, *The Autobiography of a Parader Without a Permit*, and *Homebound*.

Set in Chicago during the late 1920s, *Miss Ida B. Wells* opens as sixty-six-year-old Ida B. Wells walks through the Loop one late autumn afternoon. Upon meeting a young admiring fan, she promises to send the girl a maiden copy of a book about her life. Surveying her life, Wells recalls key events: writing for T. Thomas Fortune's *New York Age*; her 1894 effort to ride in the white train area out of Memphis and her subsequent lawsuit against the railroad; her dismissal from her teaching post; Black Reconstruction politicians; and the rise and the rampage of the Ku Klux Klan. She dwells on the subject of lynching—the focal point of this dramatic biography—where the analysis of her life begins.

Wells learns first hand the inefficacy of seeking legal protection against racist lynchings when she unsuccessfully appeals to the sheriff to intervene on behalf of her three friends whom the mob burns before everyone's eyes.

Presenting an eye witness account of her friends' murder, she states: "I saw
... the hot fire eating into Mr. Montgomery's body ... I heard Mr. James beg-
ging for somebody to help him ... I saw the very life leave Mr. Brown" (Holland 307). Wells then observes how lynching politically, economically, and
spiritually controls African Americans. For not one black spectator ventured
forward to assist the burning victims. She explains that every eye witness
was paralyzed with fear of the white citizens of Memphis, who formed a
terrorist mob and went on a rampage in the black community at the com-
plaint of a white businessman who did not want African American competition. Possibly because this particular lynching claimed the lives of her loved
ones, Wells is especially overcome by the present expression of racist violence.
She comments on both the injustice of this specific lynching and on those
preceding it. With mounting rage against Memphis, which is indifferent to
the welfare of its black citizens, she denounces the city. Wells adds that
Memphis will not protect black lives, nor give African Americans a fair trial
in the courts. What Memphis does, she continues, is to allow black citizens
to be slaughtered—on the word of *any* Caucasian. Inaugurating her anti-
lynching campaign in response to the law's failure to protect African Americans—particularly her three friends, Wells officially vows that she is "this
day taking up the banner to put a stop against lynching" (Holland 307). She
further vows to employ her newspaper and any other available instrument
to indict lynchers everywhere.

Indeed, Wells kept her pledge and vigorously employed her newspaper
to stem the plague of lynching. She published the mob's method of operation,
revealing—to their embarrassment—that they usually appeared at night,
leaning upon each other for support while they pillaged, killed, and ram-
paged. She also exposed their justification for lynching African Americans.
One "reason" she noted was to end race riots: "Several Colored people con-
gregating is a race riot to them. Another excuse is that if Colored people try
to vote—they're trying to take over" (Holland 308). However, the principal
purpose for lynching African American men and certainly the most famous
is white women, as earlier noted. Providing statistics, Wells states "in a
twenty-year period, two thousand sixty-odd Colored people was lynched on
account of these threadbare lies" (Holland 308). Taking issue with these prevarications, she used her press to speak out against "the so-called" virtue of
white women.

History reveals that Wells's notorious editorial incensed the white community to the point where a "committee" of white businessmen in pursuit
of her destroyed the journalist's press, devastated her office, and threatened
her life. This pivotal incident sent Ida B. Wells fleeing to the North, where
dissatisfied with confining her campaign to the Colored press, she addressed
the urgency of lynching in a lecture delivered at the 1893 Columbian Expo-

sition in Chicago, Illinois. In her speech, she graphically depicted the horror of African American men being dragged from their houses in the middle of the night. She stated that after being taken from their homes the men are then hung from trees and burned to death. She added that this massacre occurs amid large silent crowds of people who offer the victims no help.

It was also while in the North that Wells indicted the area for not aiding the anti-lynching campaign. She clarified the North's reason for withholding help and explained that it was because it believed the South's justification for lynching blacks. She also targeted one prominent religious leader and two eminent feminists/reformers to illustrate the futility of seeking support from social pillars who supported and practiced racism. In conversation with the British Lady Somerset, Wells stated that neither the Rev. Dwight Moody nor Frances Willard condemned lynch-law. More particularly, she added, that the zealous Moody encouraged segregation in churches by preaching on separate days to African Americans on his tours throughout the South. Wells then observed that Frances Willard, president of the Women's Christian Temperance Union, went even further in practicing racist discrimination. At a meeting in the South where people were suppressing the African American vote, she put herself on record and stated: "When I go North—there will be no word wafted to you from pen or voice that is not loyal to what we're saying here and now" (Holland 310).

Further illustrating how various reformers/activists practiced racism and discrimination, Wells noted that while Susan B. Anthony fired her stenographer for not taking dictation from the black activist/journalist, that Anthony asked Frederick Douglass, who supported women's suffrage "like no other man—White or Negro," not to attend the convention when it was held in Atlanta, Georgia. She was afraid "that the southern White suffragettes wouldn't attend—if they had to sit on the same platform with Mr. Douglass—a former slave" (Holland 311). Wells's final case in point involved Hull House founder Jane Addams, who made a caustic remark reflecting her belief in the South's justification for lynching African Americans: "We will send this message to our fellow citizens of the South. Who are once more trying to suppress vice by violence. The bestial in man, which leaves him to pillage and rape—can never be controlled by public cruelty and dramatic punishment—which too often cover fury and revenge" (Holland 311).

However grieved by the prejudice of her fellow reformers and activists, Wells was not deterred from her mission to abolish racist lynchings. As reflected in Holland's dramatic biography and as recorded in her life history, Wells persisted with her campaign despite personal, public, and legal setbacks. She brought much needed attention to the issue of racist violence and to the rationale behind it. Spearheading an historic crusade to end the reign of terror, Ida B. Wells inspired subsequent generations of women and men to both devote and endanger their lives to and for the purpose of acquiring freedom and civil rights. Her life and anti-lynching campaign continue to be the focus of current drama as expressed in Michon Boston's *Iola's Letter*.

Iola's Letter (1994)

Michon Boston's *Iola's Letter* addresses the historic lynching of three prominent African American businessmen, all of whom were close friends of Wells As earlier noted, it was their brutal lynching that galvanized the activist to inaugurate her own anti-lynching crusade. In examining the martyrdom of her friends and in courageously seeking to redress it despite violent opposition, Wells is portrayed as being deeply human, deeply compassionate, and deeply committed to justice. *Iola's Letter* also examines the issues and ideologies crucial to Ida B. Wells' times and finds a deep analogy between the activist's era and the present time. More particularly, the play recalls the perennial problems of jealousy, gender conflict, and intraracial prejudice within the civil rights movement. It presents diverse confrontational modes and celebrates the courage of a daring and unconventional activist.

The initial public staged reading of *Iola's Letter* was produced in 1994 by the Source Theatre in Washington, D.C. Howard University student Jackie Carter directed the reading, and fifteen-year-old Yendi Yarborough played the role of Ida B. Wells. *Iola's Letter* earned second prize for drama in the Larry Neal Writers Competition Awards sponsored by the D.C. Commission on the Arts and Humanities in 1994. The play was a finalist for a Chesterfield Film Company fellowship at Universal Studios in Los Angeles. *Iola's Letter* has received readings sponsored by Playwrights Forum, The Capital Hill Arts Workshop and the Source Theatre (1994 Summer Theatre Festival). In addition to *Iola's Letter*, Boston's dramas include *Stained Glass Houses* and *Anthropology*, which debuted at the Source Theatre, Washington, D.C.

Iola's Letter is set in 1893 in New York City where Ida B. Wells lives, in exile from the South. In act 1, the prologue, she sits in the photographer's chair posing for a publicity picture that she will take with her to England where she will rally support against lynching in the United States. As the photographer adjusts her poses, Ida B. Wells reflects on the events that have brought her to this point. She flashes back to an important conversation that she has with three significant people in her life, including Isaac, who runs the printing press of the *Free Speech* "colored" newspaper that she co-owns; Mr. Fleming, her partner and business manager of the paper; and Thomas Moss, her best friend, and one of the three businessmen who was lynched by a mob. The dialogue is crucial because it reinforces the argument for the legal protection of African Americans and indicates that the law neither protects black people from the violence of whites nor from that of fellow blacks.

The conversation reveals that a highly revered senior citizen in the African American community was robbed by a local, unemployed thug the previous night. The victim is identified as Old Sam Johnson, whom the assailant, Black Judas, severely cut on the leg. Ida learns that with the help of a physician, Sam Johnson is now recovering. To her outrage, she also learns that no arrest has been made for the crime committed. Explaining the reason for this injustice which blacks have historically sustained, Thomas Moss states, " As long as Judas stays in the Negro section of town, no law-man's going to waste his time tracking him down (Boston 375). However, Ida, who believes in justice for all, responds that there is no reason why African Americans cannot insist upon protection from lawmen. She then resolves to visit Mr. Johnson to acquire additional details.

In act 1, scene 3, Ida arrives at Sam Johnson's home where Mr. Carmack, reporter for the white *Memphis Commercial* newspaper has interviewed Sam. Carmack, who seeks to paint the incident only to skew it for the purpose of further justifying the lynching of African Americans, berates black neighborhoods and black conduct before Ida. More particularly he states that the black districts are unsafe because they contain hordes of ignorant and dangerous characters who lurk around to perpetrate crimes. Using Sam Johnson as an example of an African American who was assaulted by a fellow black, Carmack points out that this specific crime cannot be blamed on the white man.

Ida, however, is cognizant of the fact that the denial of protection and justice promotes criminal activity. Furthermore, she knows where to properly place the blame and replies that the men who are entrusted to uphold the law are culpable for not catching and punishing the robber. Foreshadowing the racist lynching that will claim the lives of her three friends, Carmack responds, "Don't worry. He's gonna get caught. These niggras get cocky and that's when *we* get 'em. Just like those friends of yours at that People's Grocery.... That other grocer's about to loose his business because of those boys and he ain't too happy about it" (Boston 380).

The assaulted Sam Johnson then narrates the circumstances of his attack to Ida, telling her that he had $50 on him from a bank withdrawal to purchase an organ for his wife. Returning home in the dark, "This man jumps from behind this corner ... had a knife, cut my leg ... and went through my pockets and took every cent I had, including my good pocket watch" (Boston 380). In describing the villain, Sam Johnson notes that the offender was coal black in complexion, and that he is known in the African American community as "Black Judas." Unlike preceding lynching plays, *Iola's Letter* is more vocal on the issue of intraracial castigation. Sam Johnson, who has worked long and hard for every penny he possesses is devastated when he is robbed by an African American predator "who feels that what's mine should be his" (Boston 380). Outraged, he calls such people low life, a disgrace to the race, and no good. When he makes the observation, let Black Judas attack a white man the same way that he did me and see what happens, Boston calls attention to the inefficacy of turning to the law for protection against both inter- and intraracist violence. Interestingly, Black Judas is never punished for assaulting Sam Johnson, but Tommie Moss and his colleagues will be executed for the crime of success.

The focus moves to Black Judas, who is a self-loathing, race-hating human being who has internalized every ill effect of white prejudice. Making a statement that suggests that he has subscribed to the financial limits whites have imposed on African Americans, he scornfully calls Sam Johnson (and ambitious blacks like him) stupid. He then asks what are they doing having a large sum of money—implying that such African Americans have risen above their prescribed place. Judas especially hates "the society blacks," commenting "these bastards wouldn't be half as uppity if it weren't for some white daddy or something" (Boston 381). Literate and intelligent, he brags to his friend Toby that he can read, because he is not stupid like him. Black Judas is even somewhat cultured. For as he reads the newspaper in search of evening entertainment, he editorializes: "Fisk singers. Niggers trying to sing like white folks. No sir. The Mika-do, a musical set in Ja-pan. What's that doing here?" (Boston 381). Wanting to laugh and relax, he chooses an all African American minstrel show and exits to enjoy it.

In the meantime, Ida and her friends Tommie and Betty Moss read Carmack's false and malicious description of the People's Grocery in the *Memphis Commercial*. Inciting racial hatred, the description states that The People's Grocery is the gathering place of illiterate African Americans and those who are morally depraved. Tommie, who is a letter carrier and the first African American selected to serve a position in the federal government, explains the reason why such a lie was published: "They're ... upset that the colored people don't have to pay double the price anymore.... They're unhappy because we're a success ... now they want to intimidate us and find some reason to run us out" (Boston 385). This white economic jealousy over black prosperity easily anticipates the notorious 1923 Rosewood, Florida, incident in which whites massacred and decimated the homes and property of African Americans because of a fictitious rape allegation. At the root of this racist slaughter was white jealousy over African American affluence that was exacerbated by the possibility of black voting rights.

While black enfranchisement is not the immediate issue that Ida and her friends must address, asserting their right to be prosperous in their own city is. Consequently, Ida is opposed to the idea of running anywhere. She reminds her friends who are eager to flee Memphis of her fight with the railroad when the conductor threw her off the ladies' car. Evidencing an indomitable spirit that demands legal justice and protection, she tells her friends that they have the right to hold the legislators accountable to the laws that protect their freedom. Ida maintains that they must believe that African Americans can have a grocery, a newspaper, and a family, friends, and children—posterity to carry on after them.

In act 1, scene 5, which takes place in a Mississippi train station, Ida learns about the lynching that claimed the lives of her three friends: Tommie Moss, Calvin McDowell, and Henry Stewart. Details of the murders are provided in act 2, scene 1, at the grave site where Ida and eye witnesses give an account of the genesis of the historic lynching. Highly significant, this act illustrates how the law perverts justice for African American citizens, as it initiates and ensures their destruction. Isaac, the *Free Speech*'s young assistant, is the first to recount the series of incidents culminating in the lynchings. "It all started with some colored and white boys fighting ... outside the People's Grocery store ... the colored boys got the better of the fight, but when the father of the white boys saw what was happening, he came out and whipped one of the colored boys" (Boston 387). Avenging this injustice, Calvin and all the black bystanders trounced the whites, who threatened to come in Saturday night to clean out the People's Grocery. That night, Tommie, Calvin, and Henry shot two of the trespassers and wounded one, while the other interloper escaped from the store. The following morning, policemen arrived at the People's Grocery and unjustly arrested Tommie, Calvin, and Henry. Sam Johnson adds that the law raided decent African Americans' homes and dragged citizens out on suspicion.

Ida poignantly relates how her three friends—moral giants—were kidnapped from jail and horribly shot to death for fighting white men in self-defense. She states that when her friends' bodies were found, "Calvin McDowell's fingers had been shot to pieces.... His eyes were also gouged out. Henry Stewart had a bullet hole in the neck" (Boston 388). She states that as Tommie died, he said to tell African Americans to go west, since there was no justice for them in Memphis. Becoming increasingly impassioned by the murder of her friends and by the lack of justice for black citizens in Memphis, Ida cries, "There is only one thing left to do—save our money and leave a town that will neither protect our lives and property, nor give us a fair trial in court.... Go west! (Boston 388).

In act 2, scene 2, Ida is obsessed with avenging Tommie's death through an investigation of all reported lynchings. Undeterred by Mr. Fleming who tells her that she cannot possibly force a judge's hand, because the criminal court judge himself was part of the mob that night, Ida forges ahead. She remains determined despite the fact there will be no justice, no trial, and no jury. To Isaac's query why the mob did not lynch Black Judas who was also with her friends, Ida explains the actual reason for lynching African Americans: "They found an excuse to get rid of Negroes who're acquiring wealth and property [as were her three martyred friends]. It's a way to keep the race terrorized and keep the nigger down" (Boston 390). During her lynching investigation in the deep South, Ida continues to alienate jealous black males, who accuse her of stepping out of a woman's place and not allowing them to act. The extent of their effort to abolish lynching is confined to their criticism of her. Most black males of the period, including Booker T. Washington, eminent college presidents, newspapermen, "race men," and prominent ministers of large, flourishing black churches were afraid to go against the wishes of whites and remained docile and mute on issues of racist violence.

Upon her return to the *Free Speech*, Ida writes her famous column containing the latest lynching data with its indictment of white female chastity. Ida is duly punished by the white mob for attacking white female virtue. As history and the preceding play indicate, in her absence, the *Free Speech*'s offices were bombed by a designated committee that sought to obliterate her, too. Fleeing to the North for safety, Wells changes and expands the course of her anti-lynching crusade. She goes from a local newspaper woman who exposes the truth behind lynching in a "neighborhood" paper to an international figure who exposes the evils of lynching on lecture platforms around the world. To her credit, she experienced great success in raising the social consciousness of many people, who joined in her campaign to abolish racist violence.

Patriotic Dramas

Mine Eyes Have Seen (1918) and *Aftermath* (1919) address the dilemma of choosing to defend a nation that neither protects African American citizens nor African American veterans. The plays share an exhortation to take a specific action. One drama encourages young African American men to participate in America's campaign to free Europe, while the other urges black men to avenge the racist violence that their country perpetrates against them.

Mine Eyes Have Seen (1918)

"Must I go and fight for the nation that let my father's murder go unpunished? That killed my mother—that took away my chances for making a man out of myself?... No, if others want to fight, let them. I'll claim exemption (Dunbar-Nelson [1918] 1974, 175).

Chris, the young black draftee in Alice Dunbar-Nelson's *Mine Eyes Have Seen* (1918) asks this question as he debates "participating" in World War I. Additional injustices that include his brother's maiming and the racist burning of his family's home further deter him from complying with the military order. Viewed from this perspective, where he and his family suffer the anguish of both physical and psychological racism, Chris has no reason to willingly serve in the armed forces.

Mine Eyes Have Seen, a one-act play, is Dunbar-Nelson's contribution to the Negro Participation campaign that black intellectuals, including W.E.B. Du Bois, waged to persuade African Americans to support World War I. Hoping that black involvement in the Great War would earn African Americans enfranchisement and respect from whites, black savants like Dunbar-Nelson and Joel Spingarn, chairman of the board of the NAACP, urged African Americans to endorse it and to engage in combat when possible.

Mine Eyes Have Seen grew out of Dunbar-Nelson's work as a member of the Women's Committee on the Council of Defense where she helped organize Southern black women in nine states for the war effort. Responding to the question of whether black men owe military allegiance to a nation that offers them neither loyalty nor citizenship, Dunbar-Nelson advocates black patriotism as one means to win the attention and sympathy of whites as well as one way to mitigate the period's racist violence that afflicted the African American community.

Staged on April 10, 1918, at Dunbar High School in Washington, D.C., *Mine Eyes Have Seen* was published in *The Crisis* that same month and same year. Dunbar-Nelson's niece Pauline A. Young, recalled in a 1973 interview that her aunt "produced her play and we all took parts. The audience loved it" (Hatch and Shine 1974, 173).

James V. Hatch remarks that the appearance of this play during wartime had a double edge. On the one hand, it warned white America that the black soldier would fight only for a "do right" nation, while on the other hand, it assured America that the black soldier would revenge German atrocities—including the crucifying of children and the raping of girls (Hatch and Shine 1974, 173). *Mine Eyes Have Seen*, which heralds the beginning of published plays by African American women, had a propitious publication date. As World War I approached an end, the black community became acutely aware of and incensed by the many indignities that black service men sustained in Europe at the hands of their white American commanding officers. Neither the atrocities suffered by the black soldiers abroad nor those endured by black civilians in the States abated during the war years.

It was still a time when great violence was being done to African Americans through white mob action: when the African American's life was being cramped and confined by laws and the custom of Jim Crow; when American society seemed to choose every occasion to humiliate black people. Moreover, it was a time when black anger was not always contained, and violence, related to the treatment of African American soldiers, erupted in several parts of the nation (The 1918 execution of the black soldiers of the 24th Infantry Regiment who were involved in the Houston race riot provides a case in point). Addressing this racist injustice, *Mine Eyes Have Seen* explores both the issues surrounding the abusive use of power against black people and the ways in which African Americans can search for autonomy and human dignity in the face of oppression. Recalling Grimké's *Rachel*, the themes are those of autonomy, human dignity, and the abuse of power, as they affect lives of African Americans (McKay 1987, 144).

The action of *Mine Eyes Have Seen* occurs amid a vivid background of human squalor, intersecting at race, class, and economic oppression. A description of the kitchen, located in a tenement of "a manufacturing city in the northern part of the United States" vivifies the filth that permeates the apartment (Dunbar-Nelson [1918] 1974, 174). Moreover, the site of all the play's action indicates that: "All details of furnishing emphasize sordidness—laundry tubs, range, table covered with oil cloth, pine chairs" (174). Mirroring the devastation of American injustice that has been inflicted upon its inhabitants, the environment emits the bitterness, the despair, and the hopelessness of formerly genteel and prosperous people. The portrait of the first victim (and the subsequent ones of his siblings) bears testimony to this statement. At opening, the "curtain discloses DAN," who sits in "a rude imitation of a steamer chair propped by faded pillows, his feet covered with a patch-work quilt" (174). Although only thirty years old, "his hair is prematurely grey" and his thin pinched face bears "traces of suffering," engendered by a paralyzing accident at a factory, whose management devalued human life. While Dan sits brooding in the kitchen, his sister, twenty-year-old Lucy—a "slight frail, brown-skinned" girl who "walks with a slight limp"—bustles about the stove, preparing a meal. For reasons to be imminently discovered, she wears "a pathetic face" (174).

The two siblings are awaiting the arrival of their brother Chris, and in the interval, they reflect on their former middle-class lifestyle. Evidencing selective amnesia in their conversation, one sibling highlights the sweetness of the past—with its comfort and prosperity—while the other emphasizes its racial bitterness. Nostalgically, Lucy begins the conversation, recalling the family's little house with the garden and Dan returning home from work with their father, while she and Chris studied at the table as their mother prepared dinner. When Lucy adds that the family did not have to live and eat in the kitchen in those days, Dan interjects his memory of "notices posted on the fence for us to leave town because niggers had no business having such a decent home" (Dunbar-Nelson [1918] 1974, 174). He also recalls how the terrorists burned down their house and destroyed their future plans. As Lucy reminisces about being petted because she injured her foot, Dan remembers his father, who was "shot down like a dog for daring to defend his home," and his mother, who died of pneumonia in the cold and cutting climate (174). Turning attention to himself, he notes his paralysis, which resulted from his work at a Northern factory's wheel. Overcome by his incapacitation and uselessness, Dan begins to cry. Lucy, who is interrupted from her trance, runs to him and begs his forgiveness for dwelling on the prosperous past.

Amid her apology, the long-awaited Chris enters—roughly and unceremoniously. Explaining his delay he informs his siblings that he has been drafted. Alarmed that Chris's absence will dismantle the family's tenuous economic unit, Lucy exclaims, "Oh, it can't be! They won't take you from us!... What will Dan do?" (Dunbar-Nelson [1918] 1974, 175) Dan, however, is far too proud and much too unwilling to be anyone's justification for negligence. He counters Lucy's fear with: "Hush! Have I come to this, that I should be the excuse, the woman's skirts for a slacker to hide behind?" (175) But heedless of Dan's protest, the draftee insists that he is not going to war. Chris maintains that his duty is with his family and that he owes none elsewhere. Furthermore, he vows not to pay duty elsewhere. When Lucy replies "Chris! Treason! I'm afraid!" he confirms the validity of her fear: "Yes, of course you're afraid, ... why shouldn't you be? Haven't you had your soul shriveled with fear since we were driven like dogs from our home? And for what? Because we were living like Christians" (175). Recounting the physical and psychological abuses that other family members have sustained, Chris offers the earlier quoted (and justifiable) reasons for resisting the draft. He adds: "Look at us—you—Dan, a shell of a man.... And me, with a fragment of an education ... only half a man.... And you, poor Little Sister, there's no chance for you" (175).

During Chris's speech, his Jewish friend Jake enters. Applauding Chris's recitation of the Socialist ideology, he sarcastically shouts, "Bravo! You've learned the patter well. Talk like the fellows at the Socialist meetings!" (Dunbar-Nelson [1918] 1974, 175). Jake's caustic remarks explain Chris's mind-poisoning to Dan, who presently "indulges" his brother's philosophy. Mockingly, Dan coaxes, "All right, go on—any more?" However, Chris's answer is forestalled by Jake who demands to know the occasion of his outburst. Upon learning that Chris's recent draft has elicited the row, he sardonically advises him to get exempt, since he does not want to fight. However, the entrance of an Irish matron, Mrs. O'Neill, interrupts Jake's advice with its allusion to his own willingness to fight for America. When this widow—whose husband died in fighting for Ireland learns that Chris has been drafted—she insists, "Ye've got to fight" (177).

Despite her exhortation, Chris remains adamant in his refusal to support America's campaign. To further advance his argument for resisting the draft, he points out that black men fought in America's wars of 1776, 1812, 1861, and 1898—only to be denied their freedom at home and "to have their valor disputed" (Dunbar-Nelson [1918] 1974, 176). As the debate progresses, he is moved neither by Jake's sympathetic entreaty and patriotism nor by the trench horror and atrocity stories that Bill Harvey, the incoming muleteer reports. However, when Chris learns "they crucify children," he exhibits an interesting response. Comparing their massacre of foreign children to that of his "own" in the United States he replies: "They're little white children. But here our fellow countrymen throw our little black babies in the flames— as did the worshippers of Moloch, only they haven't the excuse of a religious rite" (176).

When Jake implies that Chris is a complainer who is ashamed of his race, Dan "rises" to the occasion and demands "Stop! Who's ashamed of his race? Ours the glorious inheritance; ours the price of achievement. Ashamed! I'm proud. And you, too, Chris, smoldering in youthful wrath, you, too are proud to be numbered with the darker ones, soon to come into their inheritance" (Dunbar-Nelson [1918] 1974, 176). At this point, Dan is overcome by patriotism. Tearing himself from the chair, "the upper part of his body writhing, while the lower part is inert, dead" he articulates the platform of the era's black intellectuals: "Oh God! If I could only prove to a doubting world of what stuff my people are made!" (177). Totally consumed with loyalty for his country, he delivers a speech on Christian charity that penetrates even Chris's heart: "Love of humanity is above the small considerations of time or place or race or sect. Can't you be big enough to feel pity for the little crucified French children—for the ravished Polish girls, even as their mothers must have felt sorrow, if they had known, for our burned and maimed little ones? Oh, Mothers of Europe, we be of one blood, you and I!" (177).

A neophyte patriot, Lucy sums up the turning tide, assuring Chris that the family needs him, but that America needs him more. She adds, "Your race is calling you to carry on its good name, and with that, the voice of humanity is calling to us all" (Dunbar-Nelson [1918] 1974, 177). Swelling to the strains of the "Battle Hymn of the Republic," the play ends with an awakened Chris, whose eyes have seen the glory, and a "martial crash."

In evaluating this play, Nellie Y. McKay (1987) writes: "With its ironic twist on the Battle Hymn of the Republic, *Mine Eyes Have Seen* is a biting satire on the political blindness that keeps people from seeing how they participate in and help to perpetuate their own oppression"—as becomes evident when Chris enlists in the armed forces. Moreover, that his military compliance is predicated on groundless patriotism illustrates the fact that the play is also a satire "on the power that supports that blindness" (14). Chris's resolution to give his life for a country that is adamant in denying enfranchisement and protection to his people exemplifies this sad fact and points to the play's inherent message, which "emphasizes the need for a perceptive personal analysis of the ways in which moral and political choices are made" (14). It is noteworthy that the themes of this 1918 drama violently recurred half a century later in the 1970s when significant numbers of American young men refused to participate in another United States foreign war. Like Chris and the African American draftees of World War One, they protested against the sacrifice of their lives in a conflict, which for them, seemed established on the tenets of domestic and foreign racism (14).

Gloria Hull notes an additional satirical element in *Mine Eyes Have Seen*. She writes that in tone, the play is almost jingoistic—a fact that might suggest a possibly satiric reading. Like many Americans who supported World War I, Dunbar-Nelson favored pacifism over a second major conflict. Yet, it is also true that she—sometimes opportunistically—attuned her public utterances to the pulse of the times (Hull 1987, 72). In commenting on the drama's characterization, Hull writes that the Jewish character and interracialism accorded with the current thrust of the National Association for the Advancement of Colored People and its organ *The Crisis*, as well as with Dunbar-Nelson's own integrationist ethics. It can be observed that the Socialists are blamed for poisoning Chris's mind: "Bravo! You've learned the patter [Socialist ideology] well. Talk like the fellows at the Socialist meetings!" (175). If its intense pitch can be forgiven concludes Gloria Hull, *Mine Eyes* is a fairly good play. Certainly dramatic, it presents a tight situation, a variety of characters and interesting dialogue (175). After reading the drama when it was first published, Caroline Bond of The Circle for Negro War Relief pronounced it "splendid."

Elizabeth Brown-Guillory remarks that Chris's earlier mentioned statement: "Must I go and fight for the nation that let my father's murder go unpunished?" reflects two important attitudes of the playwright. "Not only does this passage indicate Dunbar-Nelson's indignation about soldiers who are forbidden to bask in glory, but it alludes to her disdain for the American lynch mob and, particularly, for the Southern tradition that includes active and overt racism." Chris's reference to his father is poignant because his father was shot in the South while trying to save his home, which was being burned down by a mob. Yet black men who gladly fight for their country (despite being oppressed) should not have to face degradation when they return to find that the freedom they fought to maintain for America is for white Americans (Brown-Guillory 1988, 8).

Aftermath (1919)

Where Alice Dunbar-Nelson treats the African American soldier as he deliberates entering World War I, Mary P. Burrill addresses his reception by America after he has fought her campaign. In *Aftermath*, Burrill vents her outrage at the injustices committed against black veterans of World War I, men who had fought abroad to keep America safe and free only to return to a nation that denied them their constitutional rights. Burrill champions the cause of black veterans by calling for violent retaliation against their oppression and by equipping her play's hero John Thornton with a revolver so that he can avenge his father's burning.

In *Their Place on the Stage* (1988), Elizabeth Brown-Guillory writes that *Aftermath* initiated a host of plays that advocated "Hammurabi's code of an eye for an eye" (9). Written within the contexts of the anti-lynching campaign and post–World War I furor of racial violence, *Aftermath* also echoes an editorial by W.E.B. Du Bois, the editor of *The Crisis*. Du Bois encouraged African American soldiers, upon their return, "to marshal their wartime courage to fight 'the forces of hell at' home" (Burrill [1919] 1974, 56). Burrill's play was part of the losing effort to stem the rising tide of postwar lynchings in the South and the race riots in the North. In its precise depiction of the reaction of an African American veteran to his father's lynching and of the soldier's own murder, *Aftermath* also contributes to the contemporary realist movement in American theater. That is, the homicides are important to theater history for their graphic presentation of the brutality and the immorality of lynching.

Aftermath first appeared in published form in *The Liberator* in April, 1919. It was produced on May 8, 1928, by the Krigwa Players Little Negro Theatre in association with the Manhattan Worker's Drama League at the Frolic Theatre as part of New York's National Little Theater Tournament (Hincklin 1965, 194). Encapsulating *Aftermath*'s plot, a reviewer for *The New York Times* wrote: "It tells of a young S.C. Negro who comes home from France a war hero to find that his services to free mankind have gone for nought in so far as his own state is concerned. While he was overseas his father had been burned at the stake by whites, and when he learns the truth he goes out to wreak revenge only to be shot to death" (Hincklin 1965, 24).

Through the young South Carolinian John Thornton, Burrill dramatizes the hostility that engulfed and dehumanized returning black soldiers and their people. She establishes Thornton as a war hero who endured physical and psychological pain fighting for the freedom of others: "Lots of times ... in the trenches ... I wuz dog-tired an' sick, an' achin wid the cold," he recalls (Burrill [1919] 1974, 59). Despite his sacrifices, at home Thornton's government still considers him to be subhuman and denies him his civil rights.

John represents both a distinct black individual and every black soldier. Almost any black World War I veteran could have returned home to find that America had hanged, burned, beaten, cut, drowned, or shot his "brother," with the sanction of the courts. But this particular black soldier who won a medallion because "he fought off twenty Germuns all erlone an' saved his whole comp'ny"—resolves to avenge his father's murder, thereby championing African-American self-assertion in the face of racism (Burrill [1919] 1974, 57). At one point, Thornton bitterly articulates his determination: "I've been helpin' the w'ite man git his freedom, I reckon I'd bettah try now to get my own!" (61). In comparing John's drive for "freedom" to the American military victory in World War I, Burrill validates John's personal quest for retribution, rendering it emblematic of the black struggle for justice in America. He seeks "freedom" for himself and his community through violence, just as the United States fought for democracy's survival in the just concluded Great War.

Since he can win no legal redress for his father's murder, John assumes the role of avenger. To his sister Millie's warning, "They'll kill yuh," John courageously replies, "Whut ef they do! I ain't skeered o' none of 'em.... To Hell with 'em!" (Burrill [1919] 1974, 61). Through John's courage, strength, and defiance, Burrill contributes to the counterimage that black dramatists of the 1920s and 1930s created to efface the stereotypes of ignorant, childlike blacks late nineteenth- and early twentieth-century plantation novels and minstrel shows entrenched in American literature and white psyches. A dark-skinned, physically impressive adult—noble, courageous and proud—John projects an image dominant in the black protest dramas of the 1920s and 1930s. Ultimately, however, John becomes a martyr, thereby embodying Burrill's indictment of American postwar society for the false promise of equality it held out to the black veterans.

The irony of John's fate epitomizes the plight of the African American who fought in World War I . When he went off to battle in Europe, he constantly risked death, and yet he returned alive. When he returns to his homeland during peacetime, however, his attempts to assert the rights granted to all citizens make his death inevitable. John's death is virtually guaranteed once he learns of his father's murder: not only does he carry pistols, which blacks were prohibited from owning—"No cullud man bettah be seen wid dem things"—but he plans to use them to avenge his father's burning—an act of revenge that no U.S. court at the time would approve (Burrill [1919] 1974, 60). As Burrill knew too well, early twentieth-century America was unsafe for rebellious African Americans who demanded equality, and white Americans often regarded black veterans with fear, hostility, and resentment. Yet John has experienced first-class citizenship in Paris, where "the fines' people stopp't him when they seen his medal, an' shook his han' an' smiled at him" and allowed him to go everywhere with "nobody all the time a lookin' down on him, an' a-sneerin at him 'cause he's black." It is only on foreign soil that John "[for] the firs' time evah in his life felt lak a real sho-nuf man" (57). After such treatment abroad, he reacts strongly against American racism, which has become only more virulent in response to his military service.

John initially appears as the soldier who champions his own civil rights, but he exits the stage—and life—as one who champions the rights due all humanity. This valiant soldier serves as a foil to family members Lonnie, Mam Sue, and Millie each of whom responds differently to racism. John is militant where Lonnie is accommodating; he is worldly and practical where Mam Sue is "religiously passive"; and he is direct and belligerent where Millie is evasive and peaceable.

Lonnie, John's cowardly younger brother, allowed the hoodlums to over-power his father without resisting and remains too frightened to avenge his father's death. "This sturdy ... boy of eighteen" is primarily concerned with staying alive, avoiding all potentially dangerous encounters (Burrill [1919] 1974, 57). When he arrives home later than usual, he explains, "I seen a whole lot of them w'ite hoodlums hangin' 'round de feed sto'—I jes felt dey wuz jes waitin' dah to start sumpin, so I dodged 'em by tekin' de long way home." To this, Millie replies, "Po' Lonnie! He allus dodgin' po' w'ite trash!" Yet Lonnie defends his cowardly behavior with, "Well, yuh see whut dad got by not dodgin ' em" (Burrill [1919] 1974, 58). Lonnie's cowardice is not due to ignorance, but is largely founded on his personal knowledge. A product of his Southern environment, Lonnie knows that the white men he fears do not hesitate to use violent means in order to keep African Americans sub-missive. His fear and docility, then, illustrate that submissiveness is a socially produced response found among those who live in a hostile and oppressive environment. Whereas John personifies bravery and assertiveness and trum-pets those qualities advocated by civil rights activist W.E.B. Du Bois, Lonnie embodies an extreme version of the accommodationist qualities promoted by the race leader Booker T. Washington.

While Lonnie represents the submissive black man who "knows his place," Mam Sue, the family's cornerstone, personifies the pious African American who has historically trusted God to sustain blacks through hard-ships and racism. Burrill highlights Mam Sue's strong tie to black American history by having her open the play with the crooning of a spiritual, a prophetic song that both references African American slavery and foreshad-ows the coming of her grandson John: "Yonder comes mah Lawd/ He is comin' dis way/wid his sword in his han.'" Like Mam Sue's "Lawd," John seeks justice and uses a weapon to avenge wrongdoing. Mam Sue's faith pre-vents her from falling prey to both fear and rage. For instance, she explains to her nervous granddaughter, "Yuh git skeered 'cause yuh don' put yo' trus' in de good Lawd!" (Burrill [1919] 1974, 60). However, none of Mam Sue's young descendants shares her faith. When she tells John, "Pray to de good Lawd to tek all dis fiery feelin out'n you' heart," her grandson replies, "This ain't no time for preachers or prayers" (61). He then explains: I ain't fu'got God, but I've quit thinkin' that prayers kin do ever'thing.... The Lawd does jes so much for you, then it's up to you to do the res' fu' yourse'f. The Lawd's done His part when He's done give me strength ... I got tuh do the res' fu' myse'f!" (60). Thornton and his young counterparts criticize the use of religion as a panacea to make them forgive and forget racial injustices committed against them (Turner 1968, 108).

Mam Sue's devotion helps her to endure hardship; yet she weds a curious superstition to her piety and depends upon her folk beliefs to disclose, affect, and explain events. Mam Sue's dogma facilitates God's revelations to her, for in burning fires—"jes lak he sen to Moses"—the Lord prophesies John's father's death as well as John's return from war (55). She tells her granddaughter, "See dat log dah, Millie? De one fallin' tuh de side dah wid de big flame lappin' 'round hit? Dat means big doin's round heah tonight!" Darwin T. Turner (1968) in *The Negro Dramatist's Image of the Universe* suggests another explanation for Burrill's use of "magic" in the play. He writes: "Negro playwrights of the Twenties and Thirties who pictured superstition as a characteristic of the race used it for three purposes: local color, criticism, and comedy. Significantly, however, by associating such dogma with the older characters in plays, they identified it with the past rather than with the future of the race" (111). Mam Sue's mysticism, like her singing of the spiritual—which associates her with biblical as well as African American history—links her to an older time from which the younger blacks attempt to distance themselves.

Mam Sue and her granddaughter Millie are important not only for the pious and the passive response they embody, but for the noteworthy images of early twentieth-century black womanhood they present. A closer examination of Mam Sue as a cornerstone shows her to be "very old. Her ebony face is seamed with wrinkles; and in her bleared, watery eyes there is a world-old sorrow" (Burrill [1919] 1974, 55). This description suggests the image of the powerful, but aging black matriarch who keeps the family together despite personal and community hardships. Furthermore, the illiterate Mam Sue may be seen as the particularized female victim of racist forces that have historically conspired to keep her and her people ignorant. She depends on younger, more educated blacks like her granddaughter Millie to conduct her correspondence and to interpret printed matter for her.

In addition to being illiterate, eighty-year-old Mam Sue is care-worn, having accumulated many heartaches, including the murders of fellow African

Americans. Now, however, her two grandsons preceded by their father stand on the verge of increasing the casualty list. Like many grieving black mothers, she resigns herself to her impending loss, hoping that God will someday make things "right." Her prophetic song—"Yonder comes mah Lawd ... wid his sword in his han'"—assumes a poignant relevance (Burrill [1919] 1974, 55). The warrior deity heralded in her spiritual will be the only one to vindicate the wrongs committed against her and her people, for Mam Sue recognizes the terrifying obstacles to John's quest for justice. As the play closes, Mam Sue remains the same religious and faithful woman whose crooning opened it. She has, however, in the murder of her son and grandsons, acquired another sorrow peculiar to those who are black, Southern, and female.

Younger than Mam Sue by two generations, Millie regards her grandmother's superstitiousness with a skepticism associated with youth. Like her brother John, she rejects religion as the cure-all for social injustice. As far as she can tell, it does not empower her to love those who hate, kill, and abuse her and her fellow African Americans. As the play's peacemaker, Millie represents a different kind of non-confrontational response to racism: the educated African American's attempt to ignore or downplay the pervasive effects of oppression. This "slender brown girl" who "jes hates the thought of John comin' home an' hearin' 'bout dad" indirectly causes the catastrophe that claims the lives of her two brothers (Burrill [1919] 1974, 55, 57). As the family's direct correspondent with John, she refrains from informing him of their father's murder. She explains her deception: "I couldn't write John no bad news w'ilst he wuz way over there by hisse'f. He had 'nuf to worry him with death a-starin him in the face evah day" (57). Motivated by her desire to minimize John's anxieties, she only discloses the fact and the reason for their father's murder at John's insistence, explaining that white hoodlums "burnt him down by the big gum tree" because "Ole Mister Withrow ... called dad a liar an' struck him—an' dad he up an' struck him back" (61).

Like so many of her sister African Americans confined to menial occupations during the early twentieth century, Millie works as a laundress to supplement the family's meager income. At sixteen, she is the family's junior homemaker and the heiress to Mam Sue's influential position. Previous events, however, suggest that her approach to life's harshness, including its religious and educational restrictions will be different from her grandmother's. The fact that for six months Millie has vehemently refused to tell John of their father's murder suggests that her response to harsh realities might be evasive and indirect—an approach most unlike Mam Sue's directness. (Note that Mam Sue makes Millie write to John about his father's death after initially complying with the younger woman's desire to withhold the information in her correspondence with her brother.) In addition, the fact that she questions religion suggests that Millie will replace Mam Sue's devout and tenacious beliefs with skepticism. Millie's literacy will afford her more independence and a wider perception of the world, for unlike Mam Sue and the older illiterate generation, Millie will not have to rely on others to conduct her correspondence or to interpret printed matter for her. Millie is the new black woman, who relies neither on omens nor on God to forecast and improve her lot. Although she accepts racism, violence, and oppression as inevitable facts of life, she attempts to sustain her family and herself by refusing to recognize the limitations placed upon them.

NOTES

1. Another system that explained and justified the relegation of African Americans to a nonhuman category and led to the sexual abuse of black women was the Great Chain of Being ideology that established a hierarchy of life forms within the universe. This philosophy maintained that God occupied the highest position of the chain, which descended downward to the weakest, most unintelligent and inferior life form. In reference to slaves, one contemporary author wrote:

If the order of nature was divinely appointed, any attempt to subvert that order must run counter to the providential order explicit in the nature of things. Thus any attempt to alter the present condition of the Negro which was ordained by providence would destroy the very fabric of the universe. If the Negro was, as strongly suspected, a form of being mediate between the higher animals and man, his enslavement was justified and the social order of the South was the only social order in which was shown the will of the Divine Creator [Erno 62].

In specifically considering the black female slave, philosophers, scientists, lawmakers, scholars, physicians, and laymen all subscribed to the notion that the African American's position located somewhere between man and the higher animals (i.e., apes) was especially born out in the black woman. They concurred that orangutans showed a special attraction to the African American woman; and that at some unspecified time in history, the black woman who was considered dissolute and always "ready" for any sexual encounter, had mated with the orangutan. This notion, which was used to explain the creation of the African American race was expressed by Thomas Jefferson, who in citing "the preference of the orangootan for the black woman over those of his own species," justified this coupling of animal intelligence and human form as desirable eugenics: "The circumstance of superior beauty is thought worthy of attention in the propagation of our horses, dogs, and other domestic animals, why not in that of man?" (Jordan 458).

2. In the abolitionist novel *Clotel* (1853), William Wells Brown echoes Mrs. Marston's anxiety about the precariousness of the black woman's virtue and well-being. He juxtaposes factual with fictional narrative and illustrates through the experiences of his eponymous heroine the tragic fate of countless fair-complexioned black women—Mara's sisters in distress. James Mellon in *Bullwhip Days: The Slaves Remember* (1988) renders a compilation of the actual life stories of former slaves who narrated some of their pre-emancipation experiences. His work is replete with examples of the sexual violence to which black women were forced to submit and the Marstons seek to avert for Mara. In a case in point, bondsman James Green remembers:

De nigger husbands weren't de only ones dat keeps up havin' chillun. De mosters [masters] and de drivers takes all de nigger girls dey want. One slave had four chillun right after de other, with a white moster. Deir chillun was brown, but one of 'em was white.... Just de same, dey was all slaves, and de nigger dat had chillun with de white men didn't get treated no better [296].

In the same text, slave woman Mary Peters states:

My mother's mistress had three boys—one twenty-one, one nineteen, and one seventeen. One day, Old Mistress had gone away to spend the day. Mother always worked in the house.... While she was alone, the boys came in and threw her down on the floor and tied her down so she couldn't struggle, and one after the other used her as long as they wanted, for the whole afternoon ... and that's the way I came to be here [Mellon 1988, 296].

Yet another bondswoman, Tempe Pitts, recounts:

I ain't sayin' nothin' bout my white folkses, but sometimes I does wonder why I's red-headed, when my pappy an' mammy wuz black as tar. Maybe I is part white, but I ain't sayin' nothin "bout my white folkses, as I done tole you" [Mellon 1988, 297].

But it is Sarah Grimké—feminist, abolitionist, and great aunt of Angelina Grimké—who summarizes the position of the female slave as "breeder" mistress in *Letters on the Equality of the Sexes and the Condition of Women* and crystallizes the legacy of sexual violation to which Mara and many generations of African American women became heir:

The virtue of female slaves is wholly at the mercy of irresponsible tyrants, and women are bought and sold in our slave markets, to gratify the brutal lust of those who bear the name of Christians. In our slave states, if amid all her degradation and ignorance, a woman desires to preserve her virtue unsullied, she is either bribed or whipped into compliance, or if she dare to resist her seducer, her life by the laws of some of the slave states may be and has actually been sacrificed to the fury of disappointed passion [S. Grimké 17].

3. Harriet Jacobs (pseudonymously named Linda Brent) in the autobiographical slave narrative *Incidents in the Life of a Slave Girl* (1861) bears testimony to Ellen's well-founded fear in the statement when she writes, "If God has bestowed beauty upon her [the black woman], it will prove her greatest curse. That which commands admiration in the white woman only hastens the degradation of the [black] female" (Jacobs [1861] 1969, 28).

Conclusion

Here, then, is a gender-focused analysis of the social protest plays of nine female African American playwrights who denounced nearly eight decades of injustice. They principally spoke out against the mounting racist violence of their time and illustrated in their dramas how lynching is a terror to the African American family, to African American marriage, and to African American motherhood. Through *Rachel*, Grimké dramatized the devastating effects of prejudice on a refined and sensitive young black woman, who abjures marriage and maternity because of racism. She also demonstrated the important facts of generation removal and generation prevention that occur in the aftermath of racist violence—showing that with one assault, which claims the life of a father and his son, lynching destroys an existing home and prevents the creation of a new one. Further delineating the destruction, Grimké exemplifies how lynching disorders two generations of marriage and decimates countless generations of children. Moreover, in *Rachel* (and in *Mara*), she invited white women to see what meaning the sacred institution of motherhood might have for African American women, who were forced to choose between abjuring motherhood or producing another potential victim for the lynch mob.

The pioneer women writing with Grimké and the later generations of African American women who continued the theater's protest against lynching mirrored its same deleterious effects on the lives of black citizens in their plays. They also set about the task of countering harmful stereotypes of African Americans, which whites used to justify lynching blacks and denying their constitutional rights.

Recalling Grimké, Johnson also demonstrated in *Safe* the important connection between racist violence and African American women's reproduction. In her exploration of this link, she brought some much needed attention to the desperation to which some black women were driven in their effort to protect their children from racist murder in the absence of anti-lynching legislation and just laws.

Like Johnson who preceded her, Alice Childress employed poor and uneducated African Americans to denounce racist subjugation. In *Trouble in Mind* she primarily targets the issue of racial stereotyping and works to dismantle the negative and erroneous images of black people. Resolving to have African Americans viewed both authentically and objectively by society, Childress meticulously strips away the white-imposed facades on the black characters in *Trouble in Mind*. The most noteworthy object of her demolition is the play's ignorant and passive mother who surrenders her child to the lynch mob. Childress corrects the myth of the unmaternal, indifferent black mother pervasive in white minds, clearly illustrating that no African American woman would both blame and refuse to help her endangered child.

Several of the anti-lynching plays—i.e., Grimké's *Mara*, Livingston's *For Unborn Children* and Johnson's *Blue-Eyed Black Boy*—address the issues of miscegenation and the sexual violation of African American women by white men. Grimké's *Mara* was written to counterattack white literary distortions of black character, specifically that of the morally lax African American woman, who consciously solicited sexual acts, including rape. Grimké used the image of the black woman ravaged by a white man to refute the allegation that sexual immorality is exclusive to the behavior of African Americans.

In *For Unborn Children*, Livingston reverses the traditional pairing of a southern Caucasian man and African American woman. Through this coupling, she expresses the black female perspective on the African American man's preference for white women. Marion, the lynch victim's sister ventilates her anger (and that of Livingston) with the black man's spousal choice: "What is to become of us when our own men throw us down?" Livingston further expresses her anger when she has the "transgressing" Leroy embrace his punishment for interracial mixing (Livingston [1926] 1974, 184). In illuminating the violent and inhumane repercussions of interracial mixing, *For Unborn Children* levied a strong indictment against American racism. It very particularly underscored the vulnerability of contemporary African American males to white women and illustrated the fact that cautionary commentary from African American women was just as imperative in the 1920s as it was in the 1890s. Investigations by Ida B. Wells disclosed the well-known fact that black men frequently and willingly ruined their lives by choosing white women for wives and lovers. Influenced by the activist/journalist, Livingston renders a scathing critique of Leroy's forbidden love relationship.

In *Blue-Eyed Black Boy*, Johnson employed the traditional pairing of the victimized white girl and the demonized black man as her attacker. Incensed by the legal system that denied African Americans protection from the period's racist violence and black women protection from rape by white men, Johnson protested these injustices in her play. More particularly, she articulated her especial outrage at the laws that exempted white men who fathered black children from supporting and defending them. *Blue-Eyed Black Boy* draws upon the African American female's history of sexual abuse as it features an African American mother, who for the sake of averting her son's lynching, reveals that she was raped by a white man. The play recalls this painful personal subject in order to politicize it—i.e., to insist that the forbidden topic of the sexual exploitation of the black woman by white men be included in the public debate for anti-lynch legislation. *Blue-Eyed Black Boy*'s distinguishing features include an aborted lynching and its portrayal of an assertive black femininity. Pauline Waters ushers in a new kind of African American womanhood and motherhood. Proactive in her resistance to her son's lynching, she secures the requisite help to save her child. With this work, Johnson officially declares active intervention as the only possible way to prevent lynching and to preserve black family life.

Alice Childress' *Wedding Band: A Love/Hate Story in Black and White* further expands the theme of miscegenation and its treatment of forbidden liaisons. It focuses on a biracial love affair, which is destroyed by white and black prejudice. The predominant theme of this protest play is that African Americans and whites should learn to judge each other on individual merit, instead of blaming a whole race every time a biracial relationship, intimate or casual, ends.

Johnson's *A Sunday Morning in the South* and Sandra Seaton's *The Bridge Party* are two plays that address the inefficacy of turning to the American judicial system for protection against lynching. In *A Sunday Morning in the South*, Johnson expresses her fury at the lack of federal anti-lynch legislation to secure the well-being of African Americans and illustrates how black American males in particular were regularly lynched for crimes that they did not commit. This play is highly significant in that it also delineates with a piercing and frightening clarity the fact that the black woman is the center for the intersection of racism, classism, and sexism. A look at the dialogue between Grandma Sue and the prejudiced policeman who disrespects and mistreats her substantiates this claim, while also reflecting the insignificance, the abuse, and the legal powerlessness of African Americans in general as well as that of African American mothers in particular. Interestingly enough, this pattern of police brutality against women is replicated in Sandra Seaton's *The Bridge Party* when the officer grabs Pett Mae by the arm and speaks disparagingly to her and to all the other women present. Seaton's *The Bridge Party* is a unique anti-lynching play in that it treats a segment of the African

American experience which has been long ignored. She examines the lifestyle of Southern middle-class blacks living before the modern civil rights era and dramatizes the manners in which middle-class African American women respond to racial crisis in the absence of black males.

The Ida B. Wells' plays (*Miss Ida B. Wells* and *Iola's Letter*) explore the life and the times of activist/journalist Ida Bell Wells-Barnett, who was born a slave in 1862. They examine crucial events in the genesis of her civil rights career and highlight the lynchings of her three friends, whose murders impacted her analysis of lynching and propelled her to launch her own anti-lynching campaign. Ultimately, the dramas present acts of resistance committed by a woman whose very life is an argument for justice, equality, and anti-lynching legislation.

Mine Eyes Have Seen and *Aftermath* address the dilemma of choosing to defend a nation that neither protects African American civilians nor African American veterans. The plays share an exhortation to take a specific action. One drama encourages young African American men to participate in America's campaign to free Europe, while the other urges black men to avenge the racist violence that their country perpetrates against them.

All of the dramas under scrutiny in *African American Women Playwrights Confront Violence* may be appreciated as literary munitions of bold African American women who rebelled against the hierarchies of power that were based on race, class, and gender. In their defiance of white male hegemony, the pioneer dramatists as well as the contemporary playwrights penned dramas that exposed and denounced the sexism, racism, and economic exploitation, which formed convoluted systems of savage oppression. One needs only to recall Johnson's *A Sunday Morning in the South* to observe an illustration of this painful tri-intersection in the life of Sue Jones.

In addition to appreciating these plays as literary munitions, these works may be valued as a compilation of liberational voices that talk back in defiance of white America's violent campaign to re-enslave post World War I African Americans. As previously noted, these plays were all part of a losing effort to stop the rising tide of lynchings in the South and the race riots in the North as white Americans sought to suppress African Americans, who challenged the nation to give them the enfranchisement which their war participation had earned for them. In their feature of African American characters who protest racist oppression and who demand complete equality, the plays of the pioneer dramatists promote the radically new and positive black image, who emerged after World War I.

Finally, *African American Women Playwrights Confront Violence* may be appreciated as a study that recognizes, explores, and documents the literary activity of women who have written in spite of their political, economic, cultural and social marginalization, and oppression. This book provides concrete evidence of nine particular writers who transcended and produced literature amid these "shackles." The fact that these important writers have for too long been under-acknowledged for reasons primarily due to their race and gender underscores the significance and the timeliness of investigating their dramas and their impact.

Bibliography

Abramson, Doris E. 1969. *Negro Playwrights in the American Theater 1925–1959*. New York: Columbia University Press.

Belcher, Fannin S. 1945. "The Place of the Negro in the Evolution of the American Theatre, 1767 to 1947." PhD diss., Yale University.

Bell, Bernard W. 1987. *The Afro-American Novel and Its Tradition*. Amherst: The University of Massachusetts Press.

Bennett, Gwendolyn. 1926. "The Ebony Flute." *Opportunity*, October, 322.

Benning, Victoria. 1997. "2 Held in Va. Decapitation, Burning; Police Investigating Whether Race Was a Factor in Black Man's Death." *Washington Post*, August 1, 5.

Boston, Michon. 1998. "Iola's Letter." In *Strange Fruit: Plays on Lynching by American Women*. Eds. Kathy Perkins and Judith Stephens. Bloomington: Indiana University Press.

Brown, Sterling. 1969. *Negro Poetry and Drama and The Negro in American Fiction*. New York: Atheneum Press.

Brown-Guillory, Elizabeth. 1988. *Their Place on the Stage: Black Women Playwrights in America*. New York: Praeger Press.

_____, ed. 1990. *Wines in the Wilderness: Plays by African American Women from the Harlem Renaissance to the Present*. New York: Praeger.

Bruce, Dickson D. 1993. *Archibald Grimké, Portrait of a Black Independent*. Baton Rouge: Louisiana State University Press.

Burrill, Mary Powell. (1919) 1979. "*Aftermath.*" In *A Century of Plays by American Women*, edited by Rachel France, 55–61. New York: Richards Rosen Press.

Campbell, Karlyn K. 1989. *Man Cannot Speak for Her*. New York: Greenwood Press.

Carby, Hazel. 1987. *Reconstructing Womanhood: The Emergence of the Afro-American Woman Novelist*. New York: Oxford.

Childress, Alice. (1955) 1971. "*Trouble in Mind.*" In *Black Drama in America*, edited by Darwin T. Turner, 293–346. Washington, D.C.: Howard University Press.

_____. (1966) 1994. "*Wedding Band: A Love/Hate Story in Black and White.*" In *New Worlds of Literature, Writings from America's Many Cultures* (second edition), edited by Jerome Beaty and J. Paul Hunter, 652–693. New York: Norton.

Cohen, Adam. 1999. "A Life for a Life." *Time*, March 8, 28–32.

Cooper, Anna Julia. 1951. *Life and Writings of the Grimké Family*. Copyright Anna J. Cooper.

Cripps, Thomas. 1993. *Slow Fade to Black: The Negro in American Film, 1900–1942*. New York: Oxford.

Cunningham, Virginia. 1947. *Paul Laurence Dunbar and His Song*. New York: Dodd, Mead.

Davis, Theresa Scott and Charles Y. Freeman. 1931. "A Biographical Sketch of Georgia Douglas Johnson and Some of Her Works." YMCA Graduate School Thesis.

Dover, Cedric. 1952. "The Importance of Georgia Douglas Johnson." *The Crisis*, 59:635.

Drake, William. 1987. *The First Wave: Women Poets in America 1915–1945*. New York: Macmillan Publishing Co.

Drummond, Tammerlin. 1999. "It's Not Just in New Jersey." *Time*, June 14, 61.

Dunbar-Nelson, Alice. (1918) 1974. *"Mine Eyes Have Seen."* In *Black Theatre U.S.A.: 45 Plays by Black Americans 1847–1974*, edited by James V. Hatch and Ted Shine, 173–177. New York: Free Press.

Duster, Alfreda, ed. 1970, 1972. *Crusade for Justice: The Autobiography of Ida B. Wells*. Chicago and London: University of Chicago Press.

Ellington, Mary Davis. 1934. "Plays by Negro Authors With Special Emphasis Upon the Period from 1916–1934." PhD diss. Nashville, TN: Fisk University.

"Endesha Ida Mae Holland, 61, Dies." *New York Times*, Feb. 1, 2006. http://www.nytimes.com/2006/02/01books/01holland.html

Fields-Meyer, Thomas. 1998. "One Deadly Night." *People Weekly*, June 29, 46–51.

Flanagan, Sylvia P. 1999. "Black American in Uproar Over Police Brutality." *Jet* 28 (June): 4–12.

France, Rachel. 1979. *A Century of Plays By American Women*. New York: Richards Rosen Press.

Giddings, Paula. 1984. *When and Where I Enter: The Impact of Black Women on Race and Sex in America*. New York: W. Morrow.

Gregg, Howard D. 1980. *The History of the African Methodist Episcopal Church: The Black Church in Action*. Sunday School Union: Bishop Henry A. Berlin, Jr.

Grimké, Angelina Weld. (1916) 1974. *Rachel*. In *Black Theatre U.S.A.: 45 Plays by Black Americans 1847–1974*, edited by James V. Hatch and Ted Shine, 137–172. New York: Free Press.

Grimké, Sarah. 1838. *Letters on the Equality of the Sexes and the Conditions of Women*. Boston: Issac Knapp.

Hamalian, Leo, and James V. Hatch, eds. 1990. *The Roots of African Drama: An Anthology of Early Plays. 1858–1938*. Detroit: Wayne State University Press.

Hatch, James V. and Ted Shine. 1974. *Black Theatre U.S.A.: 45 Plays by Black Americans 1847–1974*. New York: Free Press.

Hicklin, Fannie F. 1965. *The American Negro Playwright, 1920–1964*. University of Wisconsin microfilm.

Holland, Endesha Ida Mae. (1997) *From the Mississippi Delta*. New York: Simon and Schuster.

Huggins, Nathan Irving. 1973. *Harlem Renaissance*. New York: Oxford University Press,

_____. 1995. *Voices From the Harlem Renaissance*. New York: Oxford University Press.

Hull, Gloria T., ed. 1984. *Give Us Each Day: The Diary of Alice Dunbar-Nelson*. New York: Norton.

_____. 1987. *Color, Sex and Poetry: Three Women Writers of the Harlem Renaissance*. Bloomington: Indiana University Press.

_____. 1979. *"Under the Days: The Buried Life and Poetry of Angelina Weld Grimké."* *Conditions Five*, Autumn: 17–24.

Hundley, Mary Gibson. 1965. *The Dunbar Story 1870–1955*. New York: Vantage Press.

Jacobs, Harriet. (1861) 1969. *Incidents in the Life of a Slave Girl*. Edited by Lydia Maria Child. Detroit: Negro History Press.

Johnson, Georgia Douglas. (1925) 1974. *"A Sunday Morning in the South."* In *Black Theatre U.S.A.: 45 Plays by Black Americans 1847–1974*, edited by James V. Hatch and Ted Shine, 211–217. New York: Free Press.

_____. (c. 1926) 1990a. *"Blue Blood."* In *Wines in the Wilderness: Plays by African American Women From the Harlem Renaissance to the Present*, edited by Elizabeth Brown-Guillory, 16–25. New York: Praeger Press.

_____. (c. 1930) 1990b. *"Blue-Eyed Black Boy."* In *Wines in the Wilderness: Plays by African American Women From the Harlem Renaissance to the Present*, edited by Elizabeth Brown-Guillory, 33–38. New York: Praeger Press.

Jordan, W.D. 1968. *White Over Black*. Chapel Hill: University of North Carolina Press.

Kellner, Bruce. 1984. "Grimké, Angelina Weld." *The Harlem Renaissance: A Historical Dictionary for the Era*. Westport, CT: Greenwood.

Killens, John O. 1974. "The Literary Genius of Alice Childress." In *Black Women Writers, (1950–1980)*, edited by Mari Evans. New York: Anchor Press/Doubleday.

Krause, Sascha. 2005. "The Anatomy of Resistance: The Rhetoric of Anti-Lynching in American Literature and Culture, 1892–1936." Ph.D. dissertation, University of Regensburg, Germany.

Lerner, Gerda. 1967. *The Grimké Sisters from South Carolina*. Boston: Houghton Mifflin.

_____, ed. 1973. *Black Women in White America: A Documentary History*. New York: Vintage Books.

Lewis, David Levering. 1981. *When Harlem Was in Vogue*. New York: Knopf.

Lincoln, Eric C. 1969. *The Negro Pilgrimage in America: The Coming of Age of Blackamericans*. New York: Praeger.

Livingston, Myrtle Smith. (1926) 1974. *"For Unborn Children."* In *Black Theatre U.S.A.: 45 Plays by Black Americans 1847–1974*, edited by James V. Hatch and Ted Shine, 184–187. New York: Free Press.

Lott, Eric Paul. 1995. *Love and Theft: Blackface Minstrelsy and the American Working Class*. New York: Oxford University Press.

McKay, Nellie. 1987. "What Were They Saying?: Black Women Playwrights of the Harlem Renaissance." In *The Harlem Renaissance Re-examined*, edited by Victor A. Kramer, 129–147. New York: AMS Press.

Mellon, James. 1988. *Bullwhip Days: The Slaves Remember*. New York: Weidenfeld & Nicolson.

Miller, Jeanne-Marie A. 1978. "Angelina Weld Grimké: Playwright and Poet." *CLA Journal* 21: 514–519.

Minot, Stephen. 1965. *Three Genres: The Writing of Fiction, Poetry, and Drama*. Englewood Cliffs, NJ: Prentice-Hall.

Mitchell, Koritha. 2006. "Anti-Lynching Plays: Angelina Weld Grimké, Alice Dunbar Nelson, and the Evolution of African American Drama." In *Post-Bellum, Pre-Harlem: African American Literature of Culture, 1877–1919*. Barbara McCaskill and Caroline Gebhard, eds. New York: New York University Press, 2006, 210–230.

Mitchell, Loften. 1967. *Black Drama: The Story of the American Negro in the Theatre*. New York: Hawthorne Books.

Perkins, Kathy A., ed. 1989. *Black Female Playwrights: An Anthology of Plays before 1950*. Bloomington: Indiana University Press.

"Sandra Seaton [biography]." http:www.grad.cmich.edu.edu/seaton

Sharpton, Al. 1999. "Making Local Police Misconduct a Federal Case." *Essence*, June, 162.

Shockley, Ann Allen. 1988. *Afro-American Women Writers 1746–1933: An Anthology and Critical Guide*. New York: Meridian.

Smith-Rosenburg, Carroll. 1986. *Disorderly Conduct: Visions of Gender in Victorian America*. New York: Oxford University Press.

Stephens, Judith. 1990. "The Anti-Lynch Play: Toward an Interracial Feminist Dialogue in Theatre." *Journal of American Drama and Theatre* 2, no. 3:59–66.
_____. 1992. "Anti-Lynch Plays by African American Women: Race, Gender, and
Social Protest in American Drama." *African American Review* 26, no. 2:329–339.
_____, and Kathy Perkins. 1998. *Strange Fruit: Plays on Lynching by American Women.*
Bloomington: Indiana University Press.
Stetson, Erlene. 1982. "Studying Slavery: Some Literary and Pedagogical Considerations
on the Black Female Slave." In *But Some of Us are Brave*, edited by Gloria T. Hull,
Patricia Bell Scott, and Barbara Smith, 61–82. New York: The Feminist Press.
Tolnay, Stewart E., and E.M. Beck. 1992. *A Festival of Violence: An Analysis of Southern
Lynchings, 1882–1930*. Urbana and Chicago: University of Illinois Press.
Turner, Darwin T. 1968. *"The Negro Dramatist's Image of the Universe, 1920–1960."* In
Black Voices, edited by Abraham Chapman, 677–690. New York: New American
Library.
Wall, Cheryl. 1991. *Changing Our Own Words: Essays on Criticism, Theory, and Writing
by Black Women.* New Brunswick and London: Rutgers.
Wells-Barnett, Ida B. 1969. *On Lynchings: Southern Horrors, a Red Record, and Mob Rule
in New Orleans.* New York: Arno Press and the New York Times.
Wesley, Charles. 1977. *Henry Arthur Callis: Life and Legacy.* Chicago: The Foundation
Publishers.
White, Jack E. 1999. "The White Wall of Silence." *Time*, June 7, 63.
Wiley, Catherine. 1989. "Whose Name, Whose Protection: Reading Alice Childress'
Wedding Band." In *Modern American Drama: The Female Canon*, edited by June
Schlueter, 184–197. Madison, NJ: Fairleigh Dickinson Press.
Wilkerson, Margaret B., ed. 1986. *9 Plays by Black Women.* New York: Mentor.
Zangrando, Robert. 1980. *THE NAACP Crusade Against Lynching 1909–1950.* Philadel-
phia: Temple University Press.

Collections and Unpublished Material

The Camille Billops and James V. Hatch Archives, Emory University, Robert Woodruff
Library, Atlanta, GA.
Roscoe Conking Bruce Collection, Moorland Spingarn Research Center, Howard Uni-
versity, Washington, D.C.
Glenn Carrington Collection, Schomburg Center for Research in African American
Culture, New York, NY.
Archibald Henry Grimké Collection, Moorland Spingarn Research Center, Howard
University, Washington, D.C.
Angelina Weld Grimké Collection, Moorland Spingarn Research Center, Howard
University, Washington, D.C.
Montague Grimké Collection. South Carolina Library, University of South Carolina
(Columbia)
Francis J. Grimké Collection Moorland Spingarn Research Center, Howard University,
Washington, D.C.
Miller, Carroll Dean. Personal Interview with Emeritus Professor of Howard Univer-
sity, Washington, D.C., 6 August 1992.
Lucy Diggs Slowe Collection, Moorland Spingarn Research Center, Howard Univer-
sity, Washington, D.C.
Theresa Scott Davis and Charles Y. Freeman. "A Biographical Sketch of Georgia Doug-
las Johnson," 1931. Written for the now defunct YMCA Graduate School in
Nashville, TN.

Charles Chesnutt Collection, Fisk University, Nashville, TN.
Cullen-Jackman Collection, Robert W. Woodruff Library, Atlanta University, Atlanta, GA.
Georgia Douglas Johnson Collection. Oberlin College Archives, Oberlin, OH.
Schomburg Center for Research in African American Culture, New York, NY.

Selected Periodicals

Afro-American (Baltimore, PA)
Colored American
Crisis
New York Age
Opportunity
Pittsburgh (PA) Courier

Index

2/13